MANAGING *CHALLENGING* BEHAVIOUR

A BRITISH CARIBBEAN PERSPECTIVE

Dr. Roselle Antoine MBE

First published in Great Britain in 2009
by Roselle Antoine

Copyright © 2009 Roselle Antoine

Names, characters and related indicia are copyright and trademark
Copyright © 2009 Roselle Antoine

The publisher has asserted her moral rights
to be identified as the author

A CIP Catalogue of this book is available
from the British Library

ISBN 978-0-9542325-7-3

Cover design by ~GarviDesign.uk

CHANDLER
BOOK DESIGN

Typeset in Gill Sans 11½pt by
Chandler Book Design
www.chandlerbookdesign.co.uk

Printed in Great Britain by the MPG Books Group, Bodmin and Kings Lynn
The publisher's policy is to use paper manufactured
from sustainable forests

CONTENTS

PREFACE

If the primary motive was to add to the list of books on Caribbean literary criticism and the volumes of post-colonial literatures, this book might never have been written.   On the contrary, the urgency of a book on behaviour management from a British Caribbean perspective amounts to a testimony, a personal mission, a political statement of the dire need, at this particular time in the 21st century, to document and to confront the ignorance and complacency which exist about the relationship between Caribbean peoples and their culture, their experiences in the Diaspora and the resulting impact this has on them and their children in the UK. The consequences are to do with present concerns around social, political, historical, educational and psychological development and progress, evident on all levels of thinking and discourse in Britain today.

Where so-called Caribbeanists and theorists continue to concentrate on the post-colonial epoch, this ultimately creates a focus on the Metropolis as the centre and the Caribbean as the periphery. But the pre-colonial period, identified the peoples of the Caribbean in their New World environment, (one which gave us Creole peoples, the calypso, Caribbean Anancy, reggae music, *su-su*, **box-hand, partnership**, or **conubite,** to name a few; with their richness of culture. However, the focus of such history seems to be slipping by, almost imperceptibly, allowing the dominance of post-colonial enquiry, Euro-American imperialism, and diasporic Caribbean memory to project dilutions of what Caribbean cultural traditions and behaviours are.

This form of projection is often employed in order to provide an alternative to the hegemony of British formulations. In fact, underlying this, is what I would call an inconspicuous attempt to dilute Caribbeanness in favour of Black British identity, and therefore make it seem more acceptable in a British context. The closest one gets to defining Caribbean culture in Britain is the Notting Hill Carnival, reggae music, dances, Rapping and negatively, activities associated with gun and gang crimes.

What is evident, as a result, is the absence of a consistent and organic focus on understanding the Caribbean person and his Caribbean cultural make-up. In other words, the definition shifts as often as the question, (**What or where is the Caribbean?**), is asked, and is as varied as the many answers to the questions. What then is the result of such a limitation? The natural recourse is to have many theories on the literatures (the written word, although the culture has been based on the spoken word). Many of these theories are propounded by non-Caribbeans, so that what is packaged and sold as "**Caribbean**", can often be seen as Eurocentric, or Western bourgeois perspectives, which cannot adequately help us deal with grass-roots problems of underachievement, negative stereotyping, a lessening of self-esteem/self-worth among the youth, and lack of positive paths to solidify the future developments of our youths.

One of the aims of this book is to highlight the abject lack of a coherent text dealing with Caribbean heritage, and in particular, the impact of this on behaviours among young people of such heritage in Britain. There is, however, a preoccupation of texts highlighting problems to do with race and the Black British setting. Such preoccupations do not appear to provide all the answers, since they only deal with a **part** of the story, and are dysfunctional in the context of Caribbean peoples with a **past** that began hundreds of years ago, and thousands of miles away.

Therefore, to negate a Caribbean starting-point, (a period which guides and inform the psychological levels of thinking and discourse of Caribbean peoples in Britain), will have implications for understanding the Caribbean family in British society as a whole. The same strategy can be applied to Caribbeans in other diasporic settings, especially where travel to other parts of the world – Africa, Indian Sub-continent, Russia, Cuba and America, continually influences their thought processes as well as their behaviour patterns.

What is urgently called for, is rigorous action to highlight Caribbeanness , from the foggy and abstract posturing which lead to ignorance and misinterpretation. Nowadays, the label "**Black**" which, in political terms, identifies dark-skinned minority ethnic groupings, is acceptable to some, when it serves a political purpose. For example, when it is politically expedient, Asians appear to accept the identification of the term "Black", though this never identifies their cultural, religious or language status. Therefore, what seemed ideal in the 1970's, with the spread of the Black Power Movement across America, the Caribbean and among Black people in the diaspora – the "**I'm Black and I'm proud**" sentiment - has become the very rod which will break our present cultural backs in Britain.

From a Caribbean point of view, being tarred with the same political brush as other minority groupings for political expediency, is myopic. Where it might work for the Indian population who are intermittently Asians, it is not so for the Africans or Caribbeans, since it tends to be counterproductive on several fronts.

For example, from a religious perspective, there is no such thing as a "black religion". For the Indians who are "*Black*" politically, theirs is a Hindu, Islam, Buddhist, Sikh or Brahma Kumaris one, and this subsequently guides and inform their culture in every way.   Linguistically, they are identified as speakers for whom the English language is their second and additional one (ESOL or EAL). Therefore their language strengthens the identity quest, and is inextricably linked to the cultural identification, highlighted by religion. That being so, their beliefs, customs, ways of dress, behaving, thinking, reasoning, even food preparation, are guided, if not identified, by religio-linguistic and cultural principles.   Additionally, in Britain, there is a clearly visible Indian population, in terms of business, financial management, general trade, shops, dress, places of worship, language, radio stations, TV channels, a profusion of restaurants, etc.

Therefore, my concern about the all-inclusive "*Black*" label is that there is evidence to show that the term can be used to generate income for local groups, and voluntary organizations, when convenient and at times may have nothing to do with "*Black*" culture per se.   This has become absurd when events known to be African or Caribbean or both; in tone, tempo, text and historic value, are culturally diluted with yet another term, "cultural diversity".

A case in point is, some London Borough's view of how they portrays Black History Month in October each year. This event has become an event in which all non-African groups have staked a claim for their need to join in the celebrations. A reason for this is funding is available for group celebrations and therefore it is an opportune moment to apply for money that would otherwise be targeted at "*Black*" Groups. In the example above, in 2001, "Black History Month" meant for Harrow, (a predominantly white borough, with Asians forming 28% and African-Caribbeans 9%,) a time to focus on the larger minority ethnic group (Asians), who also pronounced vehemently, the need to project "diversity", instead of Blackness. The prevailing notion behind this kind of thinking is that "Black" must be seen as an all-embracing terminology, suggesting yet another jingoistic dilution - *social inclusion*. Luckily, the reverse is the case in boroughs like Brent and Haringey, where there are undisputed contingents of black-led activities during "black history month", which embody African-Caribbean history and culture.

Unfortunately, the politically expedient "*black*" factor does not stop with activities on

[handwritten margin note: lack of identity for British Black people.]

the ground. The media must own its share in the projection of so-called "black"culture. The psychology of negatively projecting black faces on TV screens, associated with 'black-on-black' crimes, mugging, theft, prison population, benefit fraud, single-parent welfare dependency (meaning dysfunctional), underachievement, behavioural problems, and the highest percentage of school expulsions; perpetuates a myth of inferiority, while projecting an imbalance of power, between white and black peoples.

On the musical scene, black music is seen as that which is produced, sung or presented by Black people – "**Black**", connoting African descent, wholly or partly. In this instance, the Asian population does not accept inclusion, and the media does not project them as such. Asian music, like Asian food, dress, religion, language, is never called "**Black**", and in terms of crime reporting, the Asian is deliberately identified from others, and not the term "**Black**". This is so that it does not obscure a culturally specific identification, where a certain negative media-projected image is sought or desired.

The complexity of the "**Black**" image does not stop there. On the level of black consciousness, in films, where top African-Americans actors are presented in key roles which show them as authoritative figures, wielding power, and delegating the same to white "juniors", create a temporary affection for their sense of blackness, as it enhances the black image publicly and raises the status of black pride. In other words, the film producer in his myth-creating role transcends or suspends popular belief and the audience consciously imbues this.

The duration of the film and power of the imagery it projects for blackness may have a variety of consequences, depending on the individual experience of the audiences viewing the film. For some, it may elevate their sense of black consciousness. For others, it may temporarily raise their self-esteem while or as an extreme, it can create stronger disbelief in the authoritative role play of the black actor; so that the image is debunked, or received on the level of a myth – implausible and impossible; meaning that it exists only in the world of the film. This feeling is strongest where a person's day-to-day experiences greatly contrast what is being projected.

What is clearly evident, is the fact that visual imagery has a profound effect on viewers, as is seen in the music industry. British Black and Caribbean peoples emulate the musical styles, language, mannerisms, dress codes and attitudes of Black America for a complexity of reasons, some of which I have already discussed, or to fill their cultural vacuum. My view is that there is a paucity of culturally cementing elements among Caribbeans in Britain, which is necessary to infuse in them a sense of cultural wholeness rather like a compass, which would enable them to be focused in their paths to progress.

What is clearly the backdrop to the complexity of black self-hood is the history of a people for whom a deliberate whitening process began over one hundred and sixty years ago, with the kinds of consequences still being felt today. On one hand, the word "*Black*", for conscientious cultural promoters, continues to be "beautiful", projected as a counteraction to prevailing negative associations.

On the other hand, because of the complex definitions of Black and the variety of consequences of accepting it as mentioned above, the deliberate attempt on the part of the British media to break down the old "*I'm Black and I'm proud*" banner of self-esteem, to the point of degradation, fear, negativity, and showing that everything considered "black" as bad, is definitely the stronger of the competing elements for pride in self-hood. Therefore, a consistent push-and-pull factor exists between people who are keen to assert a black image of positivism, politically and culturally; against the mechanism of those who control the mass media, to break down, by erecting (push factors) alternative and stronger negativity in its place.

In the case of Caribbean culture, the word "*Black*" which, in the 1970's was once seen as the pride-boosting, self-identifying and group stabilizer, had consequences which made the word *Caribbean* almost redundant as far as identity goes. The question is, how helpful is the term "*Black*" today in accessing the cultural characteristics of the Caribbean region? What does it present to young Caribbean children, especially boys in Britain, currently publicized as grossly underachieving in schools, as far as Cultural identity is concerned? What texts exist which teach unadulterated, who the Caribbean pioneers of progress are? What can Caribbeans identify as their own religion, cultural ways of behaving, (especially associated with events and occasions), Caribbean festivals and their origins, traditions which parents use orally, as a reference point, to guide and inform their thinking and discourse?

My view is that achievement has to do with a sense of direction, based on culturally infused pride, which informs the individual/group and inspires a sense of self-worth, value, esteem, and a tenacity to maintain these in the face of the most threatening forces. Therefore, the problems of underachievement and underperformance in the classroom should find their solution in the very existence and contents of this book. In this respect, it is my insistence that the socio-economic, historical, cultural and ideological contradictions, which define the life, history and experiences of Caribbean people, must form the basis of a new and more functionally relevant approaches to and understanding of Caribbean heritage peoples in Britain.

The crucial intervention which this book sets out to make, is to bridge the ever-widening chasm between the little that parents have remembered, (with their dependence on memory – known to be selective); and culture as it is practiced in Britain. More important, this intervention sets out to highlight the need for an understanding of how aspects of Caribbean heritage have fused with other multi-cultural elements in the UK, in ways which merit an understanding of behaviours, hopes and aspirations of Caribbean families' development in Britain today.

I owe a debt of gratitude to all those in my life who have, over the years, encouraged me to strive for excellence, whatever the circumstances. In particular, I would like to thank my son, Cyrus, for his unchanging belief that I can do anything! To my mother Veronica, brothers (Dean and Willan) and sisters (Theresa and Stephanie), who expect my best always: to Dr. Christopher Johnson, my dear colleague whose patience in the repeated editing of the text, discussions and encouragement has kept me going in difficult times. To **Mapute** and my team of Advisers, who gave me strength, and the community support; for whose benefit this book was written, I thank you all.

With political will, it is hoped that we can then look at new directions in 21st century approaches to behaviour management, within the contexts of social, economic, and cultural growth, as well as academic parity. These will be done in ways that enhance, promote and stabilize positive youth and community development in the United Kingdom.

Roselle Antoine

LIST OF TABLES & FIGURES

TABLES

FIGURES

CASE STUDIES

INTRODUCTION

British Caribbean People in Context

Over the past thirty years, Caribbean families have been grappling with labels and stereotypical categories that generally place them somewhere at the bottom rung of the British social and educational ladder. You as an individual, parent, teacher, educator, social worker, Human Resource Manager, Counsellor, Clinician or other professional, may be reading this book because you want a better understanding of the range of problems associated with Caribbean families, which impact on their behaviour that seem to have emotional, social and educational consequences.

Twenty-five years ago, when I began studying and working with the Caribbean community, at various levels in society, we did not have the current profusion of behaviour management cases of pupils who were "un-teachable" because of their emotional and behavioural difficulties. However, we did have concerns regarding educational attainment levels, performance and attainment disparities together with categorization of being "educational sub-normal", (popularly called ESN), with schools similarly categorised, to house our children.

Problems which were highlighted in 1975, during the time of Bernard Coard's Book, *How the British School system made West Indian children educationally subnormal,*[1] made Caribbean families more aware that they needed a different approach to viewing the British school system; (in the current/new environment), compared with the level and reliance experienced by them from "back home" (in the old/Caribbean environment).

In the old environment, "The School" for Caribbean parents, was the bedrock of all future successes with structures of demonstrable "teamwork" in place for child, parent and school. This means that children knew the boundaries of discipline and high levels of expectation for their educational outcomes. Such expectations were linked to everyone - families (including all extended family members), individual teachers and the school as Identifying institution. They regard children's marks of achievement as belonging to the village or local community. These places in turn, amplified that pride in success, by claiming their territory to be one that produces successful protégés. Such cultural characteristics promoted community pride, which led to the highlighting and advertising successful children and their parents, (by virtue of their children). To give this phenomenon a wider frame of reference, the individual Caribbean islands too advertises their children's successes, and promotes the idea that as countries, they inspire success and excellence. With this type of competitiveness, a healthy sense of inter-island rivalry based on success-generation develops. Culturally, this high level of expectation and achievement is endorsed among the individual Caribbean islands as characteristics of pride, status, and reputation accorded to them by the efforts of their individuals in society.

It is therefore that same Caribbean parental reliance, belief and absolute trust in the Schools to engage the parents in a tripartite arrangement, that was transferred onto similar expectations in the British School setting, by Caribbean parents who migrated to Britain. Therefore, it is not surprising that when Caribbean children were labelled as *"Educationally Sub-Normal"* (ESN); their parents were not only shocked at the label but were at a loss as to how this could be; their expectation being the school/authority is at the helm of the success boat. So what of this legacy? The fact is, ESN schools were set up for Caribbean children, some who are now parents of our present generation of school children! Bernard Coard's conclusion was that such categorizations were destructive, since a child was labled as "ESN", based on assessments that used social class, language, family structure and the British context, to measure academic intelligence.

You are probably one of the past unfortunate parents reading this book now for many reasons, trying to come to terms or find ways of understanding the legacy of your experience and its linkages or relevance to your children's or grand-children's situations. One the on hand, you may be reading this book because you have children who have been labelled as **EBD** (in some cases ESBD – Emotional and Social Behavioural Difficulties), and want to know what this additional label means to you as a parent or family member. On the other hand, you may be a professional whose occupation brings you into contact with those from a Caribbean heritage background, and have a minimal grasp of what you are experiencing, in terms of historical and cultural references to

Caribbean people. Therefore, understanding the legacy of British Caribbean people's entry to Britain and their experiences in context, is important to providing workable and relevant behaviour management strategies.

My standpoint is that a special responsibility rests on those who know, and have experienced our community's current state and aspirations against the backdrop of its history, to record it for our present enlightenment and our future advancement. I sincerely believe that the informed insider and practitioner are more reliable than a bystander or observer. It is from this standpoint that I chose to interrogate behaviour management from a perspective that is rooted in the experience of the Caribbean community in Britain to which I belong. For that reason the focus is a British Caribbean one.

The Caribbean community has been a vibrant and contributory segment of British life, since the early 20th century. Since that period, there have been conflicting situations during this community's presence in Britain, which have led to a misunderstanding of the British Caribbean phenomenon. It is with this in mind, I have decided to add to the debate, as both an insider and practitioner in the field of education, with first-hand knowledge and experience of educational developments within this community.

Methodology

There are four themes that provide the foci in this book, which provide the backdrop for the study and its conclusions. Firstly, the research methodology used. Secondly, I examine the factors which provide the context of the British Caribbean community in Britain and thirdly, I provide an expose of the nature of Caribbean historical development against a background of cultural practices. The fourth and final theme is a presentation in, *The Antoine Behaviour Excellence Model©* [2], and my place within that context.

The main methodology applied in this study is that of a participant observer. From this I make use of ethnographic techniques, within a contextual educational framework. According to Claire Selltiz et al, (1980) [3] the purpose of research is to discover answers to questions through the application of scientific procedures. This can be achieved from a variety of means i.e. structured, semi-structured and unstructured methodologies. In conducting the study of the British Caribbean segment of the population in Britain, in the context of behaviour management and an educational framework; this study used semi-structured and unstructured research methods. I have played the part of participant-observer throughout the research, a role which is located within the discipline of ethnographic research methods, as stated by Tim May, "*Participant observation is about engaging in a social scene, experiencing it and seeking to understand and explain it. The researcher is the medium through which this takes place.*" [4]

I adopted this approach because my personal and professional interaction with the "subjects" of this study made such an approach more appropriate. In fact, my 25 years of experience in education among the British Caribbean community, has made me an observer, participant and listener.

In the 1980's, I began research into the failure of young black children in local mainstream schools to express themselves, and the resulting consequences of their apparent identity crises, and underperformance. The Schools visited in West London, (mostly Primaries), were the ones which had decided to champion the cause of the emerging "multicultural education". At the same time, they were desperate to find reasons for the high incidence of underachievement, among black children in their schools.

This anomaly fired my curiosity and at university, during my first degree (a single honours degree in English), I explored aspects of the Caribbean oral and literary traditions in an effort to understand the impact of Caribbean cultural backgrounds (in particular, Caribbean oral traditions), on a literate society, such as Britain. The reason is that during my observations in schools, I had noticed that Caribbean children were embarrassed and ashamed to refer to themselves culturally. There was also confusion as to how they identified themselves. In fact, they attached a certain amount of shame to their cultural icons – Caribbean food, and names of cultural products.

Additionally, there was open resentment among the eight year old children, for my exposure, of *their secret* – publicising avocadoes, yam, sweet potato, breadfruit and my talk about Caribbean cuisine such as Chicken Creole. Clearly for them, this was to remain a secret. In contrast, I had witnessed more comfort with talk about sausages and mash, baked beans and names in stories like Tom and John, (not Brer Anancy). In attempting to break down these barriers to an acceptance of self and a feeling of comfort among the children, especially with their participation in our workshops, made me realise that the job of understanding and appreciating culture and identity among young Caribbean children in Britain was urgent – 25 years later ,the situation is still urgent today!

This was going to be a mammoth task, I realised, but being a part of this multicultural movement in Britain, and later through a Master of Philosophy degree, I decided to interrogate the impact of Caribbean culture, from the point of a fusion of the oral (Caribbean based) and literary (Western based) traditions, to look at its impact on the Caribbean community in the Diaspora. It's a phenomenon I call *Caribbean Orature* (2006)[5]. At that time, I had not studied a behavioural underpinning of this perspective within *Orature*. However, because *Orature* provides an understanding of the Caribbean community in diasporic communities, it means that cultural and historical backgrounds provide the praxis of the community's development and therefore affect all aspects of their determination. This includes their psychological levels of thinking, discourse, behaviour, and sense of self. I therefore decided early on, to channel my initial interest into interrogating the development of Caribbean people in Britain, by providing an educational setting; a private school (3yrs to 11yrs), within which to examine closely the developing concerns of underachievement, in the context of children, their family, and their social and economical setting. A primary aim was to look at the impact of this on education and behaviour in general. The Primary School was open to all nationalities, but I narrowed my initial interest in the British Caribbean community, to focus on the ethno-educational experience of Caribbean children in Britain. Five years later, I expanded my education provision to include Secondary-aged children, in order to test the cultural significance of behaviour management models among Caribbean pupils and their parents.

I looked at *Representation* (Hall 2003)[6], as a theoretical approach to British Caribbean development in the Diaspora. This was because (in Britain as elsewhere), it is the ethnicity, history, socio-economic, cultural and political attributes that most define them, and which are most pertinent to investigate and study. Finally, I decided that the study would work best if located overtly within the hermeneutical framework of "contextual education". The model used in this study is based on *The Antoine Behaviour Excellence Model, (1994)[7]*, which I later developed. Such an approach suggests that in-depth situational analysis, then identifying a contextual framework, produces new behavioural contexts. In doing so, I concluded that such a narrower focus on the Behaviour and Education of the British Caribbean community in the context of educational development would produce the desired result for this study, rather than the wider context of British Caribbean community development per se.

To achieve my aims in developing *The Antoine Behaviour Excellence Model*, I pursued 3 research initiatives. These were a mixture of structured and semi- structured initiatives, and are highlighted in **Chapter 7.** Among these initiatives were visits to local schools – secondary co-eds (private and mainstream); youth projects, local community organisations; regional and national, *Celebrations of Achievement* events, Seminars and Social events, involving a wide range of Black-led and a mixture of cultural participants and observers from the British community as a whole.

As an insider and participant, I have been mindful of the dangers of the covert or insider research, as highlighted by Martin Bulmer[8]. He warns against missing some of the pertinent issues or of being biased in one's selection. In doing so, I believe that a reasonable balance has been struck on the issues highlighted and that the methods chosen, semi and unstructured methods were suitable for this research in this context.

The contextual model provided in-depth studies, critiques and evaluations of British Caribbean's development in Britain in ways that draw on their history of the people. To do this end, I interrogated literary, oral and personal sources from within the British Caribbean community. However, in order to ensure breadth and depth, I used case studies and other reliable and relevant available data. My main objective was to ensure that this research was rooted in experience within the context of British Caribbean determination, for in-depth study, critique and evaluation. In other words, it must be understood, noted, and provide a greater understanding of this community.

I am encouraged also by instructive titles of books, in particular, Paul Grant and Raj Patel's anthology, *A Time to Speak*,[9] in my determination to articulate a British Caribbean perspective on behaviour management in educational settings. Therefore, the grass-roots elements of the method of research provide localised sources, some set up specifically for this study, (in both Britain and the Caribbean), as a means of self-articulation.

Another aspect of the research is to bring together two perspectives of community development (the Caribbean and Britain), from the in-depth study of British Caribbean's education in Britain. This is squared against the backdrop of parental education in the Caribbean, (a colonial one), in a dynamic interplay, that produces a new contextual reality. This means that British Caribbean education is brought into dialogue with British education per se, and the resulting situation is crystallised in what one has to say about the other. For example, British Caribbean behaviour in the UK has to be understood in the light of history and migration to Britain. Therefore the main outcome is the interplay of the two elements above and the resulting conclusion for **The Antoine Behaviour Excellence Model (1994),** in our situation presently in Britain. The next step therefore, is to examine the nature of aspects which provide the context of British Caribbeans and behaviour management in Britain.

Context

Generally, a contextual approach in this study means examining the parts which relate to a whole. In other words, analysing the shared arena in which different influences interact, and in which old and new co-exist and are reconciled. The challenges that arise from such differences create a plurality of life that manifests as British Caribbean as lived in Britain. In my previous work on the subjects in question, (Antoine 2006). I refer to Stuart Hall's Theory of **Representation** (2003), in particular, the essence of communication via shared conceptual maps and constructing a corresponding link or chain between people and ideas to create meaning. This means there is inter-contextual diversity between communities (here, **the host** which is Britain and **migranst,** which are Caribbean peoples). This merits understanding for relevant knowledgeable perspectives. For example, I am a member of the ethnic minority groups in Britain, black, female, Caribbean, Grenadian, Principal of a Private College (my own), President of a charity **The Roselle Antoine Foundation,** (civic responsibility), a mother, employer, friend and colleague. It also means that I am all of those and more, and each has its turn to be a prime identity, at different, which relate to me.

Therefore, there is a dynamic process taking place with interrelates within my life that may pose a challenge in understanding who I am. From this perspective also, it is complex to attribute a single identity to British Caribbeans all of the time. In fact, examining the socio-historical, political and economic backgrounds evidences a complexity of identity that is based on a variety of experiences. While the historical, political and economic factors are very important, the social dimension is central to the development of behaviour management in an educational setting in this book.

Introduction – British Caribbean People in Context

The Introduction summarises the British Caribbean people in the context of their existence in Britain. It links the phenomenon of challenging behavioural difficulties to a wider frame of reference and concludes that the insider and practitioner are more reliable than presumptions and present general stereotypes. It suggests that behavioural difficulties is rooted in the experiences of the Caribbean community in Britain, since there have been periods during their presence, which have led to paradoxes, inconsistencies and the enduring legacies of adverse personal histories. These have impacted on their behaviour and attitudes towards a system which they have come to view with mistrust and with less allegiance, compared to the early Caribbean migrants of the 50's.

Chapter 1   Where is the Caribbean?

This chapter examines briefly the origin, growth and development of the Caribbean Region and the fusion of multi-layers of racial groups against the backdrop of slavery, indentureship, colonisation, independence and migration – Europe, North America, Canada, Africa and other Diasporas settings.   Factors which affect the landscape environment are also analysed to show the impact these have on Caribbean settlers at home and abroad. The chapter also argues that despite being a physical place, the Caribbean can also be viewed as a mental construct or a state of mind. There is also a focus on the quest for a Caribbean identity that the levels of cultural, historic and other related influences have brought to bear on the overall conditioning of British Caribbean peoples in the host society. The fusion of various cultural influences, origination from a melting pot environment, makes it difficult to pin down.

Chapter 2   Caribbean Family Structure

This chapter analyses at length, the composition of the Caribbean family and the dynamics that interplay between this social unit and the rest of society – be it civic or otherwise. The roles of women are highlighted, to document their contribution to the strong matriarchal family pattern in the Caribbean and the resulting impact this has for their settled life in Britain. This section also shows the migratory movement from the region to the *Mother Country'* (Britain), which accounts for the range of survival strategies employed by families to co-exist in its multicultural setting.

Chapter 3   Who's Afraid of the Big Bad Youth?

This chapter examines the position of young people in Britain, through the prism of the law, the media, welfare and other mainstream institutions that tend to criminalise young people. It also explores the constructed stereotypes associated with youths and questions the imagery of perpetrators of crime compared with them being victims of crime.   It argues for a set of appropriate measures to alleviate deep-seated cultural, socio-economic problems experienced by the youth in Britain today.

Chapter 4   British vs. Caribbean Settings

This chapter analyses the levels of exclusion in mainstream British schools, compared with the negligible and/or non-existence of permanent exclusion of children in Caribbean schools. Based on the fact that behaviours can be socially constructed, a comparative analysis of both settings highlight differences that are socio-economically and culturally determined. The chapter also focuses on the different behavioural conditions of pupils, types of curricula and the socio-cultural factors that traumatise young children in mainstream education, with a recurring huge cost to the British economy. The chapter endorses the need for individualized learner-based curricula with a socially sensitive and culturally specific approach to learning.

Chapter 5   Competing Educational Philosophies

This chapter looks at the education systems involving the Caribbean Region and Britain, detailing the philosophies that underpin the behaviour in both regions of the individual, society and have resonance in the sharing of a global environment. It argues that migrants who have moved from one setting to another have philosophies that may be viewed as paradoxical in a host society. Outlining the different philosophies supports an understanding of Caribbean people's ideological thinking, discourse, and behaviours. These have wider implications for Britain in a global environment.

Chapter 6   The Dichotomy of the Black Presence in Britain

This chapter illustrates profoundly, the historic and present generational attitudes and lifestyle responses reflected in the behaviours of British Caribbean people; including families and young people in general. It examines the types of influences that affect the conduct of young people in a variety of settings and presents anecdotal evidence to explain specific behavioural forms. These are psychological in origin, having been affected by migrants' aspirations, a legacy of trauma, a developing black consciousness in Britain, and community approaches to problem-solving.

Chapter 7   Coping Strategies

This chapter explores the various strategies employed by members of the community and the government in coping with social disorder. The chapter looks at various viewpoints and methods employed by individuals and groups to deal with aggressive, violent and persistent trouble-making youth. The Chapter explores why youths join gangs and looks at the psychology behind gang formation that makes it attractive to young people. The chapter also looks at the wide variations and types of gangs, and looks at the strategies employed nationally and locally to intervene in gang activities.

Chapter 8   The Antoine Behaviour Excellence Model (ABEM) ©

This chapter presents the ABEM via an ethnographic approach to educational underachievement, affecting children who are underachieving and/or display challenging behaviour. It argues that by applying a culturally sensitive and socially specific approach to pupils' learning, they can develop on a scale that ranges from adverse behaviour displays to a model of excellence that enables access to the curriculum. Aspects of the model embody a community participatory approach to teaching and learning that results in increased attainment levels. This is achieved via a range of activities and events that also involve adults other than teachers in the classroom. *The Antoine Behaviour Excellence Model* is the praxis on which one is able to capture pupils' confidence, motivate them to full potential, develop a continuous devotion to learning, imbue self-esteem and confidence, and inculcate a commitment to participatory citizenship and educational achievement.

Chapter 9   Developing Your Own Adverse Behaviour Reduction Programme

This chapter presents programmes for evaluating and reducing adverse behaviours. The programmes are underpinned by the goals set by the *Antoine Behaviour Excellence Model, (ABEM)*, in reducing adverse behaviour rates by identifying the causes of behavioural problems and implementing effective intervention to deal with them. The design of the exemplar programmes address risk factors that help with improving school attendance, academic outcomes, students social and emotional lives, students and their families access to services in the community and a reduction of juvenile delinquency and youth offending.

Conclusion

This final section envisions a renewed approach to teaching and learning development in Britain, underpinned by a code of ethics revolving around civic, cultural, economic, moral, legislative and spiritual praxis, and showcasing the equitable nature of education in the 21st century in Britain. It recommends a strategic vision for education in the 21st century founded on both the British Government's strategic action plan and the author's expert interventionist approaches.

There are also good behaviour management techniques which need to be highlighted and shared that reflect the broad principles of quality and good practice. If we take the view that a classroom, its managers and pupils are a microcosm of society, then we are experiencing a range of diversity increases that signals innovations and approaches to match the scale in some localities. It therefore means that labelling should not be the pre-requisite for categorising any specific group, or deciding how we tackle adverse behaviours in the classroom. It also means that diagnosis needs to be directly linked to the educational solutions (it is a current practice in cases of Special Educational Needs -SEN), and should be a measurement for looking at opportunities and not a means to an end in itself.

It may be that decisions regarding continuing inclusion of the Emotional Behavioural Difficulties (EBD) or Emotional and Social Behavioural Difficulties (ESBD), pupil in mainstream school could be based on "market forces" i.e. the view of outsiders on the school in terms of league table results, and competition for high exam profiles. With the EBD and ESBD pupil, two things can happen:

(1)   He can be pressured into maximizing his performance causing great stress to his fragile imbalance, and thereby increasing his level of disruption which could possibly lead to further exclusions or

(2)   This can mean encouraging a continuation in the mainstream environment as their grades may be lower and discouraging the pupil from taking many subjects that are considered "difficult". This then reduced the self-esteem and confidence of the pupil and can cause disaffection and disengagement with education altogether: E.g., those pessimistic Year 11 pupils (15+/16 yrs), who think they *will fail anyway so what's the use of trying*.

My experience is that teachers are caught between considerations for the few disrupters and allegiance to the majority of pupils in their classes. There is a dominant professional dilemma – does one negotiate, and design individualized learning paths for the minor group(s), at the expense of providing more teaching time for those who are not disruptive?   A key factor here is the recent trend towards inclusion of special needs learners into mainstream schools. Putting aside the controversies as to whether to go for special needs inclusion or not, the fact is one has to question whether classroom teachers are adequately prepared for this task.

Another social factor is countering discrimination and prejudice, namely in convincing stakeholders that the ethical and educational imperatives is that *Every Child really does Matter!*[10] Whilst giving evidence of achievement of what I call" real success"; that is, looking at the child's and the school's starting point, rather than where the League Tables have placed them. There are also innovative practices that pioneering educators are implementing, which provide solutions for young people with even the most extreme forms of behaviour disorders. These successes need to be highlighted and it is for these reasons that *The Antoine Behaviour Excellence Model* © as practiced at the TCS Tutorial College, is being alluded to in this book: With the socio-cultural and professional imperatives, advances are being made in behaviour management as follows:

- Understanding cognitive development and learning with regard to socio- professional sensitivity and culturally specific approaches to behaviour management;
- Recognizing that school-based education is a platform for lifelong learning;
- Adopting an educational paradigm for behaviour management and special needs education, rather than one which is predominantly psycho-medical;
- Using multi-disciplinary approaches to teaching and learning that involves a community participatory approach;
- Use of a culturally diverse network of learners, stakeholders and professionals, globally;
- Using alternative behaviour management appraisal tools such as soft outcomes and hard data outcomes to accommodates diverse achievements; and
- These are underpinned by a national agenda that Every Child Matters benefiting from equal opportunity and equal access to the national curriculum.

In Britain, unlike the Caribbean, what seems to be lacking is a sharing of good, workable professional practices based on integration of professionals via networking. This integration can be achieved and maintained through supporting and sharing grassroots practices across the UK.   The single key element appears to be the need to manage behaviours in a multi-cultural Britain among all teachers because it is the way that one can ensure that policies are converted into practice among educationalists, policy-makers, parents, community leaders/teachers and researchers.

It has become apparent, over the past 25 years, that concerns about rates of exclusions, generated by adverse and extreme forms of behaviours are more marked. This is so despite the fact that SEN and EBD/ESBD are in the minority of the school population. The fact is, this minority has become a larger proportion and hence its focus in this book. It may be that this rising trend is a transitional problem, with the enlargement of minority groups in the UK, the expansion of Europe/European Union, and changes in immigration laws in Britain. What is urgent, is a recognition of the need for solutions at this early stage, to lesen marginalization of minority groups. At the same time, teachers would need to consider whether they have the relevant knowledge and skills in order to do so

I am in full agreement with Jean-Baptiste Moliere,[1] who states that we are responsible not only for what we do but also what we do not" as teachers. This means ensuring that whether pupils with adverse behaviours are in a mainstream or segregated school, their behaviour management takes cognisance of the fact that they are truly included, not just side-lined or excluded, because its easier to get rid of them, but that policies ensure that they are pedagogically and fully included to eliminate divisions among professionals as to what works and what is recognized at government level.

Given the complexity of the issues involved in behaviour management a question to ask - Is **The Antoine Behaviour Excellence Model** © creatively, an exemplar embodied in the maxim, *necessity being the mother of all invention*? For the many thousands of pupils that it has provided behaviour management solutions for, the answer is, **yes**. Sometimes the solutions to problems arise from developments, based on a personal and localised need to identify with, and provide solutions to problems which are, evidently, workable. It is hoped that this book will be a step towards further enquiry and consolidation of such expertise in the not too distant future. It is also hoped that the **Model** will do justice to the complexity of the issues around behaviour management solutions, not just for Caribbean children but for the aspirations of all SEN and non-SEN pupils everywhere.

The inclusion of all children.

SELECTED REFERENCES

1. Coard B. (1975): *How the British School System made West Indian children educationally subnormal,* New Beacon books, London.

2. Antoine Roselle (1996):   *An Introduction to Caribbean Orature: A fusion of oral and literary traditions*", unpbl. book MPhil thesis: London Metropolitan University.

3. Selltiz et al Claire: (1991): *Research Methods in Social Relations:* Published by Wadsworth.

4. **May, T**. (2002): *"Qualitative Research in Action*", Sage Publications. London

5. Antoine Roselle (2006): *Understanding the Development of Caribbean Orature*: MPhil. Thesis, London Metropolitan University

6. Hall S. (2003): *Representation: Cultural Representations and Signifying Practices,* Sage Publications, London.

7. Antoine Roselle (1994): *The Antoine Behaviour Excellence Model,* developed at the TCS Tutorial College and its Special Education Needs Unit, Harrow, London (1994-2009).

8. Bulmer M. and Solomon J (2004) 'Researching Race and Racism' Routledge, [London

9. Grant P. (1992): *A time to Speak: Perspectives of Black Christians in   Britain,* Kairos.

10. *Every Child Matters: Change for Children*, Published by TSO (The Stationery Office) and available Online:www.tso.co.uk/bookshop

11. Nelson R.J. Critical Essays: "The Unreconstructed Heroes of Molière," in *The Tulane Drama Review,* Vol. IV, No. 3, March, 1960, pp. 14-37.

| | Where is the Caribbean?

Introduction

This chapter examines briefly the origin, growth and development of the Caribbean Region and the fusion of multi-layers of racial groups against the backdrop of slavery, indentureship, colonisation, independence and migration – Europe, North America, Canada, Africa and other diasporas. Factors which affect the landscape environment are also analysed to show the impact these have on Caribbean settlers at home and abroad. The chapter also argues that despite being a physical place, the Caribbean can also be viewed as a mental construct or a state of mind.

There is also focus on the quest for a Caribbean identity that the levels of cultural, historic and other related influences have brought to bear on the overall conditioning of British Caribbean peoples in the host society. The fusion of various cultural influences, originating from a melting pot environment, makes it difficult to pin down. The chapter argues that the region is a cultural melee with evidence of strong ancestral consciousness of the racial groups which settled in the Caribbean.

Any study on such a vast region is problematic, as the Caribbean is not easily definable. No tidy line exists to draw around the region and many geographical variables that exist. For example, Belize and Guyana are usually included though Venezuela, which claims to be a Caribbean country (since part of her coast is on if not in, the Caribbean sea), has none of the historical and cultural factors which Suriname, French Guyana and Guyana, her neighbours possess, and which enable them to be part of the mainstream Caribbean. From a geo-political perspective Guyana is part of the English-speaking Caribbean.

Nicaragua and Belize share a history of British Colonialism and some of the influences which characterise the rest of the Anglophone Caribbean, but Panama and

Costa Rica, tend to be more aligned with Central America. As a result a geographical definition is complicated. However, it is possible to see the Caribbean as a place characterised by a variety of environments, inhabited by people with a variety of histories. The interactions between people and land, especially since the 15th century, have produced a variety of distinctive nation states.

European Rivalries in the Caribbean

The history of rivalries of European domination, since the 15th century by countries such as Portugal, Spain, the Netherlands, France and Britain, in the Caribbean, has created a complex and interesting hybridised environment, from which the mixture of traditional values take their characteristic traits. Since the 15th century, a variety of Europeans had set out on their voyages of plunder and pillage of the new Caribbean territories, in an attempt to expand their countries' political control, build their empires and economic systems, and perpetuate their cultural influence in the region, including Africa, Asia, Oceania and the Americas. The voyages of European exploitation and "discovery" began on the African continent.

In 1415, the Portuguese, being the first sailors and navigators to set out on these remarkable voyages of exploration, captured the city of Ceuta in North Africa. They also conquered the West African coast that was rich in ivory, gold and silver. The implications of such activities had far-reaching consequences because it signalled possibilities of exploring further a field. Encouraged by the Portuguese success, an explorer named Vasco da Gama, sailed around the Cape of Good Hope in 1498. He explored the coast of the African continent for the first time in history, which further strengthened opportunities for Europeans via a sea route to India. As a result, the Spanish set out to explore the oceans to the west, while the Portuguese explored the east.

Christopher Columbus, encouraged by the Arabian idea, that the world was round, set sail from Spain in 1492, hoping to reach China and India, but after a perilous voyage, he sighted the Bahamas on October 12, 1492, claiming that this could only be the new world he had set out to discover. In fact, he thought he had reached India and because of this inaccuracy, he called the people who lived in the Americas "Indians", and the islands of the Caribbean the "West Indies". The Continent was later renamed "America" by another explorer Amerigo Vespucci in 1499. However, it was Spanish supremacy in the Caribbean that the French, Dutch and English explorers followed.

The First Caribbeans

When Columbus arrived in the Caribbean, he met the Arawaks (or Tainos as they were sometimes called), who inhabited the Greater Antilles. Julian Steward points out in Native and Peoples of South America, that Arawaks were divided into fives sub-groups; Taino, Sub-Taino, Ciguayo, Lucayo and Igneri. This classification, he states, was based on differences of languages, technology and ceramic and artistic styles which had developed as a result of years of isolation.

The Taino inhabited Hispaniola, except the south-western peninsulas. It is this group which comprised the main Arawakan group, who by the time the Spaniards arrived in the region had the highest level of linguistic refinement and artistic ceramic styles. They were the first group to be colonised and destroyed by Columbus and Spaniards. Other Arawakan groups, who had spread to other islands such as Trinidad, were the Igneri Arawaks. They spoke a different language from the Taino and were more warlike than other Arawakan groups.

The Sub-Taino occupied Central Cuba and Jamaica and were said to have been less culturally developed than the Taino. The Ciguayo, found in North Eastern peninsula of Hispanola, spoke a different language from the Taino and were said to have been a mixture of Caribs and Arawaks, with dominant Arawakan traits.

Characteristically, Arawaks were relatively peaceful, lived a settled life, of hunting and gathering and did subsistence farming. Today one can still see remains of their art in the Grenada museum which shows that they were expert potters with refined artistic ceramics. Though they were a Stone Age people, they had a complex set of religious beliefs and practices. They also had a decentralised political and hierarchical social structure, with absolute power invested in the hands of a cacique (ruler or chief who presided over dances, feasts, public festivals and law courts). Bartolome de das Casas states that they believed in some of form of after-life survival, and had a well-developed system of shamanism or priesthood.

The other native group was the Caribs. Like the Arawaks, they were Amerindians who had originated from South America, some 1000 AD, After the Arawaks, because by 1492, they had spread as far north as Cuba, some 500 years before Columbus, where they remained until they were almost extinct by European colonisation.

Unlike the Arawaks, they were warlike in nature and were skilful in their military exploits. A sea-faring people, with no Arawakan-like aristocracy, their society was based on skill, bravery and military prowess – not hereditary lineage. As a result theirs was a male-dominated society.

The Fight for European Supremacy

1.   The absolute necessity of these new colonies in building their trade, wealth and economic power in their metropolises.

2.   They saw the colonies as their exclusive property, so the monopoly of political and judicial institution was given to the Plantocracy or Landlords.

3.   Colonial interests were subordinated to metropolitan or imperial interests.

4.   The establishment of a rigid class structure and as a product of that class system racism emerged.

The overriding aim, however, was to build economic interests and prosperity for the individual European nation with each in its own period of dominance, monopolizing trade. When local labour became insufficient, there was a need for extra labour forces for the growing of sugar, tobacco, coffee and other crops. It was this insatiable need which initiated a trade in humans. Initially, this included white labour (in the form of convicts from Europe). Later the inclusion of white slaves became enforced legally by "An Act for the Importation of White Servants" (The Deficiency Laws of 1703). This empowered every owner and employer of slaves, to keep one white man for every 50 African slaves. What had begun as simply a trade in gold and ivory and pepper, became a huge trade in human cargo in the 17th, 18th and 19th centuries. This trade was part of a triangular route (known as the Middle Passage), where manufactured goods were taken from Europe to Africa. The goods were exchanged for slaves who were then taken to the Caribbean and Americas. The captured Africans were exchanged for sugar and other colonial products which were shipped back to Europe.

The trade in Africans across the Atlantic was the largest and most brutal in forced human migration the world has ever known. Once on the plantations mechanisms were brought into play, designed to affect a total break with the slaves' past in order to force adaptation to the new environment. The rigid organisation of life on the plantation and its oppressive discipline destroyed the slaves' individuality, and at the same time forcefully impressing on them a new personality, identity and the creation of stereotypes of Black slaves. The importation of slaves was heaviest between 1735 and 1779, the period when sugar enjoyed its greatest prosperity. (It remained the dominant crop throughout the slave period). However, slave rebellions and resistance against the brutality of their slave system was rife throughout the region. Rebellions took many forms: acts of self-mutilation of limbs, suicide, poisoning masters, maiming or killing one's child, escape and maroonage.

Escape and maroonage as collective rebellion, was widespread throughout the region, and can be said to have accounted for the weakening of the slave system. Orlando Patterson observes that in Jamaica numerous revolts took place during 1655 and 1832, the period of British rule. He states that in 1673 a rebellion broke out in St. Ann's and in 1760 another rebellion led by the Ghanaian Tackey, in which 60 whites were killed. The planters retaliated by killing over 600 Africans, many of whom had taken their own lives rather than surrender. In Trinidad, there was one recorded major plot in 1805 in which Africans tried to "get rid of all white men by grinding them in Mr. Shand's new windmill". In Berbice, a rebellion took place in Guyana in 1763, led by an African named Cuffy, but failed in its attempt to overthrow the Dutch administration.

Michael Craton states in, **Testing the Chains (2009),** that in Barbados there were major revolts beginning in 1649, with other detailed plots in 1675, 1683, 1686, 1701 and climaxing in the 1861 rebellion which involved 5000 Africans. Four hundred were killed when fires were set to estates in various parishes. Therefore, rebellion and revolt was a major feature in resistance and it was these continual threats to the plantation economic stability which played a major role in destabilising plantation. The threats and resistance drastically affected labour and precipitated support for the abolition of slavery.

Later, several slave uprisings resulted in greatly reduced manpower on the plantations and as a result, the plantation economy began to disintegrate in the late 18th century with acceleration during early 19th century. There were other factors which were responsible for its disintegration:

1.   Developing anti-slavery public opinion in Britain.

2.   The reform of the slave system by the Colonial Office.

3.   Economic factors such as the effect of the war of American Independence which affected trading levels, shortage of goods, increased export insurance, rising prices, competition from other sugar producers, (Cuba and Singapore), and a rapid increase in imports.

The decline of the sugar, cocoa and coffee industries in the Caribbean created crises for the colonials, whose adopted measures for controlling the situations, gave way to the growing demand for the abolition of slavery throughout the British Empire. A counter-attack in the form of pressure was brought to bear by the West Indian Assemblies of British planters, (comprising representatives from Barbados, Antigua, St. Kitts, Nevis, Virgin Islands, Dominica, Demerara and Essequibo, Tobago, St. Vincent and Grenada). They petitioned against the British Government's changing attitude towards slavery. They realised that the probability of an enforced end to their privileges and dependence on slavery, was fast approaching drastic restrictions, if not a complete end. Therefore, driven to the verge of desperation at their projected losses, slave owners complained to Britain:

> *"If we are continually to be considered as aliens and outcasts; if our local privileges are forever to be disregarded, our constitutional rights trodden under foot and the hard-earned produce of our estates fettered with rigorously unequal and ruinous imposition; if no merit is conceded to us for what we have effected in improving the moral conditions of our slaves…"*

Despite the benefits of the slave-owning planter-class, and the economic benefits which Britain enjoyed, the Anti-slavery Society made the Emancipation issue a part of British government politics. It resulted in the theoretical end to slavery only. **The Imperial Emancipation Act,** which was passed by Parliament in 1834, was sent to each island to be used as a guideline for implementation of local Emancipation Acts. It was not expected that the guidelines and advice would not be followed; the practicality of administering its principles in the Caribbean were full of complexities. Consequently, the period following this Act was seen as one of neo-servitude. W. L. Burn in **Emancipation and Apprenticeship:** in the British West Indies **(1937)**: states:

> *"It was a fatal flaw in the apprenticeship scheme that while it was based on one theory, much of its operation had been left at the mercy of men who believed in and had recently practised a theory entirely different."*

The result was Slave owners, who felt they had lost their legal privileges ignored implementation so that slavery was only abolished as a legal system. The slaves themselves were not emancipated in practice. Slavery became exchanged for another system - The apprenticeship system, (1834), which continued another form of slavery as a general system of industry.

> *"The apprentice remained an un-emancipated prisoner on the estate to which he was attached, substantially liable to the same punishments and labouring under the same incapacity as before, the whip followed him at every step, hard labour at every turn."*

This therefore explains why "Emancipation Day in Grenada and the rest of the British West Indies was 1st August 1838. Although slavery had been officially abolished since 31st July 1834, not until 1838 did slaves become fully free in the eyes of the law." Ironically, in their "freed" condition many slaves continued to work in the place of enslavement as peasants, the aged and infirm, too ill to economically maintain their 'freedom' became beggars, and paupers, devoid of health care and were ravaged by diseases.

Although Brizan was relating the Grenada situation in this statement, the situation he described was symptomatic of the general condition throughout the region. Compounded by these situations, planters abandoned their estates, many of which were encumbered with excessive debts. This made it difficult to diversify their produce and provide alternative production to save the estates.

However, the declining sugar industry became more depleted by fierce competition of beet sugar prices among European countries. Eric Williams (1984), states that "In 1852-54 beet sugar imports into Britain accounted for only 5% of the market; by 1858-60 it was 8%, and by 1864-66 to 14%." Whereas Jamaica had been one of Britain's principal producers of sugar, by 1880 Germany had become the leading beet producer, "producing 594,300 tons of beet compared with Jamaica's 16,800 tons of cane sugar."

To add to the problems in the post-Emancipation period, planters had to find a way of coaxing freed men to continue working for them and measures such as Tenants at Will, and the Labour-Rent system (a system which allowed labourers to occupy their accommodation and cultivate ground rent-free in exchange for steady labour). Ex-slaves who were later able to own or lease small freeholds of land from estates adjacent to where they lived existed as peasants, but many freed men had refused to work on the estates. This caused a depletion in the supply of available labour and as a result, the Colonial office introduced and financed the Indenture Labour Scheme in order to supplement labour.

Brizan (1998), "*Grenada, Island of Conflict*", quotes Roberts and Byrne as stating the "The Indentured Labour Scheme gave immigrants – liberated Africans, East Indians, Portuguese and Maltese, a chance to migrate into the region, in order to increase the supply of labour.

> "*Of the total number of immigrants to the West Indies 8.03% Portuguese, 30.9% Indian, 53.9% Africans went to the Leeward and Windward Islands ...*"

Indentureship – Manipulation Of Indians

As a strategy for rescuing the ailing plantations in the Caribbean, Indian Indentureship, in particular, drastically changed the composition of the regional populations whilst profoundly influencing the relationship between Africans and the European planter-class.

Both liberated and immigrant Africans demanded higher wages for their labour. However, the planters who were unable to succeed in enticing the Africans resorted to coercion and legal reforms. Where these had little effect, they opted to curtail resistance by manipulating Indian cheap labour against them. Britain at that time was ruler of India and was able to concede to the planters' request for immigrant Indian workers.

This alternative solution suited the planters who, Eric Williams states, were able to "obtain 2,500 Indians to be indentured in Trinidad....By 1917 when immigrants came to a halt, some 145,000 Indians had come to Trinidad". The planters were the real benefactors though, since the Indian immigrants worked for less than African workers."

Bridget Bereton (1982), in A History of Modern Trinidad, confirms that when sugar prices declined, due to the competition from beet sugar in Europe, and Indian immigration continued unabated, by 1917, "some estates employed virtually no Creoles (Africans) competition for jobs was noticeable and blacks were well aware that the Indians depressed wages and increased unemployment. The Trinidad Workingmen's Association, the spokesman for skilled black workers, argued in 1909 that while Indian Immigrants was not objectionable up to the late 1870's, its continuation after that time had injured the interests of Creole labourers". In this environment of discontent and fierce competition for willing workers, Indian immigration developed in the region.

In Guyana, the 1848 strike by Africans for more wages was broken up by indentured Indians and Portuguese. Eric Williams confirms the wave of Indian immigrants, "by 1917 as being 238,000 Indians had migrated to Guyana. Furthermore, William Sewell, an

American journalist, noted how areas that had been almost "ruined in 1846, had been transformed by the Indian workers to prosperity by 1859".

Jamaica also had its share of imported Indians as reported by Lord Oliver's *Jamaica: The Blessed Island*. He relates how having approached a Captain Baker, a planter in Jamaica, to ask why he had sent Jamaicans to Costa Rica and instead had imported Indians, Baker replied that he was not prepared to pay the high wages which Jamaicans were earning there.

The arrivals of these immigrants (later Chinese, Libyans, Syrians especially in Trinidad), to the existing mixed environment, changed the demographic structure of the region. It influenced the socio-economic, cultural, religious and racial patterns of the whole Caribbean area with consequences which exist at present. These consequences are to do with the migratory flow of people into the Caribbean region, and the impact of this for Caribbeans migrating out of the region and then returning with influences that have affected their levels of thinking and discourse in their Diasporas.   **(see Figure 1)**

Figure 1: The migratory flow of Caribbean peoples - Push & Pull Factors

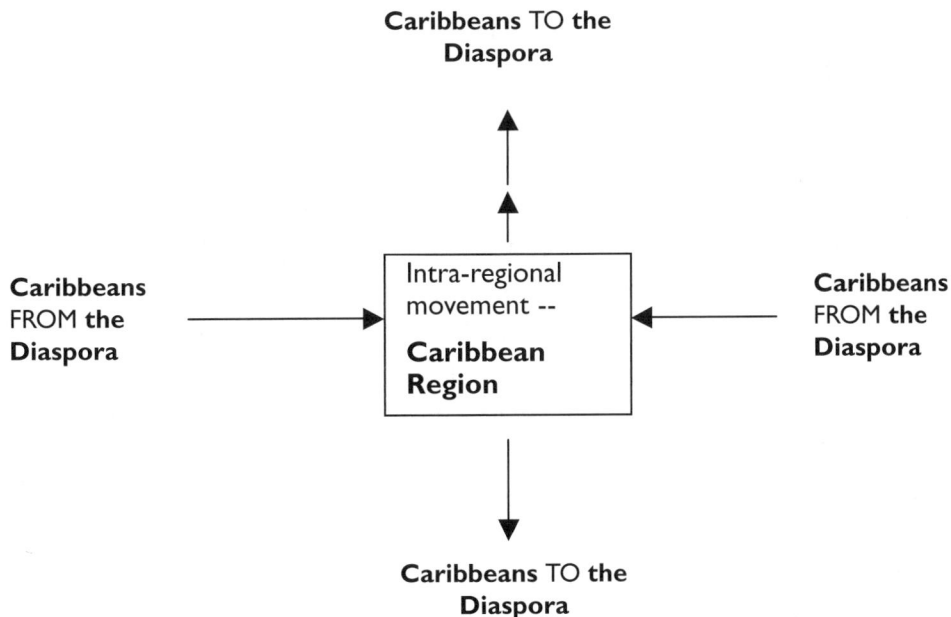

Caribbeans TO the Diaspora

↑

↑

| **Caribbeans FROM the Diaspora** → | Intra-regional movement --

 Caribbean Region | ← **Caribbeans FROM the Diaspora** |

↓

Caribbeans TO the Diaspora

Source: Adaptation from Aaron Segal's (1995):
Global Migration Trends, Macmillan Publishers, England, p. 38.

This also reflected the underlying historical, cultural, socio-economic and political experiences of the region. For example, the English language groupings in Grenada or St. Lucia are different from those of Jamaica or Barbados. The mixtures of racial influences and linguistic varieties as the chart shows is of central importance to an understanding of the development of the Creole languages, (as one example of cultural input), in the lives of millions of people in the Caribbean as well as Caribbeans across the globe.

The share in a common destiny attests to the region's plurality. Therefore, the plurality of Anglophone Caribbean culture, implicates that the region has common social features and not just linguistic connections. The processes that have created their characteristic features are largely due to exploration, trade, conquest, slavery, colonisation, immigration, imperialism and nationalism. Within this melting pot it is evident that the notion of unity exists, as well as diversity. It is also important to remember that within the Caribbean islands, there are marked differences in landscapes over distances, reflecting local responses to physical circumstances and it is this kind of individuality of quite small places, which leads people to refer to themselves as belonging to a particular place, possibly within parishes, rural or town areas and of course, not forgetting the "*big*" versus "small" island rivalries, (i.e. rivalry based on snobbery, the notion that "*bigger*" means "*better*" in every way. But how do islands such as Grenada, Barbados and Jamaica, which have their own island identity, share a common sense of Caribbean-ness in relation to a group identity? **(Table 1.1)**.

It is true that their shared interest in the game of cricket, the sun, seas and beaches, their collective attempt to form a Federation (1958), rum and coconut water, carnival and calypso, reggae music, rice and peas and so on; may be regarded as typically "Caribbean" and in a sense can be recognised as elements which make up or are part of the whole Caribbean. My view is that it can be any and all of those elements. Additionally, it may be that Caribbean people feel they are held together by a common background of historical trauma and value system which have ensured their survival up to the present day, which makes them "Caribbean" in a British setting.

What and where is the Caribbean?

We might say then, that the Caribbean is a set of islands in a sub-tropical context, curving from the greater Antilles to off the coast of Venezuela. We might include all the islands of the Antilles, Bahamas, Belize, Guyana and Suriname. However, the Caribbean is also a recognizable place in human consciousness. The identity arises from the same interaction of land and people who have similar environmental conditions, colonisation, imperialism, slavery, nationalism and super-power rivalry as well as a world economy that have contributed to their historical heritage. From these areas, migration to the UK since the 1940's, USA, Canada and the developing Caribbean countries in the Diaspora, implicates a wider Caribbean community.

Table 1:1:   Processes of Caribbean Development

TIMELINE	EVENTS
1492	Christopher Columbus 'discovered' The Bahamas
1499	Amerigo Vespucci renamed the Caribbean 'America'
1703	Introduction of the Deficiency Laws – importation of White servants
1773-1779	Importation of African slaves in the West Indies
1834	Slavery officially abolished
1838	African slaves became 'fully freed'
1917	Influx of Indians as indentured labourers to Trinidad and Guyana
1948	Establishment of the University of the West Indies
1958	Formation of the West Indian Federation
1950s-1960s	Second wave of British West Indians' to Britain
1960s-1970s	Britain grants Political Independence to most of the West Indies
1963	Creation of Caribbean Free Trade Area (Carifta)
1972	Inauguration of Caribbean Festival of Creative Arts in Guyana
1973	Founding of the Caribbean Community Common Market (Caricom)
1981	Creation of the Organisation of Eastern Caribbean States (OECS)
1981	Establishment of the Caribbean Examinations Council (CXC)
2000	Introduction of the Caribbean Single Market Economy (CSME)

Interestingly, one of the consequences of this Diaspora is that **the Caribbean** might now include **a state of mind** for many exiles and their children, with a lessening of the notion of an actual place. Certainly from the histories above, it is from these perspectives there appears to be a sense of common history of colonisation, displacement, slavery, indenture, emancipation and nationalism. All these have helped shaped the Caribbean environment, and have created a unity of experience, identified as particularly Caribbean.

Within that unity is diversity and this presents other dilemmas which gives rise to questions about Caribbean identity and its culture. So, what is Caribbean identity? There are, no doubt, problems associated with locating a uni-cultural identity in the Caribbean and attempting to do is fraught with difficulties for reasons already outlined above. Charting the various migrant flows into the region highlights the plural nature of the environment and like Caribbean identity, questions about Caribbean culture also produces a similar dilemma. Therefore, how does one determine what identity and culture are in relation the Caribbean?

Problems of Locating Culture/Identity

Paul Willis (2003), states that the concept of 'identity' has "become an important and much used theoretical and substantive category of connection and relation". This is seen as containing a variety of forms, so that one can talk of culture on several levels e.g. culture of institutions, places, sexual and ethnic groupings.

On the human level, it relates to interpersonal relationships to the norms and practices of groups, and values. However, this can be widened to embody the society, representation, social imagery, economic, political and ideological determinations since they all have cultural meaning; an originary in terms of how its formed and seen to operate.

The concept of culture, which is inextricably linked to *identity*, provides the fillip for groups and individuals wanting to take an active responsibility in the making, or indeed re-making, a sense of self, despite historically social and prescribed identity. However, it remains difficult to define - it is not a clear-cut, unified, discipline, with concepts which distinguish it from other subjects.

Aspects of culture are already studied under sociology, anthropology, literature, and a range of geographically related subjects and via regional institutions such University of the West Indies, as well as via activities of CARICOM (the Caribbean Common Market) and the Caribbean Examinations Council, (CXC). Therefore by virtue of its multi-or post-disciplinary field of inquiry, we can agree that as a concept, *culture is cantered on questions of representation*. In other words, how the world is socially constructed and represented to, and by, us in meaningful ways. Stuart Hall (1996c:439), defines it as "*the actual grounded terrain of practices, through its concern with shared social meanings, that is the various ways we make sense of the world."* Therefore, in order to understand culture, we need to explore how meaning is produced symbolically in culture as a language and as a 'signifying system' for Caribbean people. For the most part cultural studies as a subject, interrogates language at its heart, so are theories of language, representation, subjectivity, and the ethnography of lived experiences.

There are various differences within western cultural studies as to whether theory developed in one context can be workable in another. Work on this subject has been developed in Britain, USA, Continental Europe and Australia. As such, there is very little reference here to a growing body of work elsewhere i.e. from Africa, Latin America, Asia. However, it is for these reasons that since the subject under discussion is located in Caribbean cultural studies, I felt it pertinent to conduct field research in the Caribbean region to investigate the social and cultural conditions there, with regard to Caribbean culture.

Caribbean cultural representation and meanings are embedded in **sounds, images, texts, technological texts (TV, computer, audio visual, electronic**), are produced, used and understood in specific social contexts. Additionally, we have already mentioned that from a modern industrialised perspective, as well as centred on practices, the study of culture is connected with political economy i.e., with power, and distribution of economic and social resources. Therefore who owns and controls the cultural production of one country, its landscape, distribution, has implications for control of the cultural landscape.

George Lamming's characters are concerned with this very issue in his early classic novel, **In the Castle of My Skin** (1953). The novel, set in the early post-colonial era, articulates the concerns of post-colonial Barbados. A central concern for the characters is, **who owns and farms the land**, in a region where the legacy of colonialism, is in contrast with emerging national consciousness being debated among an older, and younger generation respectively.

Having said that, culture is not explainable or reducible solely in terms of another level of social formation. But the process of political economy, social relationships must be understood in terms of their modes of development. Each of these is 'articulated' in specific ways, so that context of **class, race, ethnicity, gender, sex and age,** have their own particularity, which cannot be reduced to political economy or to each other. There is a sense of overlap in the other. This is discussed in chapter 3, highlighting the role of Caribbean women within the Caribbean family structure. Therefore, to understand the notion of class is to understand that Caribbean culture is tied up with identity, but more specifically the historical processes, which have engendered the plural environments in the region.

But these processes too have implications for Caribbean people and their children in the Diaspora (e.g. Britain). The question of *what is it like to be the person who we are? How have we come to be what we are? And How do we identify with descriptions of ourselves as Caribbeans, or African-Caribbean, Indo-Caribbean, Anglo-Caribbean, Hispano-Caribbean and French-Caribbean, as well as black, white, Indian, male/female, young/old or even Caribbean-Black or Black British,* are issues that such studies explore. These have to be understood by those who give meaning to the *words, sounds, images, gestures, noises and silences* of Caribbean articulation.

Culture and Globalisation

Presently, globalisation, now at the beginning of the 21st century, has caused a reductionist appeal in world cultures. It means there is now greater ease of non-physical accessibility (via the TV and internet), as well as the speed of travel around the world. It also means that the word *'culture'*, once related to specific, settled places, and boundaries which give the impression of an authentic, pure and natural landscape, does not necessarily hold sway today. Barker's view (2003) is that "globalisation" has made it impossible to identify boundaries and "has made the idea of culture as a whole way of life Increasingly problematic".

The conclusion is that we can no longer talk of Caribbean culture as being located solely in the Caribbean region. Other perspectives on location suggest that the local is now interfered with to the point of there being trans-local processes, Robertson (1992). In other words, place is socially constructed (as seen annually in Notting Hill in Britain each year. Notting Hill becomes "the Caribbean" symbolically, territorialized by Caribbean's for the purpose of identification, historical and emotional investment) for the past 30 years. This re-enactment involves redefining the meaning of a place in that it involves dislocating authenticity claims to a place, in favour of the symbolic.

We can then begin to talk of hybrid cultural identification, endorsed by Bhabha (1994), who sees the notion of culture, identities and identifications as always a place of *borders and hybrid – not fixed*. However, based on these perspectives, there is a value in locating culture 'in-place' and as synthesis of people, language and the meeting of several cultures as an early form of "multiculturalism" in the Caribbean region.

It begins with a process known as *the Creolisation process*. Meaning, the development of an identifiable Caribbean culture in the region. The pattern of development has been a movement from indigenous or Amerindian cultures through America, having become fused with a variety of European cultural interactions. Consequently, this has moved beyond the region to the Diaspora in places such as Britain, North America, and Canada, where Dub, Rap and performance poetry, hip-hop, garage or urban music have symbolic popular cultural significance. In other words, there is a dual role. Barker (2003), sees it as "the duality of culture being both in place and of no place!

Caribbean Culture is?

Based on the above, we can agree that culture is tied up with people's ways of life, customs, dress, belief, the way they think and react, how they great each other, prepare food and the way in which they express themselves in say, art: in other words, the structure of their social life. It is also linked to a person's attitude to the world, those around him— in short, his cultural up-bringing. Therefore, one's culture can be said to identify him/her. However, whilst it may identify people, over a long time culture undergoes degrees of alteration, which affect its survival, depending on various influences, (e.g. socially, geographically, politically)..

The culture of Caribbean people is an example of this thought, from the point of view that it began from a common root, transferred to Britain and the Diaspora, and is affected by other cultural inputs in global settings. Over a period of time, this has been shown to manifest in various expressions of a "root" ideology, but metamorphosed in ways which are no longer entirely Caribbean and consequently makes Caribbean cultural development in Britain rather interesting.

We know that the first Caribbeans were Amerindians; therefore their culture is linked to the forest or natural landscape. Had this remained untouched by European contact, that culture would be unmistakably, an Amerindian folk culture? However, the picture altered drastically with imported cultures from European conquest – colonization and European expansion, making the Caribbean culture a fusion of imported cultures (i.e. plural in description because the European colonization came in the form of not only the British, but French, Dutch and Spanish). This makes the question of what Caribbean culture is one of origin and ancestry so important. In other words, Caribbean culture may be said to be a fusion of various cultural influences; seemingly originating from a model of instability, thereby making it difficult to pinpoint a pure/original cultural strain. What then do we identify the culture of the Caribbean as being, given it multiplicity of strains?

One approach is to look at the people who roughly comprise the majority, their appearance, their thoughts, their ethnic stock, their similarity of landscape and experience, in order to get a sense of homogeneity, with a plural context. Plural societies are those where different people of different cultural backgrounds live together within an accepted political framework. Britain today is an example of such a culture, popularly called a multicultural society – so is USA, East African countries and the Caribbean.

Plural societies

This means that these plural societies have resulted from cultural contact, whether by invasion, colonization, and migration or by being in close proximity to other cultures (ideas and expressions). An example of this is the case of America and the Caribbean, where the influence of the mass media can be seen to intrude, or sap the vitality of Caribbean folk culture.

The social history of what happened in the Caribbean gives a greater understanding of how the influences manifest themselves in the new environment. The Europeans came as mercantile invaders, with military might. They set up structures to ensure their "new" territory was protected from other zealous European competitors by creating structures such as forts, courts, prisons, plantations and the dominance of their languages, to the exclusion of all others, as the medium of communication. However, the Africans had bought with them their culture i.e., their ways of life, customs, beliefs, ways of thinking and discourse intact in their psyche. Therefore their religious practices, drumming, dancing, storytelling, methods of reasoning, survival strategies, were stubbornly preserved, secretly submerged and mysteriously processed among them, to ensure their survival in the face of the greatest form of brutality and suffering ever known to man – slavery.

The indentured East Indians who came into the environment after the slaves, arrived with their own brand of culture, which was less fragmented compared with the Africans. They were unwilling to mix with the Africans and therefore were able to preserve their own cultural characteristics, with less strict imposition on self-expressions. They adjusted to the Caribbean environment, whilst maintaining certain aspects of their culture intact.

It has to be remembered that the Europeans who came to the Caribbean were not of one race. Among the British colonialists were Scottish, Welsh, Irish and English men, who were forced to live and interact among the African slave labourers (The Deficiency Laws 1907). Each brought with them their own brand or style of European/Celtic culture as well as Dutch, French and Spanish cultures; all fusing to create a melting pot of many cultures.

Figure 1.2: The Making of the Caribbean – Migratory Flow

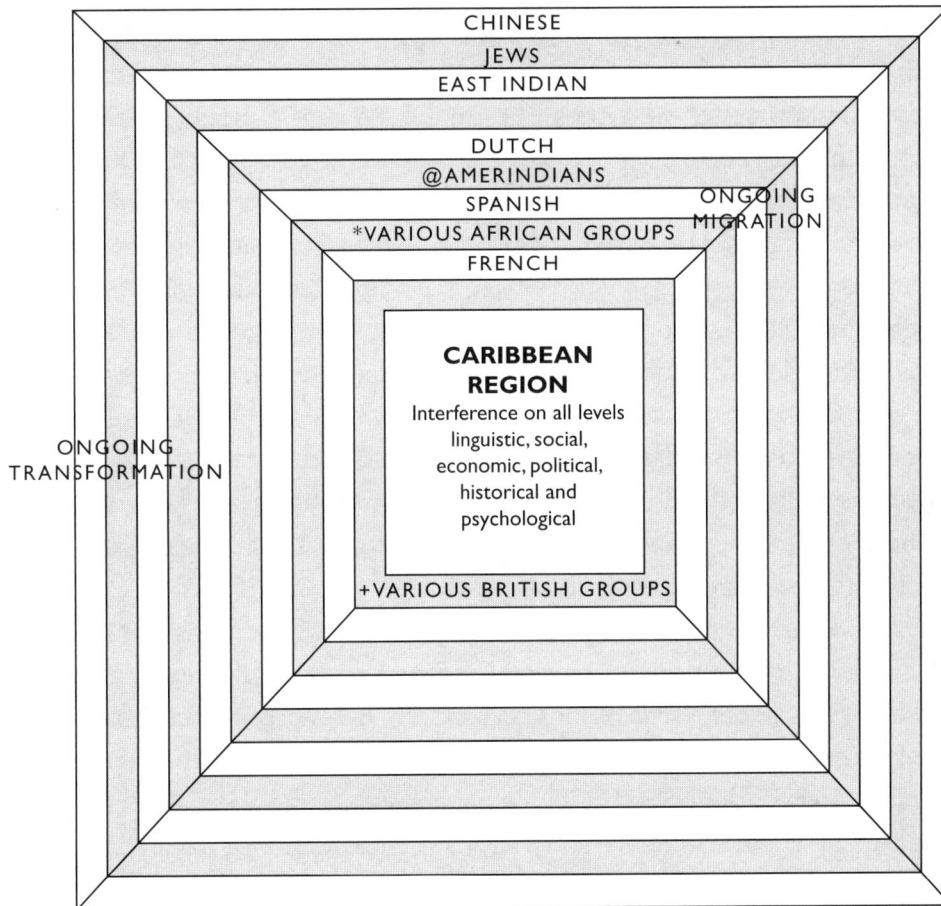

CHINESE
JEWS
EAST INDIAN

DUTCH
@AMERINDIANS
SPANISH
*VARIOUS AFRICAN GROUPS
FRENCH

ONGOING
MIGRATION

CARIBBEAN REGION
Interference on all levels
linguistic, social,
economic, political,
historical and
psychological

ONGOING
TRANSFORMATION

+VARIOUS BRITISH GROUPS

This cultural mêlée developed in the Caribbean amidst tension of body and spirit, among the entire various group the depleted Amerindians who became

Notes: The above figure represents the various ethnic and cultural layers that converge in the region leading to the Creolisation of its language and culture. .

(+) These group comprise Scottish, Irish, Welsh and a variety of local English dialects from a mixture of social classes, including ex-convicts, white slaves, planters, colonial administrators.

(*) These include Agoras, Ahantas, Akuapems, Akyems, Ashantis, Asantes, (after 1874), Borons, Congolese, Fantes, Dwanwu, Sehwi, Wasa) from both slaves and liberated Africans. @This group is divided into five sub-groups.

aloof and decimated in numbers by plantation materialism.   The largest contingent in the region – African slaves, co-existed with Indentured East Indians and European dominators; with no political pressure towards synthesis.   But what happens to a society such as the Caribbean, which appeared to be culturally fragmented, and whose submerged cultural processes were surviving among the largest racial grouping in the region, despite colonial prohibition?

The ancestral consciousness of the slave, the preservation of the essence of Africa, the deep cultural intransigence of the slave ideology, manifested itself in resistance of various kinds, song, dance, arts, in ways which are more Caribbean. The borrowing of gods from the "Old" environment and infusing them with added characteristics, lend themselves to the "New" environment. For example, the **African,** Attibon Legba, Ogun, Yemayah, Osha, Oshun and Shango are linked with Caribbean expressions on many levels. The fusion or synthesis with the **European** Christ, Lazarus, the Virgin Mary, Saint Michael the Archangel with the **Indian** Vishnu, Shiva, Brahma and the gods of the **Amerindians**, is a phenomenon which makes it uniquely Caribbean; meaning "reborn", in the region with new expressive characteristics.

The fusion of culture can be seen across the region in the congas of Martinique and Trinidad, *Kumina* or *Pocomania* of Jamaica, *Queh-queh* of Guyana, *Shango* of Grenada, the possessed white dancers (*vodoun)* of Cuba and the Bahia province of Brazil. These cultural consciousnesses transcend the carved Apinti drums of Surinam, and the painted assator of Haiti. The conclusion is that all the cultural inputs into the Caribbean region have proved to be adaptable. Today, understanding these Caribbean characteristics is vital in identifying how we make meaning of labels such as "West Indian", "Caribbean" and "black", within the complexity of such a phenomena   In more recent times, there has been further sub-categorization for study within academia, which refers to Indo-Caribbean, African-Caribbean, Anglophone Caribbean, Hispanophone Caribbean and Francophone Caribbean.(**Figure 1.3**)

When we begin to examine its infrastructure, the Caribbean we realise has its corresponding reference to indigenous and migrant input and they in turn make up the whole. The political, legal and economic structures we have inherited are Caribbean today, are clearly European Caribbean in nature. The Caribbean is divided into Nation states that represent monarchies or republics. The majority of the Anglophone or English-speaking regions have Queen Elizabeth II, (the Queen of England) as their Head of State.

While others like Guyana, Cuba, Trinidad and Tobago, Dominican Republic, Surinam have an Executive Presidency with the Prime Minister as Head of the Cabinet. Other states which have a combination of Governor-Generals and Prime Ministers have Executive powers in their countries. These structures were brought in, set up and adapted by the Europeans to suit the local environment. It is for this reason that the early imitative styles within Caribbean society suited the Europeans in the region. The imitation is infused in the infrastructure – ranging from importation of priests, styles of churches and their order of services, courts, and the education system.

Figure 1.3: Caribbean Cultural Influences

Global Mass Media	multimedia technology and traditional media
Caribbean oral and literary forms	old and new
Multiculturalism	nature of food, clothing and other consumables
Festivals	annual Notting Hill Carnival, festivities featuring other genres
Cultural Fusion	African religious spirituality, Indian, European and other traditions
Language Expressions	Creole dialect (African/Indian/European), Standard English etc

In order to understand Caribbean dances, religious practices, food preparation, ways of conducting business, songs and their meaning in a social context; we have to acknowledge the fusion of an African, European and Indian traditions in the region. For example, the "shouts" of Shouter Baptists speaking in "African tongues", the grunting and panting of Shango in religions practices are vestiges of an African culture which still exist in the region. In fact, if we delve deeper into religious practices in the Caribbean, we will realize that elements of Caribbean religious services have psycho-religious significance based on old forms of African worship. It is also not unusual to find utterances of languages e.g. Twig, Ga, Fante, (unknown to the speaker), are really vestiges of Africanisms which have permeated the Caribbean psyche and find expression in certain circumstances.

However, Africa was presented as "a dark continent" and everything associated with it was considered negatively. The psychological level of thinking, and certainly the prevailing notion, was that everything and anything European was better. In other words, education, the Euro-appearance with "good hair," suggesting fair skin with long or straight hair was more acceptable. Consequently, the flourishing of the "hot" comb for straightening Caribbean hair and bleach creams for lightening the skin became a preoccupation for social acceptance among Caribbeans. This did not stop there, European languages especially Standard English (in the English speaking Caribbean, the language of the master, was the ordered medium of communication.

Therefore words such as **dis** for **this**, **dat** for **that**, **unnou** for **you**, **nyam** for **eat** and **dey** for **they** (language derived from a fusion of languages in the region),were frowned upon. The Catholic Church and its Latin mass, (though largely not understood by its congregation), were the elements which wooed masses away from African forms of worship. Consequently, the European culture of the Caribbean was the preferred model, since it stood for 'excellence' and what was 'the best'. This was the beginning of material achievement imposed in the region. Interestingly, Caribbean culture (which was earlier submerged, in the face of colonial prohibition), continued to develop and take root and owes its survival in Creole linguistic expressions we have in the region.

It was the move towards self-government, which signalled a challenge to colonialism. Caribbean leaders began to look for alternatives forms of governance through the socialist experiment, as those in Cuba, Russia and China. It was felt that their struggles were equated with those countries, seen as class struggles. Therefore, emphasis was placed on ideology, class, culture and this signalled the beginning of the socialist experiment in the Caribbean region in the 1980's.

Interestingly, Caribbean leaders mimicked some of the cultural programmes of these countries with less emphasis on Africanisms. The trend of self-determination reached its peak in 1972; through the festival of Caribbean Arts, known as CARIFESTA. A total of 22 provinces of the Caribbean region brought together 4000 artists, an audience of 10,000, was held in Guyana, in what seemed to have been a 'declaration of cultural independence'.

The impetus for such a movement began in 1978, in Bogota, Colombia, when delegates at a UNESCO conference on culture, called for an assessment of the economic value of the cultural industries in the Caribbean region. This conference affirmed, **"Governments must invest in their countries cultural intangible, genetic ethical heritages of humanity and above all, promote creative capacity through arts, artists, and other development initiatives"**.

What was interesting about the first ever CARIFESTA in the region, was that the richness of the cultural fusion in the Caribbean, highlighted its unique characteristics. It acknowledged the plurality of the region in a myriad of ways - from the sound of deep African psyche, the Kumina/Shango drums, the Djukas of Suriname, Hindustani and Javanese dancers, East Indian music, the mellow tones of home-grown Caribbean troubadors, steel pan, soca , rapso, reggae, the wooing of the Indian sita; European classics - Beethoven and Bach, or simply a fusion of all in one.

Within all of those cultural elements are the individual methods of food preparation, children song-games, storytelling, manner of dressing, social functions and events, and a development of various linguistic varieties fusing to create a Caribbean culture in the region. A salient description of the culture of the Caribbean is defined as **unity in diversity**. More succinctly, it is expressed in Caribbean popular parlance as; *"all ah we is one! "* meaning; *we are all one people!*

This **Unity in Diversity** sentiment is less perpetuated in Britain today, given the many societal dilemmas encountered by Caribbean-heritage people in the society. The third generation strata of Caribbean migrants have a different experience, compared with their grandparents (first migrants), as will be discussed in Chapter 6. These have given rise to paradoxes within their existence and have far-reaching consequences for them, their families and Britain as a whole.

SELECTED CHAPTER REFERENCES

1. Bridget Bereton (1963): *A History of Modern Trinidad 1783-1963*:Heinemann, London.

2. Craton M: (2009): <u>*Testing the Chains: Resistance to Slavery in the British West Indies*</u>: Cornell University Press

3. Brizan G. (1998), *Grenada, Island of Conflict: from Amerindians to Peoples Revolution 1498 to 1979: Zed Books, London*

4. Burn W. L. (1937): *Emancipation and Apprenticeship: in the British West Indies* Johnson Reprint Corp (1970).

5. Williams **Eric** (1984): *From Columbus to Castro:The History of the Carib*bean 1492-1969, Harper & Row (1970).

6. Sewell W. Jr. (2005):*Logics of History: Social Theory and Social Transformation (Chicago Studies in Practices of Meaning)*.University of Chicago Press.

7. Lord Oliver: Jamaica: The Blessed Island

8. Hall S (1996*); Questions of Cultural Identity*:The Open University & Sge Publications, London

9. Lamming G. (1953): *In the Castle of My Skin,* Michael Anthony, London:

10. Patterson O. (1973):*The Sociology of Slavery:An Analysis of the Origins, Development and Structure of Negro Slave Society in Jamaica*: Sangster's Book Stores Limited.

11. Barker C. (2003):'Foreword' to *Cultural Studies:Theory and Practice*, Sage Publications, London.

12. Bhabha H. (1994): *The Location of Culture*, Routledge, London

13. Willis P. (2003):'Foreword' to *Cultural Studies:Theory & Practice*, Sage Publications, London.

14. Sherlock <u>J. H.; Philip Sherlock and Anthony Maingot Parry</u>: *A Short History of the West Indies,* (1988) Palgrave Macmillan.

Chapter Notes:

The Apprenticeship System, (1834) came about after the abolition of slavery in the nineteenth century. In the British Caribbean between 1834 and 1838, a law was passed by the British Parliament to abolish slavery throughout the empire. The apprenticeship system was designed to ease the transition from slavery to freedom by forcing the ex-slaves to remain on their plantations for a period of six years. Its main purpose was to prevent the immediate large-scale abandonment of estates by the workers. The irony was the masters, and not the slaves, were awarded compensation for the *loss* of their "property." The system proved too cumbersome to administer and was prematurely terminated in 1838. Barbados and Antigua abolished slavery without an apprenticeship system in 1834.

The Caricom Community & Common Market Council or CARICOM, was established in 1973 with the signing of the Treaty of Chaguaramas, Port of Spain, Trinidad. Currently, the regional grouping comprise 13 Member States mostly English-speaking, except Cuba and Haiti (Spanish- and French-speaking countries respectively.

The Deficiency Laws 1703: This empowered every slave owner to keep one white man for every 50 African slaves.

2 | Caribbean Family Structure: Towards A British Caribbean Identity

Introduction

This chapter analyses at length, the composition of the Caribbean family and the dynamics that interplay between this social unit and the rest of society – be it civic or otherwise. The roles of women are highlighted, to document their contribution to the strong matriarchal family pattern in the Caribbean and the resulting impact this has for their settled life in Britain.

I particularly chose to look at the role of women, in this chapter, to provide a context to the Caribbean identity and family development in Britain. This is because a large proportion of the British Caribbean family is dominated and headed by Caribbean women. A background to the Caribbean family structure and the dominance of one-parent families, headed by women in Britain, need to be understood in context. At times, this type of family structure is referred to as "one-parent families" and at other times regarded as, "fragmented or broken homes", generally meaning dysfunctional, since it does not equate with the British social and traditional view of the nuclear "family" i.e. mother, father and children living in a home as one unit..

There is therefore an anomaly in the various views of what constitute *a family* and the prevailing role of managing emotional behavioural difficulties (EBD), in Britain by a great many Caribbean females. But what has made this so? How does it present cultural conflicts and corresponding difficulties with educational achievement in Britain today?

In attempting to redress the balance of available documentation on Caribbean women's contribution to their society, and as a way of stimulating discussions and interest on this subject, this chapter will begin by focusing on Caribbean's women's collective contribution to family development in their traditional environment, in order to understand their attempts to continue in a British context. This is done in order to demonstrate the relevance of the women's position, (especially when living in societies with few natural or financial resources), in overcoming their problems of multiple dependency. Firstly, this means dependency, in the old environment in the Caribbean on industrialised countries; and counteracting poverty and unemployment, despite being part of an international economic order in which the odds are heavily against them. Secondly, it highlights their difficulties in managing in Britain today, where the structures which were available and supported them in the Caribbean, are absent. More specifically, these were to do with the roles of extended families and the community in helping to raise children.

It is true to say that there have been few individuals in each Caribbean island, whom one can attribute certain developmental roles to e.g. *Nanny of Jamaica, +Higgins of Antigua (to name a couple which relate to their individual island's history). However, the real effectiveness of women's contribution as a whole, regionally, have shown that penetrating the higher echelons of administration and policy-makers have been more visible and continue to be so by regional, collective counteraction and interaction.

Within this context, I will examine how women's contribution is expressed in the Caribbean geographical setting, i.e. the physical landscape. Within this landscape, as "man-made" construct,   I'll show how the histories which the region contains, give rise to the psychological levels of thinking and discourse, which are peculiar to the women in the region. It will also show that the effects of neo-colonialism and industrialisation in the region, have made women's contribution tenuous through a number of invidious processes. These are as follows:

1. The historical heritage of economic and political dependence on England during slavery and colonialism.

2. North American influence in the post-independence decades, (1960s - 1980s) and the Creole culture of the Caribbean.

3. Women's development in relation to Caribbean men, thereby charting a sociological process as it affects them, in terms of power and resistance to suppression.

4. "Contribution" seen as a metaphor for a "journey of discovery" of themselves, their strengths and potential, in the Caribbean region.

No doubt this social development would have implications for the women's view of themselves, their abilities, and expectations of their individual and family advancement in Britain. As members of the diverse minority communities in London, there are times when, on the personal level, the clash of cultures would have caused a sense of confusion for these women and their families. For example, certain Caribbean traditions which formed part of their early life principles, were either not accepted in Britain, not popular or gave a negative impression to the host community. This is best described by looking at the foundation or Caribbean life-principles, compared with situations where they failed to find their correlative in England.

Caribbean Life Principles

1. **RESPECT FOR ELDERS.** Firstly, this is most important to Caribbeans, and is firstly evident in forms of greeting to everyone, known or unknown and in ALL places. Many migrants talk of the difficulty of continuing this tradition in England simply because to continually say, "*Morning*" to a total stranger, would result in strange looks and questions about one's sanity. Therefore, even to this day, I would consciously refrain from greeting people and limit this to Caribbean older people, who always acknowledged you with raised eyebrows and a smile, the fact that you still adhered to the old traditions.

    Of course it causes a certain degree of confusion because on returning to the Caribbean one had to be consciously become aware of this requirement on a a full-time basis. The refreshing admiration comes when on entering a bus, one person says, "*Good morning*" and absolutely everyone on the bus replies! This invigorates the Caribbean past and confirms the present reality with absolute admiration.

2. **EDUCATIONAL EXCELLENCE** is instilled as the ultimate personal goal and therefore a competitive spirit exists among children in schools in the Caribbean. The complexity of expectations of a Caribbean migrant child in Britain has to do with surviving and wanting to excel in an environment where this does not necessarily hold the same significance among children. The reason for this is the many competing ideologies in society, the difference in family structure and teacher expectation, mean that one is left to drive their own determination to succeed.

Difference of education in the Caribbean v's U.K.

3.   **RESPECT FOR AND BELIEF IN GOD.** The Caribbean child is taught to believe that the centre of one's life is Godliness and going to church is compulsory. The manner of dress, and importance attached to this activity is not one which children had a choice in. Additionally, this activity was seen as the means of moral and spiritual development – a family undertaking which is a MUST. The challenges in a British environment, in the 1960's had to do with the choice to stay at home, the lack of cultural activities in the church, styles of worship, the racial composition of the congregation and their different attitudes to foreign worshippers.

Additionally, **praying as a family** unit (e.g. All family members are regarded as immediate Carers, and extended members could administer discipline and reprimand when necessary), and associated with religious principles is the strong sense of **discipline. This is accepted as** an all-embracing responsibility for ALL adults (whether blood related or not) who can reprimand any child. This is similar to the African proverb that *a child is raised by a village*. As a result, it is the accepted norm that a child would never challenge an older person's advice openly or answer back. In a British environment, because the educating principles are different, this allowable behavior across the cultural divide in Britain, has confused Caribbean parents and is a major source of conflict in the home. Added to this conflict is that physical **punishment,** which is seen as corrective and imbedded within a cultural framework in the Caribbean but is not acceptable in Britain.

4.   **RESPECT FOR INSTITUTIONAL AUTHORITY – ACCEPTANCE OF THE STRUCTURES OF SOCIETY –** encourages one to be a part of them and fosters individual aspirations. On the personal level, as this was part of my life principle, I found the indifference among people, did not distract me from appreciating the importance of this aspect of my life.

5.   **EDUCATION** in the Caribbean is seen as a development process which has to be revered because it changes the status of individuals and their family. More specifically, the fact that it engenders pride in whole families. My grandmother called it *"raising the family's nose"*! It is therefore understandable why she instilled in me the necessity of my present motto, *"I am Somebody Great!"* I have, throughout my life in England, adhered to this affirmation and have instilled in many thousands of people, whose lives I have been fortunate to touch, the same principle of belief, and high aspirations.

As Founder and Principal of the TCS Tutorial College for the past 15 years, I have made it the College Motto. Therefore, I am happy to say that this same principle has been responsible for the many successes of those past and present students of the College. This is a life principle, born in the Caribbean some half a century ago, which I hold very dearly because of its life-changing qualities and the encouragement and hope it gives to those who dare to believe in it. The converse in the Caribbean was that failure is seen as reprehensible or an anathema to our tradition of excellence and achievement. That is why to this day, **success is** recognized and celebrated – within families, among locals who share in the pride, regionally, nationally and with full involvement of media (from school achievement to competitive activities beyond educational establishments). Without these in place in the UK, one has to draw on his/her own strength and life principle to overcome their absence in a host community. In fact, it is my belief that if the objective conditions do not exist, one has to create them.

6. **INVOLVEMENT WITH CRIME AND THE LAW:** in the Caribbean a family has a sense of shame attached to any family member associated with forms of lawbreaking. This is because there are repercussions for the individual, family members, and their immediate local community members (e.g. village). This is one aspect of Caribbean moral that has been evaporating almost imperceptibly in the past century. This is evident by the levels of crime and criminal activities among the younger generations in Britain. It is also an area of Caribbean life in Britain which concerns me greatly, despite understanding the difficulties on both sides of the cultural divide. There are many challenges which face young Caribbean children in the UK , which will be alluded to later on in this book,

7. **FELLOWSHIP & TOGETHERNESS** – local groups gathering, sharing and developing cultural mores. In a British setting, given the spread in demography of Caribbean peoples in Britain, this proved difficult in the 50's and 60's, limiting one's sense of cultural development. It is easy to see how this aspect of Caribbean life has taken other forms, as a means of survival. The early Caribbeans had "blues parties", to create cultural gatherings, in the absence of churches which were predominantly or wholly "white". This accounts for the rise in "black" churches in Britain today, where Black and Minority Ethnic (BME) communities can re-create their known forms of worship with overwhelming numbers in their congregations.

8. **CARIBBEAN CHILDREN ARE BROUGHT UP TO SHOW RESPECT FOR PUBLIC PROFESSIONS** (nurses, teachers, doctors, clerks, etc) – usually it is a first career aspiration, because they provide role models which are immediately available outside the home. Additionally, a similar expectation is **respect for the law.** In the Caribbean context, (though circumstances may have changed), all families shared in upholding the law. And because of the respect associated with the law, representatives of the law were not seen as contentious and oppositional.

    as opposed to now they are viewed in Britain.

9. **FAMILY KINSHIP** is important – whether as a nuclear unit or extended, the same importance and respect is attached to *absent* parents. Other principles are associated with the correct **dress code. This is** extremely important to Caribbean children who will have specific clothes devoted to particular occasions and events. **Cleanliness too is accorded the** state of being *next to Godliness* – a maxim every Caribbean child learns and applies with pride to one's appearance.

10 **ADDRESSING PEOPLE** – absolute respect for seniority (in age, is shown in forms that prefix peoples names, e.g., *Mr. Mrs. Miss, Uncle, Aunty, Brother, Sister and Teacher.* This culture of respect and formality has been perpetuated by the strong matriarchal arrangement in the Caribbean. In England, this is likely to be laughed at, so a challenge to a Caribbean child is that initially this is extremely uncomfortable, if not confusing to let go, until full conformity to the British non-adherence. Perhaps the greatest difference for Caribbean families is the lack of grandparent involvement in the bringing up of children in the British Caribbean family. In the Caribbean, grandparents are pillars of a family unit, and are the ultimate reference point for all conflicts and disharmony. They represent the Peacemakers who hold cultural wisdom and knowledge and are the recipients of unconditional respect from all younger people.

    Perhaps the biggest challenge for the migrant Caribbean woman in the UK, is the lack of equal participation of women in all sections of British society. Women in the Caribbean have for some time, been instrumental in many of the region's changes - from *cultural archives* to Heads of government; heads of industry and Churches; leaders of communities and organizations, in ways that are very different in Britain. The call for gender equality and Equality Laws in the recent past in Britain, are not new facets of society for Caribbean peoples. The Caribbean female's sense of unbridled power, probably accounts for the fact that Caribbean women have the highest rate of business start-ups in Britain, at 25%; compared to the UK national average of 22%. It confirms the Caribbean woman's ideal, that nothing is out of her reach, a life principle that is an integral part of life in the Caribbean **(See Figure 2.1)**. This belief has been challenged many times - firstly by the gender disparity in Britain and secondly as not only as a female but also the added component of racism – being female and black crate its own monumental challenges among all sections of British society.

Figure 2.1: Caribbean Life Principles

Respect for Elders	greeting and addressing people in a courteous manner
Education Excellence	inculcation of ultimate personal goal
Respect and belief in God	prayerful mediation was integral to families
Respect for institutional authority	the law and other authority-figures
Fellowship	social interaction among individuals and groups
Respect for Professions	teachers, lawyers, doctors and clerks were looked up to
Family Kinship	unity among families was vital whether nuclear or extended

Since the celebration of **International Women's Year in 1975**, followed by the **United Nations Decade for Women 1975-85**, there has been a greater awareness of the contribution that Caribbean women have and continue to make in their societies.

It is evident that available documentary or other media of women's contribution have, on a global scale, more to do with aspects of society's structures. This includes how the balance of power is distributed firstly among individual countries, and secondly among individuals in each society. Moreover, the existence of documentary evidence on women's contribution is affected by world trend-setters, and often these are leaders, history-writers and the notion of what is "civilised", (given that the economically stronger societies receive more recognition globally). This means that in our hierarchical world "strength" is measured by notions of "power" or superiority on socio-economic, political, cultural and nuclear might.

In such situations, the functioning of that "powerful" society is often given more global exposure; a fact which can be confirmed, for example, in a British setting. Depending on what aspects of British life one is referring to, names which come readily to mind are Florence Nightingale, Emily and Christobel Pankhurst, the Match Girl strikers, etc. If, on the other hand, "Caribbean women" and "contribution" are referred to, it is possible that because the region is not seen as a *First World*, from a global perspective, that there could be less readily recollected data, without having recourse to consult with available documentation on the subject.

Furthermore, the ease of available data on women in general, have a lot to do with the kind of societies they belong to; in terms of capitalism, communism, socialism, colonialism, imperialism and super-powerism. Often *where* women fit into the schemes of things among such tiered structures in society, reflects their own society's levels of thinking at any one time. Therefore, if one were to say that in European societies, the paths of women's contribution to society have been more clear-cut than in the Caribbean, this would probably immediately be met with a resounding "No!" However, when seen from a comparative viewpoint, with the Caribbean's scarcity of available documentation, the suggestion could be an accurate one.

There certainly appears to be more available information among developed countries, as opposed to the "Developing or Third World". This is partly due to the worldwide attention which living in Metropolitan centres afford such societies, compared with countries existing on the periphery of the Metropolis. It is also possible that the term "developing" has an underlying assumption that things are not yet matured or reached the level which merits global attention, or at any rate, seen as not fully developed (equated with power).

However, if unravelling layers of biases against European women over the years, when they have attempted to redress the balance in relation to their male counterparts is problematic, my view is that a far more complicated issue is to talk of Caribbean women's contribution to their individual societies. The reality of Caribbean complexities is compounded by their socio-economic, political and historical legacies, which affect them and which is not clear-cut.

Anomalies abound! The term *"Caribbean"* for example, is problematic. Who do we include in this description of "Caribbean women?" given the diversity of colonial, imperialistic powers which have affected the region; (having been spearheaded by European patriarchy).

Moreover, the complexities of attributing "*contribution*" to women in the area, is further compounded by drawbacks which have stemmed from European domination of the Caribbean peoples and the introduction of foreign ideologies which have retrogressed the development of both men and women; though women have suffered greater marginalisation. Therefore, one has to look at the notion of identity, ideology and women's development in relation to men in the region and how they face up to situations which constantly challenge and undermine their independence.

It will be seen that asserting themselves and focusing attention on what they have done to develop their Caribbean society, has to do with stripping away many layers that have suppressed them into extreme forms of marginalisation. There has been an obvious need to re-orientate the education of women and to eliminate sexual stereotyping (this is being done in schools) so as not to reinforce the inequalities of career opportunities between males and females, and to debunk prevailing attitudes of society which force them into traditional roles. It will be seen also that the women have championed their causes collectively, from island to island, and have succeeded. Additionally, the Black Power Movement of the 1970s marked a change in people's consciousness, which affected both men and women's attitudes to each other. It asserted self-identity, pride in blackness, and in a sense highlighted the wider context of their regional problems.

However, it must be said that Caribbean women are not a homogenous group. In many Caribbean and South American societies, women of African descent vary in colours that determine their status as well as cultural associations. The majority of women are black, either of African descent or of mixed race. For example in Trinidad and Guyana, approximately 45% of the population are of Indian descent. In each island, there are small numbers of local whites, descendants of ex-colonials, as well as expatriate whites who have settled there. Smaller ethnic groups such as Chinese, Syrians, and Portuguese exist as well as very small pockets of native Amerindians, (Guyana, Dominica and St. Vincent). Therefore, "Caribbean women" will be regarded as women from the Caribbean region who, regardless of skin colour, are perceived as and who perceive themselves as Caribbean.

Much of what has been written about the women have been by the women themselves. Early documentation took the form of research projects, newspaper articles, literary works, magazines, poems, short stories, novels and plays. However, more attention has been paid to the black women in rural areas, who are at the bottom of the socio-economic ladder, with less opportunities than those in the middle and upper classes. Through education, women from these rural areas have been able to achieve social mobility, by becoming teachers, nurses and few have gone into the Civil service.

Perhaps the two most dominant values traceable through a time perspective are analyses of the women's developing survival strategies and methods of encouraging self-reliance through female networks which have brought about legislative reforms and improved socio-economic status for them.

The Family & Support Systems

It is important to look at the dynamics of Caribbean family patterns and interactions, since this not only play a major role in helping to shape identity but reflect how women (and men) perceive their roles in their society.

Early Caribbean history shows that controlling women has been integral in maintaining the power of the oppressor group; be it among colonials or native groups. Carib Indians are said to have raided Arawaks settlement and captured the women to make use of their agricultural skills. Added to this was the divisions of language differences and labour between Carib men and women - they each had their own language.

Later the European colonials, during slavery, used women as concubines, which created social divisions of colour, and as a result of the complex sex-gender relationships of the colonials with the oppressive slave society, Caribbean male bias saw their women as treacherous; and colluding with the slave-owners. However, despite their sexual roles to their masters, the women had to work alongside the men in the field, performing the same physical tasks so that there was little sexual divisions of labour between them.

European Concepts of Households vs Caribbean Formations

It was not until after the abolition of the slave trade that the introduction of European concepts of household organisation began to be adopted into the region. Previously there had been a diversity of family unions, ranging from the most dominant arrangement single parent families (those headed by females), forming 30-40% of the population, to various adopted East Indian versions of family patterns. Such high proportions of female-headed households indicated that, unlike many other societies, the women were often the major economic providers for their families. This meant that many of them worked outside the household, and were employed in low-status/low-paid jobs, were experiencing great stress and hardship in agriculture, as well as in the service sector.

The women were responsible for child-caring and rearing and a high value and status was attached to the mothering role.

Relationship with men ranged from common law unions, visiting relationships (a man in a half permanent relationship when the visits to the household, were varied in frequency and duration of stay), to forms of marriage as those organised by East Indian populations especially in Trinidad, Guyana and Belize - countries with significant East Indian population.

The prevailing importance of motherhood provided women with a great deal of influence, authority and respect, and generally they adapted their family structure to suit their economic situations. It was not uncommon to have family members who did not necessarily live in the same household and the concept of family often went beyond blood relations, to include friends, neighbours and God-parents. Shared-mothering enabled them to bring up their children often without the support of the male, since full-time mothering and house-minding had been seen as ideal.

However, the introduction of European concepts of marriage and the nuclear family, with its patriarchal ideologies of male dominance, encouraged greater sexual divisions of labour in the region. Men began to be offered better paid jobs, with fewer jobs available for women. As a result, women worked less regularly, but left to combine work with household production for survival, as well as the raising of their own children and little male support.

In her paper on *Male/female Socialization Career Counselling and Jobs for Women and Men*, Norma Shorey-Bryan recorded that 70% of cases brought before the Jamaican Family Court related to problems of obtaining child support from fathers. Shorey-Bryan states:

> *"In-depth interviews carried out with individual women in the **Women in the Caribbean Research Project** (WICP), emphasised the importance of friendship ties with other women in times of emotional stress and difficulty".*

Relationships suffered conflicts where the imported ideal of male dominance and economic responsibility for the household did not fulfil the realities of family needs. Consequently men, not able to fulfil their duties, left in search of job satisfaction and/or regular pay, leaving the female to maintain her situation.

It is thought that one reason for the absence of men could be attributed to unstable economic conditions in the region as a whole, but another reason points to a psychological factor of male marginality, their feelings of alienation stemming from a subconscious guilt in not being able to live up to their own and society's ideal of being the provide. Consequently, the ambivalence which men face is not being economically strong affected their self image and the resulting paradoxes and conflicts have caused male domination of their women and children, in some cases, through violence or curtailing their women's freedom by refusing to let them go out. Such complexities of the socialising process is a circular one. since values and attitudes are transmitted to generations consciously and unconsciously. Children who observe these patterns of interaction, internalise what roles and behaviour are appropriate to their sex, later perpetuate the vicious circle.

Interestingly, Shorey-Bryan's research in 1982, among a variety of adults and young people in Barbados, Jamaica, Grenada and Dominica, revealed that top on their list of their socialising principles were the stereotypes relating to gender expectations, namely:

- Boys do not do housework, (perhaps sweep the yard).

- Girls cook, clean and wash and could cry where boys should not.

However, women explored ways of coping with their situation for survival and adopted a variety of strategies and social networks which provided support and functioned as support systems on which they were able to draw in times of emotional and economic need,

GROUP AFFINITY then, as practised today, helped to meet practical needs of individuals. For example, very basic community banking such as "*giving hands*", "*throwing a partner*", or "*Susu*" as it is called in Jamaica and Grenada respectively, or otherwise called "the box" in Guyana, "*partnership*" in Barbados, "*sociedad*" in the Dominican Republic and "*conubite*" in Haiti. This very old form of banking, involves groups of individuals who are able to pool funds together on a weekly or monthly basis, and the total sum given to an individual in the group and this lump sum of giving to a group member is repeated weekly, until everyone has had a turn).   Therefore, if 20 people put together £20 per person per week, the total of £400 a week is given out each week, based solely on trust of each group member to continue the circle of giving until each person has had £400, then it all starts again. This way it's easy to plan, based on finance which is readily available, without charges tied to it. This extremely old form of banking, began in the Caribbean as a way of helping freed blacks in post-slavery times, achieve a degree of economic stability. Such measures helped to ensure a social structure which depicted an individual's obligation to the community and demonstrated the cultural similarities within the region, but also the strength of their shared solidarity.

In Britain today, these economic, survival strategies continue, to help relieve poverty and deprivation. Given such experiences, the word "social" can be said to embody a wide range of issues that have impacted on the experiences of British Caribbean women in general. In Britain, these issues are to do with categories such as education, employment, housing, health, religion, ethnicity, gender, and by virtue of these, are regarded as a minority group. It means that as a minority group, they are adversely affected by all measurable social indicators, making any attempts at equality with the majority group, an almost impossible task.

In the UK, British Caribbean families' existence is influenced by political decisions. This began with the British Nationality Act 1948, which granted Caribbean people the right to enter Great Britain as British citizens (holding British passports), from her present and former colonies. This meant that Caribbean people had opportunities to better themselves economically in Britain in the fact of the depleting economies in the Caribbean islands – a move which benefited the migrants and Britain. The post-war destruction and a need to re-build Britain's infrastructure, was a primary reason why Caribbean peoples were invited to Britain.

Young men and women arrived in Britain and tried to upkeep family members from their wages. When this was accrued, children who were left behind with extended family members were able to join hitherto "absent" parents. Partners also joined (usually the male entered Britain first), followed by women and they were then able to share and reduce the burden of the economic pressure, - trying to maintain double households (in Britain and the Caribbean). The majority of Caribbean migrants settled in inner cities, which means children joining them were faced with the reality of having come from highly agricultural environments to join parents, (with home some had no bonding), and who were in the heart of industrial settings. One could say that given the odds against them in a British setting, their survival strategies are an interesting phenomenon and highlights vestiges of a sense of cultural appreciation and lifestyles, which they constantly draw on.

The Black Presence in Britain

Although most people today date the West Indian or Caribbean presence as beginning from the *SS Empire Windrush* era, Peter Fryer states that the presence of black people in Britain dates back to a time before the English arrived! He states that there were

African soldiers in the Roman imperial army that occupied southern England during the 3rd century AD. However, little is known about the black presence between 3rd and early 6th centuries. After the 16th century the presence of Africans and Asians were more evident, predominantly as slaves, servants and entertainers, (1989). Fryer refers to 3 Africans; the first being Olaudah Equiano, a Nigerian who arrived in Britain in 1757, aged about 11, as a slave. He became a journalist, author and anti-slavery campaigner, in *Staying Power:TheHistory of Black People in Britain*, stated that:

> *"To kidnap our fellow creatures, however they may differ in complexion to degrade them into beasts of burden, to deny them every right but those and scarcely those we allow to horse, to keep them in perpetual servitude, is a crime as unjustifiable as cruel."*

The second notable presence was Ottobah Cugoano, a Ghanian was captured and brought to Britain in 1772 at the age of about 13. He was a writer like Equiano, and also an anti-slavery campaigner. Fryer also states that Ignatious Sancho represented an early black presence, having been born on a "slave ship" in the mid-Atlantic and brought by two English sisters to live in Greenwich at the age of 2 years. Sancho was brought up in slavery but he dedicated himself to literature and music composition in which he excelled. He used his literary contacts to protest against the slave system. James Walvin (2007) in *Britain's Slave Empire*, states that during the time of European enslavement of Africans, London had great numbers referred to as "exotic Blacks",taken on as foot soldiers, servants, and coach drivers to the wealthy. Some of these are captured in artistic works showing slaves dressed in stylish garments, as appendages to the English household, rather like pets, and used to show off, among the gentry, their success in slave mercantilism in society,.

Other documented early black people was Mary Secole, the Jamaican nurse who worked alongside Florence Nightingale during the Crimean War. In fact Black History Month highlights the achievement among Caribbean and other Black Britons over the past centuries. There is also documentary evidence of the tremendous contribution made by Caribbeans and black people in general, to Britian. Books such as *Third World Impact* (Hansib 1988) and *Black Who is Who* (Ethnic Media Group:1999) show the defiance and determination to pursue their goals of economic freedom and advancement by their refusal to be held back by their circumstances. Black people lived in small numbers, especially in areas supported by seaports in London.

But is is important to know why Caribbean people have come to Britain. Firstly they were British subjects, coming from British colonies, headed by King George and subsequently Queen Elizabeth II. They responded to a plea from the British government to come and help re-build Britain after the Second World War, they came in the troopship Empire Windrush in 1948, in Tilbury where it docked the largest single passenger load of Caribbeans. Most of them were from Jamaica (500), and this signalled the flow of migration to Britain from other Caribbean as well as those from the New Commonwealth.

This type of migration was due to what some experts called "push" and "pull" factors. In other words social and economic situations at home in a neo-colonist New Commonwealth helped to "push" people from places like the Caribbean while Britain's post-war rebuilding programme and industrial boom created opportunities that helped to "pull" people into Britain in search of economic prosperity. The majority of immigrants were economic migrants but others were students. Sheila Patterson (1968) in Immigrants in Industry, states that by 1961 at least 19% of the Black student population (36,000) were Caribbeans. The largest group was Africans making 33% and Asians forming 13%.

There were also armed services personnel who chose to stay in Britain after World War II for despite the poor employment prospects immediately after the War. Another "push" factor for Caribbeans was the severe restriction of Caribbean peoples to the United States, (after the passing of the McCarren Act of 1952). Britain therefore provided a window of opportunity for those looking for economic advancement. It is also reported that some Caribbean peoples came as missionaries to Britain. Yet another "pull" factor, was the fact that many parents who had migrated to Britain, later settled beyond the 5 years they and projected and foregoing the expected return, sent for their children in the Caribbean instead. It was via this factor that this writer entered Britain in the late 1960's. A report by the Runnymede Trust (Heinemann 1980) remarks that:

> The growth in Britain's Black population is a post-war phenomenon. In 1951 there were 1.6 million people living in Britain who were born outside the UK, of whom only 0.2 million were born in the New Commonwealth. By 1971 there were 3.0 million people who were born outside the UK of whom 1.2 million were born in the New Commonwealth. The majority of these 1.2 million were Black workers attracted to Britain during the 1950s and 1960s by employment opportunities"

The majority of migrants to Britain from the Caribbean are Jamaicans and this has a significant influence on the ethnic balance of Caribbean peoples in Britain. Within the Caribbean region Jamaicans have a tendency to move in search of social and economic improvement and we see this adding to the fact of their being the majority among Caribbeans in Britain. In Britain while Jamaicans represented the largest group of Caribbeans, Trinidadians and Guyanese migrants were among the lowest.

Another factor of note is that whilst the majority of Jamaicans were of African decent, the Trinidadian and Guyanese migrants were predominantly of Asian descent. It is important to note that there is no exclusive classification to the island ethnic sub-divisions, since Caribbean heritage, stems from a myriad of backgrounds and can be seen in other smaller islands as representative samples of a very plural environment.

For example, it is possible to see in a Caribbean island population, a mixture of African, Indian, Arab, French, Spanish, Dutch, Chinese, Portuguese, Amerindian and European heritage peoples, which is characteristic of the only constant in the Caribbean i.e. the changing identity and composition of the peoples of the Caribbean region.

It is important to note that Caribbean migration was part of a much wider immigration phenomenon in Britain. Certainly the presence of Caribbean peoples in Britain increased the numbers of "Black" Peoples in Britain, specifically where the word "black" means African, Asian, Caribbean, and other minorities. The shifting categorization may allude to the growing pluralistic nature of British society, so that at one time they were referred to as "Coloured People", "Ethnic Minorities" "Minority Ethnic", "Black and Minority Ethnic" (BME) or just "Black" as they are politically referred to intermittently. Black now means African, Asian, Caribbean and others.

The 1991 National Census documents the total "minority ethnic population as just over 3 million. It is said that of this 0.9 per cent or 499,964 identified themselves as "Black Caribbean". By the time of the 2001 Census, there was a significant increase in the number of minority ethnic people from 5.5per cent to 7.9 percent of the overall population. At this time Caribbean heritage people represented the second largest minority ethnic group, along with Pakistanis at 0.9 per cent. The largest minority was Indian at 1.5 per cent. **(Table 2.2)**.

Important to note here is the growing phenomenon or "splintering" of Caribbean heritage peoples, initially via migration, then through inter-relationships with the indigenous population, creating added biological increases, then a category of Caribbean offspring born in Britain of Caribbean heritage parents, (some who would have migrated from the Caribbean and others who have never been to the Caribbean), making theirs a Black British identity.

Table 2.2: *Population of the United Kingdom: by ethnic group, April 2001*

Category	Number	%	Non-White population (%)
White	54,153,898	92.1	-
Mixed	**677,117**	**1.2**	**14.6**
Indian	1,053,411	1.8	22.7
Pakistani	747,285	1.3	16.1
Bangladeshi	283,063	0.5	6.1
Other Asian	247,664	0.4	5.3
All Asian or Asian British	**2,331,423**	**4.0**	**50.3**
Black Caribbean	565,876	1.0	12.2
Black African	485,277	0.8	10.5
Black Other	97,585	0.2	2.1
All Black or Black British	**1,148,738**	**2.0**	**24.8**
Chinese	**247,403**	**0.4**	**5.3**
Other ethnic groups	**230,615**	**0.4**	**5.0**
All minority population	**4,635,296**	**7.9**	**100.0**
All population	**58,789,194**	**100**	-

Caribbean Settlements in Britain

When Caribbean people arrived in Britain they settled mainly in England. Given that the main reason for migration was employment, migrants concentrated in the industrialized inner-city areas of London, Manchester, Birmingham and Sheffield. These were areas of expanding industry and could account for the fact that large disproportionate minority populations are in some areas compared with other areas in Britain overall. In fact, in places such as Birmingham, the addition of other ethnic minorities means that it possible to find that certain areas present ethnic population as a majority component of the White population.

The need for manpower in the steel and textiles industries in the north-west of England and West Midlands "pulled" many Caribbeans to these areas during the 1950's and 60s, However this began to change with the docking of *SS Empire Windrush,* when many migrants found work in railway, bricklaying, agriculture, transport, health and iron foundries in places as far as Scotland, South Wales, the Midlands, (evident in the National Census of 1991-2001 – 96.5% lived in England, 1.4% lived in Wales, 3% in Scotland, 1.2% in North (Tyne & Wear), 7% in Yorkshire and Humberside, 6.1% in East Midlands, 1.4% in East Anglia, 56.7% in the South East, 2% in the South West, 1.5% in the West Midlands and 8% in the North West" **(Table 2.3)**.

Table 2.3: UK Population by Regions

REGIONS	POPULATION PERCENTAGE
England	96.5%
Wales	1.4%
Scotland	3.0%
North	1.2%
Yorkshire & Humberside	7.0%
East Midlands	6.1%
East Anglia	1.4%
South East	56.7%
South West	2.0%
West Midlands	1.5%
North West	8.0%

(Source: *Office of National Statistics 1991-2001)*

A resultant demographic shift shows a movement of the middle class Whites from the inner-cities, where the ethnic minorities occupy, which became socio-economically deprived. Evidently they were affected by included under-performance in the job market and other areas such as education, health and housing. Whereas in the Caribbean families lived closer together, with the support of extended families the traditional responsibility of the community, in Britain they found themselves alienated by a society which cared little for their presence, and brought home the true significance of being an "ethnic minority".

Towards a British Caribbean Identity

When people from the Caribbean first came to Britain, they were ethnically identified as "West Indians". This was generally referred to because the term was used exclusively to refer to people from the Caribbean. The description owes its origin to Christopher Columbus who mistakenly believed he had landed in India, in 1492, having sailed west from Europe to the Caribbean. As a result, the area became known as the West Indies and the people referred to as West Indians. Therefore **SS Empire Windrush** had brought West Indians to Britain. It is of note also that the cricket team from this part of the world is still called The West Indies Team. But the lack of an identity which identified the migrants as British subjects, was uncomfortable in the face of increasing prejudice. Also, it means that as West Indians, without a mention of Britain, this implied a sense of un-belonging, or foreign (contrary to what was thought pre-Windrush), "British subjects some of whom had gone to fight for the motherland and had answered to the appeals for help to re-build the "**Motherland**". Increasing disquiet with the negative experiences and the notion that, as Yasmin Alibhai-Brown (2007), puts it, right-wing political thinking equated **Britishness,** (**The Independent**, Oct. 2007) with whiteness and therefore exacerbating the white vs black identity by creating "otherness".

The emerging Black Power Movement in the United States and the raising consciousness of the Blacks in Britain was spurred on by racist incidents with **Teddy boys**, **Mods** and **Skinheads** of the late 50's and 60's from sections of the unskilled working-class communities. This caused a change in the migrant community's perception of themselves in Britain as a host society, as opposed to the view of it being an extension of their island territories. (see Chapter 3, on Who's Afraid of the Big Bad Youth.) By the 1970's Black youths were projected as rude boys and the rise of Rastafarians, caused a change in the way that linked them with a resistant subculture.

By the mid-1970's the prefix **Afro** was added to **Caribbean** as a more authentic identity for Caribbean people in Britain. This laid emphasis on an Africentric thinking when Afro Americans made conscious decisions to identify themselves within a American environment and this thinking spread throughout the African Diaspora. Therefore the African descended majority in Britain, (mainly Jamaicans), who were by now very disaffected with their **West Indian** identity, which was seen as inferior compared with being regarded as **British,** meant that they readily adopted the term Afro-Caribbean. As a result, sociologically and psychologically, the region was being "Africanised", where it was once "Indianized" by Columbus and indentureship. What made this identity easy to

provide egs. of each category

adopt was also the fact that men and women were able to identity with certain icons that popularised the thinking e.g. **Afro** hairstyles, **Afro** combs, **Afro** shirts, **Afro** art (language, dance, music, poetry).

However, by the late 1970's Afros had given way to the word "**African**": as a geo-ethnic identification for Caribbean people in Britain. It is not surprising, because Black Americans had begun to refer to themselves as **African-American**. In other words **Afro-American** became **African-American** and **Afro-Caribbean** became **African-Caribbean**. It is possible to see these identity developments as phenomena which have responded to a changing society, especially that of questing for an identity of one's own by Caribbeans in a British context.

The result of this is that non-African Caribbean identity peoples were disenfranchised, a practice which leads to further "splintering" of the identity claim. For example, at university level it is not uncommon to find references to "Indo-Caribbeans" as a way of selectively claiming certain racial inheritance of the general Caribbean heritage to the exclusion of the British and African input. Examples of this quest can be seen in the re-naming of individuals, many debunking their English sounding name for African names, and donning African fashion such as dashikis and other African garments, to demonstrate their changed ideologies.

Today, the concept of Black is complex. On one hand it is synonymous with Black African and Caribbean or dark skinned peoples. On the other hand it is a politically correct terminology to identify Black and Asian minorities in Britain or what Beckford calls "those engaged in resistance of domination, or counter-hegemonic resistance".

Caribbean identity has, as a result of the above, become submerged. It runs the risk of being debunked by Caribbean heritage children born in Britain, for whom the experience and meaning of the identity is almost non-existent. Whereas those who see themselves in solidarity against white supremacy/hegemony can align themselves with Blackness, it is not so for the Caribbean terminology.

Another difficulty which is evident in relinquishing the word **Caribbean** is that of the invisibility of accurate Ethnic Monitoring, statistics and data which identifies a specific Caribbean input e.g. the British Caribbean people's contribution to business development in the UK. Added to this complex identity, is the fact that the majority of Caribbean heritage people in Britain today are born in Britain, are British citizens, and now call themselves "Black British". This is one reason why, the title of this book on behaviour management, refers to a **British Caribbean** perspective.

In doing so, such an approach avoids the problems of grappling with all of the previous identities and labels, relating to Caribbean people as discussed above. What it does however, is maintain the word Caribbean, because it is appropriately linked with the original inhabitants of the Caribbean region (e.g. Caribs). It also embraces Caribbean heritage as a primary socio-historical and geo-ethnic identification.   Furthermore, it confirms the present stage in the development of Caribbean peoples in Britain, by embracing their *Britishness,* since they are now part of the fabric of British society.

In conclusion, given the Caribbean's complex background, one could say that Caribbean families in Britain have adopted strategies for survival that have become an interesting social phenomenon and highlights a strong sense of cultural affinity and lifestyles, which they constantly draw on. The reality of some Caribbean mothers bringing up children on their own then, is not necessarily structurally 'inappropriate', (given their socio-historical background), but supporting mechanisms that they have been used to from their communities in the Caribbean region, are absent, and based on knowledge and understanding of their present needs in context, strategies must be put in place in order to assist in minimizing their present social and other problems. *The Antoine Behaviour Excellence Model*, as a case in point, responds to such essential requirements. It is for these reasons it provides high levels of parental and community interactions, necessary in the tripartite relationship (*parent(s) and children, school, and education Authority*), it engenders, for successful behaviour management both in and out of the school.

SELECTED CHAPTER REFERENCES:

Beckford R. (2006) *Jesus Dub: Theology, Music, and Social Change*, Routledge.

Black Who is Who (1999): Ethnic Media Group 1999.

Field F & Haikin Patricia (1971):. *Black Britons*, Aurora Books Ltd.
Fryer P. (1984): *"Staying Power: The History of Black People in Britain."* Humanities Press.

Patterson Sheila (1968): *Immigrants in Industry,* Oxford University Press.

The Future of Multiethnic Britain, The Runnymede Trust, Profile Books, 2000.

Third World Impact (1988): Hansib 1988.

Walvin J. (2007):   *Britain's Slave Empire*, Penguin.

Yasmin Alibhai-Brown (2007): *"Britishness" The Independent Newspaper* , Oct. 2007, London.

Chapter Notes:

National Census of 1991- 2001 - **The census in England and Wales A census is a survey of all people and households in the country. It provides essential information from national to neighbourhood level for government, business, and the community. The most recent census was on 29 April 2001. Plans are being made for the next census to take place on 27 March 2011.**

British Nationality Act 1948

(1)   Every person who under this Act is a citizen of the United Kingdom and Colonies or who under any enactment for the time being in force in any country mentioned in subsection (3) of this section is a citizen of that country shall by virtue of that citizenship have the status of a British subject.

(2)   Any person having the status aforesaid may be known either as a British subject or as a Commonwealth citizen; and accordingly in this Act and in any other enactment or instrument whatever, whether passed or made before or after the commencement of this Act, the expression "British subject" and the expression "Commonwealth citizen" shall have the same meaning.

SS Empire Windrush 1948

The steamship Empire Windrush brought the first generation of migrant workers from the Caribbean to England, and therefore played an integral part in the origins of multi-cultural Britain. The **Empire Windrush** arrived at <u>Tilbury</u> on <u>22 June 1948</u>, carrying 492 passengers from <u>Jamaica</u> wishing to start a new life in the United Kingdom. The passengers were the first large group of <u>West Indian</u> <u>immigrants</u> to the UK after the <u>Second World War</u>.

UN Decade for Women 1976- 1985

Increasing global awareness of these and other inequities between the sexes was one of the goals of the United Nations Decade for Women (1976-1985). According to Leticia R. Shahani, Secretary-General of the World Conference marking the end of the Decade, "the Decade has caused the invisible majority of humankind--the women--to be more visible on the global scene".

McCarren Act of 1952):

<u>Pat McCarran</u> was the chairman of the Senate Internal Security Subcommittee that investigated the administrations headed by <u>Franklin D. Roosevelt</u> and <u>Harry S. Truman</u>. In September 1950 he was the chief sponsor of the <u>Internal Security Act</u>. This legislation required registration with the Attorney General of the <u>American Communist Party</u> and affiliated organizations. In June, 1952, <u>Pat McCarran</u> and <u>Francis Walter</u> instigated the passing of the McCarran-Walter Act that imposed more rigid restrictions on entry quotas to the United States

* **Nanny** (or Granny Nanny as she was affectionately known), was a leader of the Maroons in Jamaica at the beginning of the 18th century who fought with the British during the First Maroon War (1720-39).

+ **Bertha Higgins MBE** a great artist from Antigua (1889-1966), who helped local steel bands gain recognition in schools and who formed the first ever Antigua Art Group.

Discourse is "*a particular way of thinking talking and writing*"- see Catherine Belsey's *Critical Practice*; New Accents: 1980, p. 5

3 | Who's afraid of the Big Bad Youth?

Introduction

This chapter looks generally at the position of young people in Britain today. There are concerns over the trend of rising criminal activities, and the kind of media focus they attract, that makes such a chapter inclusive of all youths - meaning the focus here is not racially, gender or culturally specific. Whether we choose to highlight the so-called "black on black" crime, with body counts at regular intervals, or the frequency of weapon- related crimes among school children and the high rise of children in Secured Units (children's prisons), up and down the country, we must ALL realise that these are widespread societal problems which merit more than just daily conversation points. School Heads' anxieties over safety of staff and pupils; the older citizens concern for their safety on public transport and on the street due to fear of young people's open violence towards them; parents worry over the safety of their children whom they part with daily and the young person's anxieties and secret traumas over surviving in the school and public environments on a daily basis, is both the government's and every local community's problem, which simply cannot be ignored.

It is my belief that as a developed society, our *vision* of our youth should be one in which:

1. We value youths with mutual respect and equal fundamental rights;

2. We understand and believe in the ability of our youths to shape and change society in progressive ways; and

3. We mould young people to develop self-awareness, as well as an awareness of their total environment.

Can we honestly say, without reservation, that such has been or is the case in Britain today?

During the past 5 years we have seen an increase in adult fear of, and almost an obsession with the word "**youth**", which has become synonymous with the words "**crime**" and "**disorder**". What is evident, with closer analysis and interrogation of the facts, is that adults' fear of youths is widespread; projected through media representation, political discourse and selected ways of projecting statistics; and these in the main, have perpetuated and over-inflated the reality.

Moral panic has set in on both sides and the state of youth now acts as a social metaphor for the state of society – are our streets safe, can schools control them, have parents become irresponsible, are the courts too lenient, is TV's corruptive influence to be blamed for this generation of peculiar personalities, who dress strangely, and are both promiscuous and irresponsible?

The resulting dilemma is that a young person is branded as a thug or potential criminal, who will immediately erupt into violence or attack an innocent bystander. The physical evidence, on an adult's first sight of a young person, is that a handbag or hand-held belongings are clutched closer to the body; footsteps immediately quicken away from the youth or develop into an automatic run. An emotional panic button is pressed at the ready to cry for "help", while the young person is forced to account for where his/her hands are positioned *at all times*; how quickly or slowly he/she moves; forced to create facial expressions showing 'no interest' in his/her surroundings, and especially in the adult, or express a combination of both annoyance and/or surprise in the apparent fear of him/her.

On a train or bus or even on the street, the young person is daily burdened with the fact that his youth is seen as an automatic threat to the adult world, since he/she is viewed suspiciously as the enemy (a mugger, a lout, a thief or a yob), and may be forced to adopt a stance of defence in a closed environment where his/her movement is more constrained. Psychologically, coping strategies can take the form of a number of displays e.g. surprising quietness and embarrassment, almost as an apology for being *young* and a '*suspect*', with the youth staring downwards, eyes fixed to the floor, to avoid eye contact with adults. On the other hand, brashness and loudness (orally or with mobile phones or electronic equipment), compensate for the youth's own feeling of powerlessness constructed by the stereotype. Other actions tend to confirm the stereotypes associated with youth, crime and disorder that he/she has imbued and consequently acts out – i.e. living up to the image constructed socially and politically for them – and 99% of the times, this constitutes a range of anti-social behaviour.

But what has generated this widespread perception? Are young people really to be feared and are such fears justified? How accurate are measurements which categorise our future generations with descriptions ranging from *"demons, evil beast; spawn of Satan; yobs; young criminals; deprived of proper moral standards; monsters; animals; young villains; hardcore child; super crooks; tearaway thusg; rat boy; depraved; Lord of the Flies gang"*; (reported persistently in Britain's daily press – from **The Daily Mirror, The Guardian, The Daily Mail, The Independent**), to the Prime Minister's (Tony Blair 1994), crackdown on '**bail bandits'** and his promise to '**lock up young villains'** and eradicate '**the yob culture'**.

Ironically, the youths are forced to accept and suspend belief, it seems, in their reaction, to what they see daily these days, as an apparent, insatiable, appetite for violence, organized crimes, involvement with wars and general destruction, perpetuated by adult brutality, injustices and a lack of responsibility or rationale for their representations, within the adult world, (both home and abroad). Additionally, young people in Britain are annually regarded as incapable of passing high exam grades. Instead, Exam Boards are blamed for lowering exam standards and making exams too easy. In other words, the adult community chooses to openly and publicly reject pupils' high levels of success. Such general and persistent perceptions suggest that young people are incapable of excellence, success or developmental outcomes!

If one examines adult fear as expressed through the media, policies on youth control, political and social construction of crime through relations of power, used by the State to criminalise young people, it would highlight the lengths that adults will go to allay their fears, in order to deal with their anxieties over the youth. With this **them** (youths) and **us** (adults) dichotomy of fear, any serious analysis must confront the issues of how and why certain aspects of young people's behaviour have come to be perceived as so grossly problematic. Answers would question whether youths should be categorised as needing a criminal justice system, or whether the courts are the best vehicles for dealing with them, rather than understanding and listening to young people. It will be seen that the overt focus on young people in society as offenders, highlight them as **perpetrators of crime** and rarely as **victims of crime**, as a vast majority of research documents.

My view is that young people are the custodians of our society. They hold the prosperity for future generations and can play an important role in national development, if provided with the right tools – empowerment, learning to use those tools, a supportive environment in which to use those tools and opportunities to help lead the way in economic growth. As well as creating opportunities for social and economic stability, investing in our youth is therefore an economically sound approach to take.

Conceptual Framework

In this book, the word "*youth,*" is defined as spanning the adolescent period from 10 to 24 years of age. Youth or adolescent development therefore refers to the physical, social and emotional processes of maturation that occur during the 10-24 year period. The adolescent period represents the transition from childhood to adulthood; with biological processes initiating the process of adolescent, while societal factors determines the initiation of adulthood.   (It is noteworthy that **children** are described by the **UN Convention of the Rights of the Child** as those **under the age of 18 years** but **in Britain children are defined as those of 10 – 13 years old**).   This chapter therefore looks at the linkages between:

    a.   The underlying factors which lead to a perception of anarchical and dangerous youth in Britain, via manipulative strategies used to generate such a view.

    b.   Youth outcomes as a result of the above, which become risk factors, since they increase the likelihood of experiencing the negative outcomes projected.

    c.   The questionable protective factors which should be in place to counter-balance the risks projected on three levels - the individual, the micro-environment (family, social networks, peers and role models, community and neighbourhood), and macro-environment, (mass media, the economy, public institutions, cultural and historical background, social norms on gender and minority groupings).

My standpoint is that young people are not the problem but are a product of their micro- and macro-environments, since they react to situations in which they find themselves. As an extreme example, they rationalize that if no other forms of employment exist, their family needs drive them to the drug lord who provides not only money but 'protection' and a sense of belonging. Other factors influencing their rationality are families' ability/inability to protect youth behaviour outcomes – being regarded as both the strongest risk factor and strongest protective factor. At times these provide conflicting and confusing outcomes as this study reveals.

The school environment provides a connectedness and regarded as a highly protective link against all risky behaviours, can also have devastating effects on those youths with low academic achievement and as a corollary making them feel socially excluded and "useless".

Other factors affecting youth rationality are levels of poverty for young people in disadvantaged situations. Parents, particularly single parents, are more likely to be absent from the household and frequently leave youth and children unattended and unsupervised. Youths will engage in opportunistic activities involving, petty crime, violence, alcohol, "easy money" activities, including drugs and sex – all risky behaviours within a setting which should provide a strong protective environment.

A key message in this study therefore has to be the interconnectedness of factors that predispose anti-social behaviour, risky outcomes and empirical methods of analysing or manipulating statistics to generate expedient fear-factors, and at times grossly negative stereotyping of our youth. My standpoint is that there is a complex interrelation among family, school and community in the micro-environment which impact on the macro-environment; and that challenging and changing the factors and practices which lead to negative or unfair portrayals of youths will enable significant progress to be made in the social and economic stability of Britain in the 21st century.

A Background on Youths in Britain

The problem of youth in Britain is not new. Long before the current mixtures of cultures entered the British youth arena, the 1950's fears were premised on the image of teenagers called Teddy *boys,* who had no regard for authority, lacking respect and were contrary to adult authority. '*Teddy boys*' were the first post-war, immoral, working-class youths, branded as "*folk devils*", characterised by violence, pseudo- Edwardian dress-style (a parody of the upper-class), love of rock and roll, a dislike for the new immigrant arrivals in Britain. In 1954 *The Reynolds News,* a local paper reported that *Teddy boys* were known to go Paki-bashing, and were regarded as a "grave social evil".

Ten years later, themes such as sexual promiscuity, drug usage, student revolts, football hooliganism, truancy and vandalism were fears which amplified levels of adult concern. From the late 50's onwards, British society was being interpreted by sociologists who suggested that the gap between middle and working class was disappearing, advancing to the earlier classlessness expressed by political commentators and this produced *Mods*; a new youth group of concern. *Mods* were working-class youths of the early 60's, desirous to share the benefits of the 'new affluence' in post war Britain.

Furthermore, descendants of the **Teddy boys,** and originating from East London and working class estates in the suburbs of the capital, they were characterised by their short hair, Italian suits, amphetamine (speed) takers, scooter-riders, but seen as part of a crude subculture which engaged in clashes with **Rockers** on the beaches at Margate, Brighton and Hastings in 1964 with **Teddy Boys**.

By 1968, **Skinheads** appeared in East London from sections of the unskilled working class community. They projected working-class toughness with Doc Marten 'bovver boots' cropped hair, braces and half-mast trousers. Their Paki-bashing and queer-bashing activities showed them as attempting to claim or control territory, with increased football hooliganism and violence. Their directed anger at the migrant communities projected them as having a racist right-wing sub-cultural style.

In the 1970's, **Punks** emerged as a subculture in the wake of mass unemployment and rising fascism, high inflation among school leavers. **Punks** were categorized by their 'new' musical style, and saw themselves as outsiders, unlike skinheads. They saw no future in their lives, so gravitated to building their own subculture but on their preference for heroes from the past rock culture. In attempting to create their own society, they wore plastic bin liners, lavatory chains, zips, safety pins, dyed hair, ripped T shirts, and deformed school uniforms – anything rubbishy as an attack on the previous styles. Names of pop groups at the time evidence their tendency towards disruption, perversity and abnormality. As a result, they used sobriquets as well as songs which exemplified their perverse symbol: **(Names of bands - Sid Vicious, Rat Scabies, Johnny Rotten, Poly Styrene, Sex Pistols, The Damned: Songs – I want to be sick on You, Anarchy in the UK, Pretty Vacant).**

In the late **1970,** the symbol of violent black youths as muggers, with a "resistant" subculture, developed as a response to economic inequality were projected. Black youths projected as Rastafarians, with the rising popularity of reggae music, and the image of the '**rude boy**', were seen as attempting to establish their own identity. Demonized as dangerous, fearful, based on the '**rude boy**' subculture of West Kingston, Jamaica, they were categorised as dope dealers, pimps, welfare dependents, and petty criminals and rebellious.

Given this brief socio-historical, political and economic background, it is possible to conclude that Youths appear to respond to situations they face in the adult world by trying to ascertain their own place in society. Conversely, as adults, our categorization of their activities seems to **brand** them irrevocably.

Creating Criminal Records & Statistics

Criminal Statistics for England and Wales are annually produced by the British Crime Survey (BCS), and these are sourced via 2 strands:

1. crimes recorded by the police and

2. crimes recorded based on victims' interviews.

The first BCS was carried out in 1982, (10 years after America's first National Crime Survey). Britain's criminal statistics are annually produced, involving some 40,000 interviews with the 16+ age group. These are the most referred to sources of information and data on the extent of offending in Britain. The data offers a classification of youth as follows:

1. Children – 10 – 13 years old (The UN Convention of the Rights of the Child extend this category to those under 18 years)*

2. Juveniles – 10 – 17 years

3. Young persons 14 – 17 years

4. Young adults 18 – 20 years

5. Adults 21+ over

However, what is revealed by the statistics over the past decade shows a contradictory picture of youth offending, implying that in fact youth crimes rates have *fallen* and *not rising* as dramatically reported **(See Fig. 3.1).**

Note: *This definition was made during preparations for the International Youth Year (1985), and endorsed by the General Assembly (see A/36/215 and resolution 36/28, 1981)..*

Figure 3:1: Analysis of Youth Crime Rates

●	The decade between 1992 and 2001 showed that following the Crime and Disorder Act 1998, the number of juveniles convicted, cautioned and warned actually fell by 25%.
●	Less serious crimes account for just under half of all youth crimes (theft, and handling stolen goods).
●	Violence against the person accounts for less than 14% of indictable offences (2001 50% dealt with by reprimand or warning), implying their less serious nature
●	Adults account for more than 75% of all detected crimes (while the peak age for known offending is 18 (males) and 15 (females).
●	33% (males and 9% (females) of those born in 1953 had been convicted of an offence before the age of 46 (NACRO 2003a, Home Office 2002, Simmons & Dodd 2003).
●	The Audit Commission (1996) suggested the following:
✓	Under 18's committed 7 million crimes a year;
✓	Crime probably caused by predominantly males;
✓	Youth crime is made up of less serious property offences;
✓	Violent crimes, sexual offences are rare;
✓	Drug offence rise for youth adults; and
✓	Only 3% of offences lead to arrest and many offences are not
✓	Detected or recorded by police or conviction not secured

This then presents a controversial picture of the extent and the nature of youth criminal activities in Britain. The most important fact is that the criminal statistics are not impartial – they are partially and socially constructed for several reasons; depending largely on 3 methods of reporting:

1.   **PUBLIC REPORTING** – this method depends on crimes reported to the police by the public which does not necessarily present a true picture. Reasons being that it's up to the victim to report the crime; not all crimes are reported for

various reasons e.g. no obvious victim, victim powerlessness (e.g. child abuse), distrust of the police (certain youth cultures) too trivial offences (shop-lifting or high spirited brawls, and victims may have no faith in the police to take it seriously e.g. racial harassment).

2.   **POLICE REPORTING:** With this method, the police choose to label an offence as a crime **when** it is recorded. Therefore, because discretion is exercised as to what is regarded serious enough to warrant their attention, statistics produced are highly subjective. In fact, The British Crime survey 1994, estimated 40% of offences reported to the police were not recorded whilst 8 years later, a marked increase to 70% were reported. Some argue that police recording is influenced by the political context at the time of the offence, policing priorities within the force, and how and by whom, an offence is recorded. Compare this with the 1950's, when crime was not a political issue and did not seem to have any financial implications (statistics generated for funding resources gains). An important point to note is that police practices were different, e.g. juveniles were dealt with informally.

3   **CONSTRUCTED CRIME WAVES:** It would seem that changes in law enforcement and definitions as to what constitutes a"crime" legally, decide whether the rate of crime is rising **(though this is often projected)** or falling. Evidence shows that welfare-inspired legislation which governs the treatment of young people in the 20th century, encouraged law enforcement agencies to take up cases they would have previously dealt with informally. As a result, more young people are brought before the courts, creating the impression of a "crime wave", when the reality is that more official agency are intervening. Moreover, classification of offences, (minor and major), in favour of one-fit-all category - **'known crimes',** doubled vandalism as a crime, in one year. Worse still is when police officers **'play the crime card'** for political expediency in order to increase police numbers and police powers, especially with the introduction of performance indicators in the 1990. **The Guardian** (18/3/99) reported "cuffing" of cases as a police practice, to improve clear-up and detection rates to politically acceptable levels.

In addition, there are methodological problems with the reliability of some surveys, for example, victimization surveys; a victim has to be recognised as such. Then there are 'victim-less' crimes where victims are unwilling to accept the victim status (as in the case of domestic violence, sexual acts, corporate crimes) and changes in legislation and the number of arrests and sentences represent not actual changes in the level of crime, but in the capacity of the Criminal Justice System to process individual cases. For example, "New Labour" has created 661 new criminal offences and have launched hundreds of anti-crime initiatives, and in the main, these have been directed at anti-social and non-conformist behaviours, (**Table 3.1**).

Table 3.1: Methods of Crime Reporting

METHOD	DEFINITION
Public Reporting	Depends on crimes reported to the police by the public
Police Reporting	Police labels an offence as a crime when it's recorded
Constructed Crime Waves	More young people in court for various behavioural offences
Abnormal Behaviour	Contradictory crime statistics reflecting minor offences

Typical or Abnormal behaviour?

However, given the contradictory nature of official statistics reporting, criminologists have turned to measures such as self reported crime studies, which ask people to list crimes they have committed (whether it led to arrests or not), in order to gain a more accurate picture of 'hidden crimes' (pioneered in the US in the 1940's). Most report studies revealed that although young offending was widespread, ranging from keeping something found, stealing at school, breaking the windows of an empty property, or shoplifting, the majority of reports were restricted to minor property offences. The largest survey to date involved a nationwide sample of 14,500 11 – 17 year olds in 2000/1. The survey found less serious offences such as fighting in the streets, shoplifting, but the offending was infrequent and in fact it revealed that most young people were law-abiding most of the time!

It can be concluded therefore, from such studies, that the degree of offending can be regarded as typical, rather than an abnormal form of behaviour. What is interesting from the self-reporting reports is that contrary to widely-held beliefs about the correlation between class, race and gender to criminality, middle-class children were just as likely to be involved in crime as were working-class children. In fact, *The Guardian* (25/2/01), reported that middle-class and high-income families children were more likely to play truant, commit vandalism, and take illegal drugs. If this fact was singled out and dramatised for media attention, it would result in critical and sociological actions taken to project such acts as a 'crime wave'. This therefore shows that with less attention drawn to specific acts, there is also less fear generated suggesting that official statistics reflect not so much patterns of offending, but policing strategies/methods of reporting, media selectivity and socio-political manipulation of the issues concerning the youth.

Youths as Victims

Not all young people are criminals. In fact, they are more often than not, the victims of crime! So what about crimes against young people? The bulk of attention paid to crimes in the UK, focuses exclusively on young people as offenders, rather than as victims of crime. In attempting to redress this biased priority, studies in 1979 of 11 – 15 year olds in 2 Sheffield schools found that as high as 67% were victims of crime, 25% had suffered a physical assault and 40% were victims of theft. (Mawby 1979).

Later, in 1994, studies in Edinburgh revealed that criminal acts were committed with 'alarming frequency', *against young people*, ranging from assault, threatening behaviour and theft. In fact, 52% young women and 361 young men suffered adult harassment (e.g. being stared at, indecent exposure, increasing for females as they grew older). In Addition, 30% (14-15 year olds) experienced 'touching' or 'flashing'. In 1995, further studies in Glasgow showed that 68% young women had been sexually harassed, whilst two-thirds young men suffered assault and theft. These studies led to the conclusion that young people were 'more sinned against than were sinning,' To make matters worse, research in Teeside revealed that young people endured levels of victimization that would *certainly not* be tolerated by adults. (Anderson et al).

Moreover, racial harassment and bullying are endured by black and ethnic minority youths daily with racially motivated crimes increased by 250% between 1989 and 1996. This daubs the UK as the highest for this level of crime in Western Europe, (Human Rights Watch 1997). Ethnic minority groups are more likely than whites to be victims of household and personal offences (e.g. Pakistanis - victims of vandalism of their homes, cars and serious personal threats, Caribbeans are most at risk of assaults – Stephen Lawrence's death in 1993, which resulted in The Macpherson's Report. This high media profile case, confirmed what ethnic minorities already knew and experienced – police ambivalence, institutional racism and lack of accountability. The resultant campaign by the Lawrence's family exposed racial violence and judicial harassment and hate crime to the forefront of issues addressed by law enforcement community safety agencies in the late 1990's.

Parental Victimization

So why is there a lack of attention paid to youth victimization, compared with their image as perpetrators of crime? It is not surprising that the British Crime Surveys had not included questions about young people's experience of victimization and violence in the home. The NSPCC (2003) revealed that children under one are most at risk of being murdered than any other age group (46 deaths per million of population compared with national average of 16 per million). Parents are the principal suspects of 75% of all child homicides and the extent of domestic child abuse remains largely unknown. The NSPCC estimates that 1 in 10 young adults have suffered serious abuse or neglect during childhood and noted over 600 children are added to Child Protection Registers every week. This issue was recognised back in the late 19th century, but was shrouded in discourses to do with neglect, cruelty or general concern about juvenile and delinquency. The Victoria Climbié murder by her family and the Baby P murder are cases in point. **(Figure 3.2)** The engagement with a selective aspect of such major issues by criminological research showed that little had been done to expose the routine of violence. Instead, the concern about future delinquency caused by parental neglect or the relationship between delinquency and the risk of victimization has been highlighted.

Figure 3.2: Victoria Climbié

Victoria Adjo Climbié (2 November 1991 – 25 April 2000) was abused and murdered by her guardians in London, in 2000. The public outrage at her death led to a public inquiry which produced major changes in child protection policies in the United Kingdom, including the formation of the Every Child Matters programme; the introduction of the Children Act 2004; the creation of the ContactPoint project, (a planned government database that will hold information on all children in England and Wales); and the creation of the Office of the Children's Commissioner chaired by the Children's Commissioner.

Both her guardians, Marie-Thérèse Kouao (born 18 July 1956 in Bonoua, Ivory Coast) and Carl

Manning (born 31 October 1972), were convicted of murder and sentenced to life imprisonment at their trial on 12 January 2001.

In addition, young people not only suffer from physical and sexual abuse and bullying, but are often witness to much persistent parental violence in the home as "indirect victims". **(Figure 3. 3)** Such experiences of trauma can include post-burglary or criminal damages to homes or attacks on family members. Where priority and focus is on an overwhelming concern with sexual abuse, often the welfare agencies consider it their responsibility to provide child victims with advice and support focusing on only this. In fact, an NSPCC survey on the strategies developed by Crime and Disorder partnership, found that over half did not refer to child protection or the safety of young people at all!

Figure 3. 3: "Baby P"

"Baby P" (also known as "Child A" is the alias of a 17-month old boy who died in London after suffering over 50 injuries. His mother, her boyfriend, and their lodger, Jason Owen, were all convicted of causing or allowing the death of a child, the mother having pleaded guilty to the charge. A court order issued by the UK High Court prevents the publication of the identities of Baby P, his mother and her boyfriend.

Baby P had more than 50 injuries or bruises and an attempt had been made to cover up the crime. By the end, he was unrecognisable, his curly, golden locks shaved off. He had a broken back, nine fractured ribs, fingernails and a toenail missing, a severe mouth injury, a ripped ear and extensive bruising on his body. He also had sores and puncture wounds on his head.

The Child Protection Services of the London Borough of Haringey were widely criticised in the media. Following the conviction, three inquiries and a nationwide review of social service care were launched. The nationwide review is to be conducted by Lord Laming into his own recommendations after a similar case in Haringey concerning the murder of Victoria Climbié in 2000. The death was also the subject of debate in the House of Commons of the United Kingdom.

Institutional Victimization

Moreover the alarming rate and extent of child abuse to young people are in the care of Local Authorities, is not as highlighted compared with projecting a young person as a criminal. The revelations of systemic violence to young people in care, also known as 'looked after children' by residential staff, showed that throughout the 1980/90's, there has long been a cause for concern. Instead, socially polished language has clouded such issues of victimization in terms of 'abuse' and 'mistreatment', rather than criminal violence. The conclusion is therefore a disappointment that "the vast majority of partnership prioritise dealing with young people only as perpetrators of crime and anti-social behaviour". Also a review of much of the available research on child victimization in general, has left many, such as Furlong and Cartwel in 1997, to come to the conclusion that "in many respects, the concentration on young people as the perpetrators of crimes has left us blind to the extent to which young people are victims.. While adults express concern about "lawless" youths, many crimes are also committed against young people by adults".

Given their victim status and their inability to control what is projected on their behalf, it would seem that the relative powerlessness of young people means that they have to *earn* their status as victims – whilst their status as young offenders are readily *thrust* upon them. It is my view is that as subjugated others, ironically, the powerlessness of youths account for the fact that both their "protection" and "regulation" lie in the hands of those who are the very source of their victimization, whether in an institutional setting, politically, the media or parentally! **(Figure 3. 4)**

Figure 3. 4: Process of Victimisation

Youths as Victims	young people are victims of crime more than the perpetrators
Parental Victimisation	parents also experience the impact of crime on their children
Institutional Victimisation	'abuse/mistreatment' by agencies responsible for care
Trend Reversal	Prime Ministerial 'identification' of potential criminals prior to birth

Reversing the Trend – A Way Forward

The question is how do we reverse the trend and redress the imbalance of such constructed partiality? It is painfully obvious that the yob, truant, sexually abused youth of today, will be the parent of tomorrow. For a small number of young people, offending will be persistent but what strategy for positive engagement of youths is being projected, in order to foster developmental resilience, propriety, trust, national pride, social responsibility and a sharing of good practice, whether it be socially, politically, economically or culturally? British society is clearly not poised to reverse some of the fears of crime and disorder of the youth, the fact that a good deal more prisons are being built and the former Prime Minister (Tony Blair), identification of potential criminals from the womb – at the pre-birth stage!! But is not the case that the image of threat being invested in the young people attributing to them more power than they actually possess?

If we agree that young people are a positive force for development, peace and democracy, it is therefore imperative that a set of guiding principles for youth development in both the macro- and micro-environments become the focus of attention, in order to reverse the current negative trend. As for specific policy recommendations, progress and policies as well as specific actions, these must be context-specific i.e. based on the nature and acuteness of the youth issues faced by each local/regional area in the UK (as well as the national context). However, overall my specific recommendations are as follows:

I.   USING THE MEDIA AND SOCIAL MARKETING GOAL:
To harness the potential of youth and channel them into strategies for societal change, economic development and technological innovation.

As we have seen demonstrated the media could be used to change norms and values related to key risk areas:

(a)   *The environment* – there is a need to actively involve young people in the decision making processes that relate to their environment.

(b).   *Leisure* – young people are increasingly seeking and find new ways to spend their free time, both out of necessity and interest. Local youth clubs of the 1970's have systematically disappeared and street gathering have replaced these structural bases where access to creative opportunities, personal development and social inclusion took shape.

2.   CAPACITY BUILDING AND YOUTH PARTICIPATION GOAL:

To develop strong inclusive communities and encourage active citizenship

Personal Development

a)   Develop each individual's ability to deal with a changing world.

b)   Strengthen the linkages between formal and non-formal educational systems. Minority communities have much to contribute to mainstream education, if inclusive approaches are encouraged, officially, to share in the knowledge and enhancement strategies they bring to bear, in shaping their children's educational attainment (daily/weekly) among the profusion of voluntary Complementary Schools run by the Ethnic Minority communities in Britain.

c)   Target and eradicate all forms of discrimination against young men and women.

d)   Create and promote leadership and institutional bases of youth organisations.

e)   Foster the emergence of young leaders at the grassroots level, thereby Encouraging active youth participation in civil society.

Families

a)   Making families including fathers, a top public policy issue, with more clarity in family law for equity in parental responsibilities.

b)   Put in place incentives (e.g. tax breaks), to encourage innovative parental skills development, to reflect global changes in society and to minimize inter-generational conflict.

c)   Establish youth funds to finance innovative National Youth Programmes, especially those initiated by youths and community based organisations as part of their continual social development and contribution to Youth Policy-making processes.

d)   Improve juvenile justice (establish new protocols, techniques for reaching youths and their families with less reactionary, media-generated law enforcement practices, and

e)   The government should provide a set of verifiable indicators which would allow for better and transparent measurement of progress achieved for young people in the future. (Some of these could be drawn from the United Nations Millennium Development Goals to be reached by 2015, for the benefit of young people).

Many membership-based organizations both here in the UK and around the world, are learning (too late, in some cases), that their future stability and existence depended on forward planning which should have included young people as part of their long-term goals. Sadly, some have had to accept demise because their 50 years of adult self-indulgent management, have not produced a succession of younger, interested and enthusiastic people to continue their organization's excellent work. Similarly, we, as a society to some extent, also run the risk of similar consequences of non-engagement, with our future generations.

In conclusion, strategically, there needs to be a "**New**" thinking, on harnessing youth's development, beginning with the Commission approach, in order to inform and guide government policy-makers on the above issues. A strategic approach would be to separate Youth Affairs from the current DCSF (Department for Children Schools and Families), with a focus on **Challenges, Priorities, Gaps and Potential Partner Agencies** to be involved, in creating **A vision for 21**st **century British youth** which is positive, mutually respectful and fundamentally just.

Our **Annual National Youth Conference** has been an eye-opener in that once empowered in a positive and productive way, young people have demonstrated that they can, within solutions-focused for a, respond with the solutions as they view them, to the rising problems of crime and disorder in our cities (Birmingham, Nottingham, Leicester, Sheffield, Liverpool, Wolverhampton, Manchester, Northampton and London). **(Figure 3.5)**

Figure 3.5: Harnessing Youth Potential – A National Imperative

The main Objective of the conference was to empower young people to be active participants and decision makers of their future in Britain. *"Empowering young people means creating and supporting the enabling conditions under which they can act on their behalf and on their own terms, rather than at the direction of others. It provides proof that the government listens to young people and engages them in decision-making at the highest level."*	
Aims:	The aim of **The Roselle Antoine Foundation's (RAF),** Annual National Youth Conference 2008; was to give the adult population a strategic advantage of understanding young people's vision for Britain's future in a society where they will be the drivers for peace, democracy and tolerance.
Objectives:	The conference enabled youth teams in various cities in Britain (Birmingham, Liverpool, Sheffield, Leicester and London), to work more efficiently together, to deliver a vision of youth development for Britain. Through constructive arrangements they engaged in opportunities for greater understanding among the generations, sensitive to negative impacts of conflicts, and embrace initiatives to combat crime, violence and negative stereotyping.
The Roselle Antoine Foundation October, 2008.	

We were able to bring together young people and their families around Britain, in order to create a national dialogue, aimed at bringing about change and solutions to their many localised problems. Our strategy demonstrated that if the government includes young people meaningfully in the decision-making process for change, especially as it relates to them firstly, and nationally as young people of Britain, their future and the well being of the adult population will be enhanced. The need to work with grassroots organizations in order to access young people cannot be over-stressed. In a film entitled "**A Voice of Their Own**", (October 2008), commissioned by **The Roselle Antoine Foundation** charity, revealed an empowered, articulate and creative youth force around Britain, desperate to be heard, to be included and for their suggestions for change to be implemented. They presented as young people who had a good grasp of their localised situations within a national arena and stressed the need to implement their ideas in order to change the negative image of youths in Britain. The downside, of this exercise was that the various Youth initiatives and/or Departments set up by the government did not show enthusiasm for these empowered **youth voices**.

Most importantly, no programmes or initiatives for young people would achieve its full potential or maximize its success ratio, unless the young people themselves are meaningfully and strategically involved at the inception, implementation and evaluation stages. Our interviewed young people felt that the government's erroneous view is that young people will automatically engage with the faceless and impersonal various Commissions and Departments seeming to represent them. There was much dissenting voices among the various groups who expressed a need to meet them at their level and locale to get first-hand knowledge of their plights. Certainly our experiences have shown that **the empowerment approach** is a workable strategy in harnessing the vision, creativity and value that young people can and do bring to our society.

SELECTED CHAPTER REFERENCES

Anderson, S., Kinsey, R., Loader, I and Smith, C (1994): *Cautionary Tales: Young People, Crime and Policing in Edinburgh,* Aldershot, Avebury.

Tony Blair - *A decade of Tony Blair* – Telegraph.co.uk

Furlong, A. and Cartwel, E. (1997): *Young People and Social Change,* Buckingham, Open University Press.

Mawby R. (1979): "The victimization of juveniles: a comparative study of three areas of publicly owned housing in Sheffield" *Journal of Crime and Delinquency,* vol. 16, No 1, pp.98-114.

Chapter Notes

HUMAN RIGHTS WATCH is one of the world's leading independent organizations dedicated to defending and protecting human rights. By focusing international attention where human rights are violated, we give voice to the oppressed and hold oppressors accountable for their crimes. Our rigorous, objective investigations and strategic, targeted advocacy build intense pressure for action and raise the cost of human rights abuse.

THE NSPCC was founded in 1884 as the London Society for the Prevention of Cruelty to Children (London SPCC) by Benjamin Waugh. After five years of campaigning by the London SPCC, Parliament passed the first ever UK law to protect children from abuse and neglect in 1889. The NSPCC is the only UK charity which has been granted statutory powers under the Children Act 1989, allowing it to apply for care and supervision orders for children at risk.

THE ROSELLE ANTOINE FOUNDATION (RAF); A UK REGISTERED CHARITY
First Annual National Youth Conference, A Voice of Their Own – October 2008
Using the Empowerment approach, this unique conference embodied the strategic advantage of understanding young people's vision for Britain's future as drivers for peace, democracy and tolerance. The conference enabled youth teams within various cities in Britain to work more efficiently together to deliver a developmental vision for Britain. Through a constructive approach they will be engaged to show their understanding of national issues, sensitive to negative impacts of conflicts, and initiatives to combat crime, violence and negative stereotyping.

4 | Exclusions - British vs. Caribbean Settings

"Afro-Caribbean pupils are three times more likely to be excluded from mainstream schools than their counterpart".

Introduction

This chapter analyses the levels of exclusion in British mainstream schools, compared with the negligible and/or non-existence of permanent exclusion of children in Caribbean schools. It focuses on the different behavioural conditions of pupils, types of curriculum and the socio-cultural factors that traumatise young children in mainstream education, with a recurring huge cost, running into millions of pounds, as well as a drain on the British economy.

Perhaps one of the greatest concerns for Caribbean parents today is the alarming rate of schools' fixed and permanent exclusions their children are experiencing. This is made more intense by their inability to provide appropriate and relevant solutions they so desire, when faced with this problem.

But what has given rise to this growing trend? How is such a phenomenon being tackled outside of the formality of Exclusions Appeal processes and the trauma associated with Permanent Exclusion? A more worrying aspect is the lack of knowledge of what was behind earlier indicators that had pointed to disruptive behaviours, aggressive confrontations, violent outbursts, fear, intimidation and actual bodily harm in and outside the school environment?

Those who are faced with constantly ill disciplined children and the profusion of Exclusion letters, Governing Bodies appeal procedures and/ perhaps had lacked interest in the consequences of these problems in the school environment, are often at a loss as to how to tackle these problems. Solutions are not easy to come by and the gaps in reintegration, continuation of mainstream education, reparation and changed behaviour patterns, become narrower if the time in solving these problems are long.

Special Needs

These problems often give rise to labels describing a "special education need", but what does that mean? The word "special" is used to describe something that relates to a particular individual, group or environment. The word "special" also means different from that which is considered "normal". Normal is used to refer to what is ordinary and expected. As far as behaviour is concerned, these words are problematic because they are loaded with meanings. They can imply positive or negative outcomes for the individual.

It is true that certain pupils have special needs: After all, each individual is unique and that makes him/her special. But our educational system responds to a "special need" in different ways. At times this can result in exclusion, as in the case of pupils with disruptive behaviour, as being too difficult to deal with in a mainstream environment among others and thus they are removed to environments considered more appropriate for their learning. In some instances it may be a valid response. Alternatively, one can say that it may be valid if our understanding of the factors underlying the problems were more interrogatively understood than they are now.

The arguments for looking at solutions to adverse behaviour management among Caribbean children have to be considered in relation to an understanding of the realities and newly emerging trends. Highlighted in this book, these persuasively show that there is no young person who should be excluded from his/her learning environment simply because it is in his/her "better interests". Of course there would be individuals who, on a case-by-case basis, may not benefit but the arguments for withdrawal should be made in a fully informed manner, which takes the following into consideration.

To begin with, each individual is unique, like DNA. Each individual has a different intellectual profile, and educational systems strive to accommodate these in the school environment. However, certain factors must be taken into consideration in the case of the Caribbean child. Proponents of multiple intelligence argue that it is misleading to think about "a single mind, a single intelligence, a single problem-solving capacity" (Fleetham 2006). In agreeing with this view, we can assume that there is no single approach to behaviour management which will suit the needs of any classroom of learning, whether having SEN or not.

Take, for example, the 1970's view of children's learning which branded them "educationally sub-normal". At the time, Bernard Coard, a teacher, examined in, "*How the British School System made West Indian children educationally subnormal*", (1971); why these so-called "sub normal" pupils were having considerable difficulty in learning. He identified a solution for these specifically labelled pupils, which lay in the kind of assessment tools/measures adopted and the relevance of these tools as well as the learning materials to the child's own reality. More specifically, he alluded to the concept of multiple intelligence, since Caribbean children who were labelled as "educationally sub normal", were considered achievers, and articulate in a setting which omitted the assessment/measurement criteria for educational normality.

Multiple Intelligences

The theory of multiple intelligences challenged the concept of there being a single intelligence which could be tested by intelligence quota (IQ) tests. Instead it is argued that individuals have a range of intelligences: linguistic, logical-mathematical, spatial, musical, bodily-kinaesthetic, interpersonal, intra-personal, and naturalist. Whereas work on multiple intelligence is over 20 years old, the level of work where behaviour management and the Caribbean child is concerned is largely exploratory. In fact, if we examine adverse behaviour management, we will see that these multiple cognitive resources have been exploited directly or indirectly by the teaching profession for some time.

For example, approaches via the cognitive, direct, natural, communicative, functional-notional, community, learning, the total physical response, the suggestive/affirmative approaches, can all be described in terms of how we attempt to tap into children's different "frames of mind" in order to achieve successful behaviour management.

To talk about adverse behaviour management today, is to be faced with pupils with "special needs", categorised predominantly as having emotional and social behavioural difficulties (ESBD), emotional and behavioural difficulties (EBD), and these fall within the category of SEN (with or with a Statement). The teaching profession has been grappling with pupil's diverse needs for many years. However the prevailing view that pupils with ESBD and EBD are somehow different and therefore require different educational solutions is a reality in our time. It is obviously true that some of the pupils need very specific learning approaches. But it is also true that the same logic applied to learning in general for non-SEN learners applies to those pupils with SEN, specifically those with EBD and EBSD.

For example, the resultant success gained from the range of individualised learning styles in different educational settings have proved that such approaches also signal a need for individualized learner-based curricula. ICT, and internet learning are two cases in point, where guided by their own individual "frame of mind" certain SEN pupils have made considerable progress in their learning. It has been stated that "technology is making it possible for dyslexics to gain access to information and is changing our ideas about what is worth learning and doing. A new class of minds will arise as scientists".

In fact, my experience is that multimedia has impacted on the SEN behaviour due to the fact that the visual representation and the potential of virtual it presents enable the learners to experience and "see" what is often overlooked. There has been a plethora of evidence on how diagnosed conditions influence ways of learning. In fact advances in knowledge have enabled more information dissemination and therefore diagnosis. However, there appears to be a problem with, not so much diagnosing but labelling those with adverse or emotional and social behavioural difficulties and their solutions in the educational decision making process.

Complexities arise for example with a pupil who is diagnosed with ADHD, or one specific diagnosis but may have multiple disorders linked to his diagnosis. Additionally, the case of an individual with dyslexia, who may also have emotional, behavioural and social difficulties, sensory and physical difficulties or communication and interaction disorders.

Labelling Children

A further complication arises when the pupil is not medically diagnosed with EBD or EBSD but is proving to be an extremely difficult element to deal with, especially when this impacts on the learning of others in the classroom, to the point where behaviour management becomes the focus as opposed to teaching the curriculum.

So how does the Classroom or SEN teachers respond to the educational needs of one of these learners? Which diagnosis label do they choose? Do they find out about, say Dyslexia, and then differentiate their teaching? Do they tailor-make their approach based on their own experience, expertise and insight, or follow recommendations for the diagnosis? What about EBD and EBSD diagnoses? Has our engagement with finding labels to categorise a problem presented us with more complicated issues?

The labelling issue is further complicated , because globally, rates of pupils with special educational needs differ from country to country. E.g. In the Caribbean (less than 0.3%), in Europe – 0.9% Greece, 17.8% Finland. Furthermore, the figures are not representative of a true picture, because some pupils are educated in segregated schools (0.5% (Greece, Italy, Portugal, Spain) to 6% Switzerland.

Therefore, a strategic approach to solving behavioural problems, point to the need to adopt an individualized style within the educational setting. This is relevant for all children, (whether Caribbean or non Caribbean), those who are gifted and talented or those with behavioural problems that are unclassified.

There are clearly specific reasons for successful behaviours management techniques for the classroom teacher. These are necessary in the following areas: cognition and learning, emotional behavioural and social, communication and interaction and sensory and physical. It therefore means that specific solutions are needed to achieve good practice and can be found in the subsequent chapters of this book.

Settings & Attitudes

There is no doubt that different settings – geographical and cultural, socio-economic and historical - have an impact on the ways that childrens' attitudes and behaviours. History has shown that behaviours can be socially constructed and therefore a comparative analysis of both the British and Caribbean setting will highlight differences that are socio-economically and culturally determined. Present concerns in a school setting, regarding young people's behaviour in Britain today are to do with violence and disruption. But why is violence and disruptive behaviour in schools a growing problem in among Caribbean pupils, especially boys? What are the long-term effects for the child, his parents and for society as a whole?

At TCS Tutorial College, the *Antoine Behaviour Excellence Model* © demonstrates that partnerships between schools, parents& children, role models and those who are able to impart personal histories and cultural knowledge to the young, drawn from the community, use of local government agency services, partnership with the Local Education Authorities, the community at large and others, have come up with innovative ways to reduce behaviour problems and create positive empowerment approaches to development.

Part one of this book, which formed the context and background of Caribbean people, raised questions about the cultural differences between a Black British setting and the Caribbean and attitudes to the role of the State, expectations of children and education. Any comparison of the two regions is problematic given the marked differences in the organisation and structure of education. In the Caribbean, schoolteachers are national government servants with a job for life; considered as a high status profession and a high standard of academic achievement is expected of teachers, who traditionally have taken charge of pupils' academic progress as well as being community stakeholders in their social and personal development.

Children generally go to school in their locality. Although 'government' schools are the expected norm for general admission, private education is usually accessed by middle classes, who could afford the fees, uniforms, books and travel (since they can travel across Parishes) by predominantly private owned transport. Although the concept of a national curriculum, is relatively new in Britain, the standard of education directed by the CXC (Caribbean Examinations Council), has existed in the region since the early 1980's.

Teacher Shortages

Historically, in Britain, more marked since the 1980s, teacher shortages have become the norm; teachers have had to be recruited from overseas, including the Caribbean. Added to this is the fact that schools continue to have difficulty in filling teaching posts in subjects such as mathematics, science and modern languages. The fact that there is now 'parental choice' in where they send their pupils, schools are under pressure to compete for pupils and by virtue of this, the funding allocated for the pupils. Teachers too are required to be experts in their chosen subject areas, especially where pressure on schools to produce League Table outcomes is seen as a demonstration of their educational clout.

Growing Problems

In both the Caribbean and Britain there is recognition that violence and disaffection in schools have been growing, although definitions of the problem differ. In the Caribbean 'violence' is defined not only as physical attacks, but also more broadly as the trauma that poverty causes whole families to become disaffected and socially excluded. These ultimately disturb and disrupt the educational process, forming barriers which lead to emotional and social and behavioural difficulties (ESBD) in pupils.

PHYSICAL VIOLENCE is seen as a symptom of societal deprivation and it also highlights the loss of authority which schools and teachers once enjoyed and took for granted as the foundation of teaching and learning. This is especially so for Britain since pupils can be heard to say *"I can do what I want, you can touch me!"* or *"I will make you lose your job!"* Often this is said to insinuate the pupils' power of the adult, where he feels he only has to accuse someone (whether for malice or a just cause).

PARENTS TOO, ARE VICTIMS of this type of attitude since they too feel they have loss their authority, and live in the shadow of their children's threats of reporting them to Social Services and other enforcement agencies. Because of this, whilst the importance of maintaining a civil atmosphere in schools has been the expected norm, there is now a much stronger emphasis on the problems of physical violence, leading to both social and school exclusions, **(Figure 4.1)**.

For the purpose of this study violence is defined as blows, insults, extortion, assaults on fellow pupils, commonly associated with bullying. The Social Exclusion Unit's report presented to Parliament in May 1998 summed up the situation thus:

TRUANCY AND EXCLUSIONS have reached a crisis point. The thousands of children who are not in school on most schooldays have become a significant cause of crime. Many of today's non-attenders are in danger of becoming tomorrow's criminals and unemployed.

No one knows precisely how many children are out of school at any time because of truancy or exclusion. But each year at least one million children play truant, and over 100,000 children are excluded temporarily. Some 13,000 are excluded permanently'1

PERMANENT EXCLUSIONS from school had been measured at between 2,000 and 3,000 annually in the late 1980s so the increase in the decade to 1998 was dramatic - about tenfold. School exclusion and social exclusion comes with a big price tag – not only to the individual youth but their communities and the UK economy. Counting the cost of exclusion shows a substantial expenditure to the Exchequer. For example, the total cost for the young un-employed costs £10 million each day, youth crime costs £1 billion, and underachievement cost millions of pounds, **(Table 4.1)**.

---

1 *Truancy and School Exclusion report by the Social Exclusion Unit, May 1998*

Figure 4.1 : Summary of Contrasting Settings

- Geographical, cultural, economic and social are different

- Young people's behaviour in Britain has to do with violence and disruption

- The Antoine Behaviour Excellence Model is practicable and workable

- Expectations for children to achieve in the Caribbean are high

- There are low expectations set by the British education system

- Since the 1980s British teachers have been in short supply

- There is a recognition that in the Caribbean and Britain violence disrupts schools

- Physical violence is a symptom of social deprivation in Britain

- Parents see themselves as victims with little or no authority over their children

- Caribbean schools seldom exclude children from schools

- Permanent exclusions in British schools amount to 2,000 -3,000 annually

Education! Education! Education!

The Blair government, shortly after coming into office in 1997, with their strong focus on *"Education, Education, Education"*, announced their targets for reducing permanent exclusions in England and Wales, by one third in five years. Measures introduced included clear targets given to Local Education Authorities (LEAs) to cut numbers of truants and school exclusions, with greater focus on Education Action Zones, new powers for the police and a tougher approach to parents. The aim was to get the numbers down from 12,300 in 1997 to 8,400 by 2002. (Although it was noted that in Scotland and Northern Ireland, the problem was far less severe, the rate of exclusion being about one tenth of the figures for England).

Official data on exclusions in Britain is collected and considered reliable, if too crude to be very helpful in identifying causes. In the Caribbean, exclusion is not a policy for behaviour management. In fact, schools do not remove pupils for neither fixed nor permanent exclusion periods, and pupils are not transferred from one school to another as a form of behaviour sanction. Individual schools impose their brand of sanction which never takes pupil management beyond the school and so are not classified as 'excluded'. This is the case even for outsiders or visitors, since there exists an ethos of respect and sharing good values that tend to prevent the promotion of "differences" among the populace. Therefore, no pupil is ever excluded from school, in the Caribbean. Consequently, for obvious reasons, the information which follows concentrates on the British situation.

Who is excluded?

In England and Wales the figures show that pupils in certain groups are more likely to be excluded. These are:

- Boys – in secondary schools 4 boys are excluded for every girl. In Primary schools the ratio is 14:1

- Secondary age pupils – more than Primary age pupils

- Black pupils, particularly African-Caribbean boys who, are 4 times more likely to be excluded than white boys

- Pupils with Special Educational Needs, especially those with ESBD (Emotional, Social and Behavioural Difficulties)

- Pupils from households below the poverty line and live in deprived neighbourhoods

- Children who are or have been 'looked after' i.e. in public care

- Children from travellers' communities, (Table 4.1).

Discriminatory practices & Exclusions

In 2006, The Telegraph cited an official report by Peter Wanless, who was in charge of schools performance within The Department for Education which showed Afro-Caribbean children are three times more likely to be excluded from school because of "systematic racial discrimination" against them. The discrimination, the report states is "largely unwitting" on the part of teachers but is a cause of the exclusions gap. Figures published by the Department for Education in 2004, showed that the rate of permanent exclusions for Afro-Caribbean children was four in 10,000, compared with around 1.3 for white British pupils. However, the rate for black African children was similar to the white British figure at around 1.5. Chinese pupils had the lowest exclusion rate of 0.2, followed by Indian children at 0.5, Bangladeshi at 0.8 and Pakistani at around 1.

Table 4. 1: Pupils' Exclusions June 2007

(Source: Hansard Archives Publications & Research – 4th June 2007)

ETHNIC GROUP	NUMBER	%
White	7,470	0.13
White British	7,220	0.13
Irish	50	0.21
Traveller of Irish heritage	30	0.78
Gypsy/Roma	30	0.39
Any other White background	140	0.09
Mixed	500	0.26
White and Black Caribbean	280	0.41
White and Black African	50	0.24
White and Asian	30	0.09
Any other mixed background	140	0.21
Asian	290	0.06
Indian	70	0.04
Pakistani	160	0.08
Bangladeshi	50	0.06
Any other Asian background	20	0.04
Black	670	0.26
Black Caribbean	380	0.39
Black African	190	0.14
Any other Black background	100	0.36
Chinese	10	0.02
Any other ethnic group	60	0.10
Unclassified[5]	380	n/a
All pupils[4]	9,380	0.14

n/a = Not applicable. [1] Includes middle schools as deemed. Includes non-maintained special schools. Excludes general hospital schools. [2] *Figures relating to permanent exclusions are estimates based on incomplete pupil level data.* [3] *Number of permanent exclusions expressed as a percentage of the total school population of same gender or ethnic group.* [4] *Pupils of compulsory school age and above have been classified according to their ethnic group.* [5] *Includes those pupils for whom information on their ethnic group was not sought, refused or is missing. Note: Numbers have been rounded to the nearest 10. There may be discrepancies between the sum of constituent items and totals as shown. Source: School Census.*

A Spokesman for the Department of Education confirmed that Ministers were keen not to brand the school system as racist, but concluded that "there is always more that some schools, parents and the government can do to ensure that every child fulfils their potential, whatever their background." It stated further that "The exclusions gap is caused by largely unwitting, but systematic, racial discrimination in the application of disciplinary and exclusion policies. Even with the best efforts to improve provision for excluded pupils, the continued existence of the exclusion gap means black pupils are disproportionately denied mainstream education and the life chances that go with it."

Although the report states that 1,000 black pupils are permanently excluded from school each year, and 30,000 for fixed periods, Tony Sewell, dismissed the racism theory as, "confused rubbish".   A former education lecturer at Leeds University, Sewell said: "The boys complain that there is very little discipline because teachers seem afraid to challenge them. These boys are not in an environment where there are consequences for their actions and we should be asking questions about the lack of ethos, expectations and discipline in some schools." (2003).

The Caribbean & 'Exclusions'

In the Caribbean, even if figures for 'exclusions' did exist, they could not, legally be collected according to ethnicity. A reason for this is, despite the multi-layered racially populated region, all children born in the Caribbean are regarded as 'Caribbean' and not splintered into ethnic enclaves.

A Caribbean, Head teacher will generally not exclude a pupil. As direct employees of the Ministry of Education, they are responsible for implementing government education policies, including that of compulsory schooling for all children between the ages of 5 and 16.

The UK data on what happens to pupils after permanent exclusion is said to be poor. Collecting data on permanently excluded children only began in the 1990s, even though since the 1940s it has been possible for Head teachers to remove 'troublesome' children from their school.

Exclusions – A Blight on League Tables

In fact, before League Tables began in the 1990s, there were often informal arrangements between schools, to exchange difficult children, so that formal exclusion was more infrequent. Now that admitting such children may affect a school's position in the national performance tables Heads are less willing to accept them. However, pupils may still be passed from school to school, but the older the pupil is when excluded, the less likely it is that he or she will ever return to school. Some Permanently excluded pupils go to Pupil Referral Units (PRU's) at Key Stages 2 and 3; but these, like schools, vary in quality. Some enjoy good attendance rates and succeed where schools have failed in improving pupils' life chances; others are little more than containment centres.

Prior to September 2007, permanently excluded children could spend, on average, at least four months out of school before receiving any formal educational provision. This situation has been changed by the 6 day ruling, which stipulates that an excluded pupil must be provided with alternative education after the 6 day of exclusion.

Why Are Children Excluded?

Evidence shows that the most common reason given to parents by schools in England, for permanent exclusion, is physically aggressive or challenging behaviour. (NB: *'Physical aggression'* is the preferred term instead of **"violence"**). Physical aggression is a loaded terminology and can have a whole range of meanings. In most cases, exclusion is preceded by a long history of difficult-to-manage behaviour and disruptions. Vandalism and theft are less often cited, and drugs only feature in about 6% of cases, perhaps because Head teachers exercise constraint in playing it down. In fact, 32% of excluded young people say they have been involved in selling illegal drugs and it was suggested that abuse of drugs is quite often behind anger and stress and bad behaviour, even though it does not show up in the statistics.

The Cycle of Challenging Behaviour

My experience with 50% of the pupils with ESBD confirms this latter view. The resultant dilemma is that of a pupil who is already caught up in the cycle of extreme challenging behaviour, and aggravated by drug misuse, anger and aggressive behaviours, (which give rise to bullying and violence), petty crime, and eventually involvement with the Police and the Youth Justice System.

Reasons often quoted by parents for these types of disaffected displays are, 'difficulty with school work set' and 'special needs not adequately met'. Parents frequently see bullying as an issue and are even prepared in many cases, to see their own child as the bully. Changes occurred between 1997 and 2001, when the Minister of Education, (David Blunkett), ruled that School Heads may permanently exclude pupils where malicious disruption of classes or threat or actual violence persist. This was done in response to the concerns of teachers who felt their hands were tied, especially as they had to meet government targets for reducing exclusions.

The prevailing view was that more attention needed to be paid to exclusion which stemmed from certain types of schools and LEA policies. The argument was that some schools and LEAs adopted a more heavy-handed approach, with regard to 'excluding' pupils, than others. For example, Hayden and Dunne (1998) view is that Grant Maintained schools (now called Foundation schools), are four times more likely to exclude than LEA controlled schools. There is no

doubt that exclusion figures affect the image of a School, and some Heads, not wanting to be stigmatised with the negative image, are keen to opt for "*managed moves*", (i.e., transfer to another school, rather than exclude), so that the data on permanent exclusions is shown as reduced or non-existent. The repercussion of this type of 'ghosting', is that the exclusion rates cannot be pinned down and the potential for future, higher exclusion and associated problems exist. **(Table 4.2)**

Table 4.2: Number and Percentage of Permanent/Fixed period exclusions by reason for exclusion England 2005-2006 School Census

Reasons	Permanent Exclusions (3)	% of all permanent Exclusions (3)(4)	No. of Fixed period Exclusions	% of all fixed period exclusions (4)
Physical assault against pupil	1,260	16	62,670	18
Physical assault against an adult	740	9	8,240	2
Verbal abuse/threatening abuse against a pupil	330	4	12,730	4
Verbal abuse/threatening behaviour against an adult	900	11	79,370	23
Bullying	80	1	5,270	2
Racist abuse	30	0	3,370	1
Sexual misconduct	110	1	2,620	1
Drug and alcohol related	450	6	8,360	2
Damage	170	2	9,390	3
Theft	220	3	7,770	2
Persistent disruptive behaviour	2,370	30	72,340	21
Other	1,340	17	71,720	21
Total (5)	7,990	100	343,840	100

Notes:

(1) Includes Middle schools as deemed; (2) For the 2005/6 School year information was collected via the school census for the first time for secondary schools; (3) Estimates based on incomplete pupil level data; (4) The number of exclusions by reason expressed as a percentage as a total number of exclusions; and (5) There were 2 permanent and 4 fixed period exclusions for which circumstance was not known.

Exclusions - The Caribbean Ethos

In the Caribbean, excluding a pupil would be regarded as a failure on the part of both the school and an education system, whose purpose is to provide a place for educating every pupil. The Caribbean ethos of educating children in the region is both a public and progressive one. Public, in the sense that a child is aware of the expectations placed on him by, (not only his immediate family) but the expectations of the local community, because he is also seen as their representative. There is also an even wider field of expectation, when success is generated at the local level, and thus success extends to a hierarchy of expectation, beyond a village to a Parish and eventual island competitions when highlighting both island and regional educational success. Perhaps one of the biggest differences between education in the Caribbean and Britain is the role played by the media in general. **(Figure 4.2)**

Figure 4.2: Caribbean media celebrating student achievement

(Source: Stabroek News, Guyana, August 22, 2008)

" QC students top CAPE, GCE

Anna Regina boy CSEC star **Nazana Weekes** and **Robert Mansell,** both of Queen's College, have been named top Caribbean Advanced Proficiency Examination (CAPE) and General Certificate of Education Examination (GCE) students respectively while Rahul **Neehal Lall** of Anna Regina Multilateral is unofficially the top Caribbean Secondary Certificate Examination (CSEC) student.

He secured 14 grade ones and 2 grade twos. Weekes secured the CAPE top spot with five grade ones in Computer Science 1, Computer Science 2, Information Technology 1, Environmental Science 2 and Pure Mathematics. **Samanthani Lalaram:** obtained 13 grade ones.

Meanwhile Mansell gained his spot as the top GCE student with four 'A's in Biology, Chemistry, Mathematics and Physics. Nine other students were listed as GCE top achievers while 16 other names were released as the top CSEC achievers but in no specific order.

Motivating Pupils - Media Support

The interest of the media in publishing success and recognizing achievement is part of the culture of educational advancement that reflects the ethos of created because they report and publish educational success. Each year, Caribbean newspapers devote pages to report on the achievement of students throughout the region. This means that pride of achieving becomes a motivator and competitive element in the educational setting. There is nothing more encouraging than when a local child is able to see his name published in a local paper as having achieved a measure of success. These present personal goals and strategies for publicizing achievement among pupils and the whole community.

The local radio also plays its part in broadcasting success and this culture of **expectation, recognition and celebration**, is an expected norm in the Caribbean region. It is important to note however, that corporal punishment has been a major deterrent (though outlawed in most islands), which is accepted by all involved in the welfare and upbringing of the child.

Many Caribbean parents in Britain today, attest to the benefit of having such structures in place in their childhood and in their attempts to make comparisons of the differences between the two landscapes. In fact they relate their confusion over the differences in Britain where the above do not exist.

One must bear in mind that the parents of pupils who became first generation Black British, were brought up on a dominance of radio use. This was the case for most islands, and not just those in rural areas. Accordingly, they were used to inform the community, in the same way death announcements, meetings and other important events were reported. These forms of media were the sources of communicating reliable information.

There is no doubt that Caribbean parents' childhood and history, of their own education, is seen to be at odds with their present children's educational management. This may account for the fact that Caribbean parents' high expectations of their children's educational outcomes in Britain, and their attitude to managing that education, is not necessarily a lack of interest or a lack of knowledge (although in some cases this is so). Logically this can be relevant in trying to understand parent's view that the school and the education authorities will do what is "expected" of them, in assuming full responsibilities for their children's educational welfare and development

Exclusions in Britain - Facts You Should Know

According to the Office of Standards in Education (OFSTED), as part of behaviour management, all schools should have a Behaviour Policy in place, to inform and guide pupils, parents and staff as to their individual and collective roles and responsibilities. In other words, this provides a Code of Conduct by which everyone operates.

A school should have a written policy setting out the standards of behaviour it expects. The policy should outline what the school will do if the child's behaviour falls below these standards.

Promoting Good Behaviour

Generally, all pupils in a school benefit when behaviour is good. High standards of behaviour are important in helping children to feel safe and learn well. Parents, Guardians and Carers play a key part in this. In Britain, the government advises schools to focus on promoting positive behaviour, by helping to build self-discipline and encouraging respect for others. But schools also need sanctions to deter pupils from misbehaving.

Behavioural Policies

OFSTED guidelines for schools suggest that schools should review their behavioural policies regularly and publicise them to parents, staff and pupils. These policies should include a code of conduct for pupils. Rules on conduct can apply before and after school as well as during the school day. They can set expectations for how pupils will behave in corridors, in bus stops and at lunch and break times, as well as in the classroom.

Sanctions

The Office of Standards in Education, (OFSTED), states that all schools have a legal right to impose reasonable sanctions if a pupil misbehaves. For example, some sanctions a school might use include:

- a reprimand

- a letter to parents, Guardians of Carers

- removal from a class or group

- loss of privileges

- confiscating something belonging to a child if it's inappropriate
  for school (for example, a mobile phone or music player)

- detention

Discipline & Physical Contact

The Department for Education and Skills (2003) states in their guidelines on the use of Restrictive physical interventions for pupils with severe behavioural difficulties states that Teachers can't punish pupils physically, but can physically restrain them where it's necessary to stop a pupil injuring him or herself or someone else, damaging property or causing serious disruption. Certain members of school staff can search a pupil suspected of carrying a weapon, with or without their consent. In dealing with pupils with challenging and aggressive behaviours, a risk assessment and risk management strategies are used to improve practice in relation to managing risks posed by pupils with severely challenging behaviour.

Detention

Detentions can take place during school hours, at lunchtime, after school or at weekends. If a child fails to attend without a reasonable excuse, the school may give him/her a more severe punishment.

Parents are entitled to 24 hours' written notice of a detention that takes place outside normal school hours, so you can make arrangements for transport or childcare. The notice should tell parents why the detention was given and how long the child will have to stay at school.

- If a child cannot attend the detention, parents can explain
  their reasons to the child's teacher or Head teacher. They may
  reconsider the detention in certain circumstances, such as:

- The detention falls on an important religious day for the family,

- Parents are concerned about the length and safety of the route
  between school and home ; and

- Parents cannot reasonably make alternative arrangements for
  collecting their child from school.

Fixed Period Exclusions

A child who gets into serious trouble at school can be excluded for a fixed period of time. Schools can exclude a child if:

- They have seriously broken school rules

- Allowing them to stay in school would seriously harm their education or welfare, or the education or welfare of other pupils.

Other Points to Bear in Mind

- Only the Head teacher or Acting Headteacher can exclude a child ;

- A child can't be given fixed period (non-permanent) exclusions which total more than 45 school days in any one school year; and

- If a child is excluded for longer than one school day, the school should set work for them and mark it.

The school should call parents on the day an exclusion is given and follow up with a letter including information on:

- The period and reason for exclusion;

- Parents duty during the first five days of any exclusion to

- ensure that their child is not present in a public place during normal school hours, whether in the company of a parent or not; and

- Any arrangements made by the school that apply from the sixth day of the exclusion.

Permanent exclusions

A school will usually only permanently exclude a child as a last resort, after trying to improve the child's behaviour through other means. However, there are exceptional circumstances in which a Headteacher may decide to permanently exclude a pupil for a 'one-off' offence.

If a child has been permanently excluded, be aware that:

- The school's governing body is required to review the Headteacher's decision and parents may meet with them to explain their views on the exclusion;

- If the governing body confirms the exclusion, parents can appeal to an independent appeal panel organised by the local authority ;

- The school must explain in a letter how to lodge an appeal; and

- The school must provide full-time education from the sixth day of a permanent exclusion. (Table 4. 1)

Table 4.1: Summary of OFSTED Guidelines for School Discipline

• Behavioural Policies	Rules on conduct of schools and pupils
• Sanctions	Discipline codes to deal with children's misbehaviour
• Discipline/physical contact	Physical intervention for pupils with severe conduct problems
• Detention	If a child fails to attend school without reasonable excuse
• Fixed period exclusions	For pupils who seriously break school rules
• Permanent Exclusions	A last resort when all else fails to improve the child's conduct

The trauma of Exclusion - Socio Cultural Factors

Working for the past 25 years with disaffected and permanently children, has shown evidence that many of the children who are excluded are often from socially deprived backgrounds, fragmented families or have a web of social problems that impact on their ability to function in the school environment. Many who are being brought up by a single parent are more likely to be managed by a mother. As already discussed, in the Caribbean child's case, it is not unusual to find that sometimes this parent would be working. In fact, at least a majority of the time she will leave home before the child goes to school and returns well after the end of the school day.

This accounts for the reasons why many children, attend school without a breakfast, and are unable to concentrate on school work well before the morning break at 11am or thereabouts. It is also a fact that a child will happily leave home without the correct school uniform and arrive late for school. The parenting guidelines, though loosely understood, are not adhered to as there is no monitor to enforce when they are broken. In many cases the lack of supervision at this crucial time of the day, means that a child may go to school without money for lunch and he/she is fully occupied with thoughts of how h/she is going to survive throughout the day without the means of getting food.

The child's way out of this situation is often to take what he wants from others, and this leads him to become a bully due to his/her circumstances. Such behaviour accounts for the fact that a parent may think he/she has an 'angel' at home, the child's method of coping with the home situation – appearing to comply with what is required at home and on leaving that environment, displaying the opposite behaviour in public.

It is important to note that these children may also be victims of neglect, violence & abuse (sexual and verbal, physical, drugs, alcohol), excesses (over compensation by being given material things to make up for parents' absence from home), used as mini parents (looking after younger siblings by feeding and taking the lead of doing or ensuring the homework is done, or generally mildly bullying his siblings given the power to "parent" at will). The child may also be suffering rejection (by parents/families), experiencing poverty (lack of adequate nourishment, poor parenting, financial support), bad housing, the stress of living in dangerous and violent neighbourhoods, without the support of close family or community networks.

A Cry for Help!

Adverse Behaviour can become a cry for help. A sign that something is wrong or there are areas which need to be investigated. Adverse behaviour can also be a child's way of hitting back (a "coping" strategy), a way of creating mastery of a situation when all else is going wrong. He adopts the bully stance, or reacts to boundaries and rules in a defiant manner. Often h/she can be heard saying, "*I don't care!*" – emotionally translated, really means, "*I don't care what you do to me because I feel nobody cares, nothing is right with me anyway, therefore, I might as well go beserk and be done with it.*" Exclusion probably exacerbates this situation on two distinct fronts, (**Negative** and **Positive Posturing**).

Negative Posturing

1. It amplifies the rejection – strengthens this feeling of abandonment;

2. The child adopts a revenge mission to become as obnoxious as much as possible; and

3. Mainstream school rejection intensifies the personal rejection. And being placed in an alternative school setting, (often Pupil Referral Units), is a confirmation that h/she is being given something lower or sub-standard, and is in keeping with how the child is feeling;

4. The child feels that there is now no need to try to achieve anything, so he throws whatever little caution there might have been to the wind and carries on the way h/she is used to:

    a. The resulting low self-esteem and confidence brings the child at low psychological points and the level of disaffection increases as the feeling is there is no point is proving to anyone that they can be positive or achieve anything.

    b. If you listen to excluded children, 99% of the time they would state that those who excluded them did so unfairly and as a result they begin to view all those in authority as unjust, unfair. This is usually followed by the "them" and "us" syndrome, which becomes a part of the way that they view society.

    c. Not only is the child vowed to be as obnoxious as h/she can be but there follows a determination to make others lives a misery also– that way they can make a "name" for themselves.

    d. The belief principle in who I am and what I can be reverses in favour for "Everyone judges me as a loser, nobody likes me".

    e. If rejection and underachievement is what was experienced, there becomes a need to join others who are like them. This way they can excel in this communal arena and achieve within it (e.g. a gang), without too much chances of being downgraded.

Positive Posturing

The attitude adopted once, an exclusion takes place may one of liberation and self-knowledge. Therefore it is one that engenders positive outcomes. They are centered around the strength of character and the circumstances surrounding their exclusion, and treatment in their post-exclusion status. In turning his/her situation around, such a person can use the opportunity to great advantage by examining him/herself and looking at ways to redress the imbalance which led to his/her downward trend. At times, pupils adopting this positive stance, can be heard to express the following:

- *I was judged unfairly and I will prove this;*

- *I will now demonstrate just good I can be by now taking this opportunity to excel;*

- *I will turn over a new leaf and achieve and then go back and show those who punished me;*

- *I now realise how foolish I was; there is justification for the action taken and I have learnt from it;*

- *This experience will never be repeated;*

- *I need to change others opinions about me – there is still a positive chance for me to do good; and*

- *I want to go back and show them how wrong they were about me.*

Possible Exclusion Danger Zones

1. Paradoxically, a good deal of the dangers to exclusions is associated with the positive posturing. This is because it takes a greater amount of will power and overall strength of character to succeed in the new-found endeavours.

2. The child might become unpopular with his peers if he tries to change the status quo, since there are less children moving to that side of the spectrum.

3. He will be fought, (physically and mentally), by his friends and may quickly become a victim of his own changed status – having a need

to excel or succeed.

4. His positive attitude then becomes a barrier between him and his friends, since it is not "cool" to act as what they would describe as a "nerd".

5. There is more work involved in trying to change attitudes, associated with this type of positive behavior. In other words, the child may have a need to maintain friendship with his peers, but at the same time he/she is aware of their wrongdoings and it is this part of them he/she is rejecting. This may cause tension between his peers and say, his parents, where parents have become instrumental and an active partner in the changed status. Parental intervention may not be something his/her peers would welcome and therefore reduces the child to a perspective of being weak, and needing the help of parents, where strength would indicate maintaining the present status.

6. The child may need to move (physically) away from the local area by relocating to a place where he/she is unknown and will at least be given an opportunity to start afresh.

7. Parents are less able to move their homes (to another more positive and productive area) and might feel "trapped" in the benefit system. This is so especially where they are reliant on the shortages of government and government-funded housing to change demography.

8. The child is then forced to accept "punishment", even death, is the result, as has been seen in the various incidents involving knives in the Britain, over the past 2 years.

9. There is a greater likelihood of failure, in an attempt to do good, and therefore there is a sense of," if you cant beat them, join them", syndrome occurring, which makes the need to deal with the ensuing problems complex.

10. Many gang members are in gangs not because they really want to, but because being out of a gang, is more dangerous to their well being and safety.

The Criminal Justice System & Exclusions

What follows from this spiraling, downward trend, is the certainty that the child will end up having to engage in the Criminal Justice System. Often it begins with pupils having to attend Court for petty criminal activity such as theft of mobile phones, and goods from local shops, necessitating a loss of time from school. Added to this is the trauma of the resulting arrest, charges and the likelihood of custodial periods, and the need for legal representation. There is also parental sense of shame that is associated with this for families. Parents who have to deal with the Police and the law in such situations (areas they have very little knowledge of coping with), would sometimes opt for the classic *coping strategy*, that of extreme anger and abandonment. Faced with this situation they may become so angry with the child's involvement of the entire family (by association), in their reckless behaviours, would abandon the child, unsupported in the hands of the law.

Many children, faced with this situation become victims of their own situations - are taken advantage of, and will often lose their Rights, by agreeing to misdemeanors and crimes they may not be entirely responsible for or did not commit; once pressure is brought to bear on them, in what would become fearful and compromising situations out of fear and anxiety.

Exclusions & Underachievement

There is no doubt that the cost of exclusion impacts on underachievement. In some cases it is the cause of exclusion, meaning that a child who experiences public shame and embarrassment, that draws attention to his lack of skills competence among his peers, or who is made to feel silly and incapable of projecting himself as an equal amongst his peers, is more than likely to develop low self-esteem. However, with this experience of negativity, he may resort to strategies that will help him to reverse the status quo, and find creative ways of remaking his credibility and this is often associated with his *"street cred"* or the way he is seen by others. He may use options open to him as follows:

1.   Take the attention away from his lack by providing a distraction (negative mostly), aimed at repositioning or re-identifying himself amongst his peers.

2.   Draw attention to his newly, self-appointed status, by becoming the class clown. Using humour as a way of making others feel good

about him, eases tension, creates popularity and it singles him out as someone with a particular skill i.e. a humour, comedy and branded as ' the funny guy or girl'. These indicate that a 'specialist' label is now attached to the individual.   At this stage, there may be little or no recognition that instead of laughing with him, others are maybe laughing at him. What matters is simply gaining the ability to be "known", "seen" or "singled out" as someone with an publicly known, individual "skill", increases the 'street credibility' and elevates the "comedian', in the eyes of his peers.

3.   Another route he can also take is to assert his authority or elevate his image by becoming a bully. This is a status-creating identity, which, unfortunately, more pupils with 'internal' low self-esteem tend to prefer.   It is because submitting someone to your will gives an impression of having "authority and power", leadership qualities, gained from instilling fear in others. The word 'internal' is used here to suggest that the low self esteem is something which is experienced on a personal level. What the bully then attempts to do is psychologically reverse this sense of lack, by creating a dominant 'external' image to cover up his internalized lack.

However, in groups where more than one bully exists, the criteria for leadership identification becomes a means of vying for the 'top' position and is often associated with various forms of extremes. In other words, the '*real*' leader is seen as the person who can inflict the greatest and most sinister methods of pain and suffering on others, (as is prevalent within gangs). It is important to note however, that not all bullies are created in this way. Some youngsters bully because they have been victims of bullying, aggression, ridicule and/or extreme forms of un/disclosed physical and mental abuse.

The Cost of Youth Unemployment

The percentage of 16-24 yr olds classified as unemployed in the UK was as follows:

a.   England 9%, Wales 8.6%, Scotland 10.1% and Northern Ireland 6.3%. but in each English region the cost of young people classed as NEET (not in education, employment or training), were twice as high.

b.   In England, Scotland and Wales, almost one fifth were considered NEET a very poor comparison with other countries

c.   The productivity loss to the economy as a result of youth unemployment is estimated at £10 million every day (and this is excluding those considered 'inactive'. for other reasons

d.   It costs the State about £20 million per week in Job Seeker's Allowances, a substantial cost to the Exchequer of youth unemployment and inactivity

e.   And of course the personal cost of not being in education, employment or training is priceless in the longer term

The Cost of Youth Crime

1.   The estimated cost of youth crime in Britain is estimated at around £1billior in 2004

2.   The rate of imprisonment is higher in England and Wales than in 12 other European countries. England and Wales also has the highest percentage of prisoners under 18 and the second highest percentage between 18 and 21.

3.   Prisoners are much more likely to be socially excluded than the general population. They are 13 times as likely to have been in care as a child, 13 times as likely to be unemployed, 10 times as likely to have been a regular truant and 2.5times as likely to have had a family member convicted of a criminal offence.

4.   Scotland has shown the greatest success in reducing youth crime, showing a reduction (between 1984 and 2004), of 18-21 but with partial reversal between the mid and late 1990's

The Cost of Underachievement

1.   Since the mid-1990's there has been little change in the percentage of young people 16-24 with no qualifications.

2.   In 2005, these figures stood at 12.6% in England.

3.   12% for Wales; 8.3% for Scotland and 19.9% for Northern Ireland.

4.   Compared to France the percentage of young people with low or no qualifications in the UK is very unfavourable for all ranges.

5.   There is some evidence of a relationship between education and healthy outcomes. The education of parents can affect the educational outcomes of children – indicating proof that education can help break the intergenerational cycle of poverty.

6.   Education underachievement affects the relative performance of the UK economy. (Table 4.4)   The UK has between 10% and 35% lower output per hour than France, Germany and the US. Much can be attributed to a poorer level fo skills and shortfall of capital investment.

7.   There is a growing relationship between educational underachievement and crime. US evidence suggests that social benefits from a 1% increase in the high school completion rate are equivalent to 14.26% of the private return.

Table 4. 4: Counting the cost

Type of Costs	Amount
Youth unemployment	£10 million per day
Job Seeker's Allowance	£20 million per week
Youth crime	£1 billion (2004)
Underachievement	£2-5 billion
Cost of creating a new prison place	£100,000 (2004 estimates)*
Annual cost per prisoner	£38,000 per year (2004)
Mental Health	£20 million (Nov. 2008)
Offending/Re-offending rates	£50,800 per year per offender

Source: *(The Princes Trust Data carried out by London School of Economics LSC):* ***The Kalisher Lecture,*** *delivered by The Honourable, Mr justice Penry-Davey, October, 2008.*

Conclusion

There is no doubt, that the individual setting, (Britain and the Caribbean), is faced with problems that are specific to their own environments. There are also underlying problems associated with infrastructure and specific geographical factors which make an unequal comparison of the settings. For example, Caribbean countries are part of the Commonwealth and there are targets and goals within which they operate that draw attention to those, as well as their philosophical "ideal". There is a drive within Developing Countries to meet UNESCO's *Millennium Development Goals* (MDGs). Indeed, a special reference to Goal No. 2, embodied in the *Dakar Framework 2000,* directs the achievement of *Universal Primary Education (UPE)* – a key Millennium Development Goal that*, 'Children everywhere must be enrolled in full-time primary education by 2015'.*

Whereas in the UK there are legal requirements that make this requirement an easily achievable goal, the first obstacle of *UPE* in the Caribbean, is to do with actual access by ALL children to primary education e.g. very few children with Special Education Needs are included in national education delivery, and for a variety of reasons, **(Fig. 4. 3)**. However, there are also other factors which mitigate against excluding a child from school as a behavior sanction, because the drive (as inferred above), is for *inclusion* rather than *exclusion*!

Fig. 4:3 – *Inclusion vs. exclusion - mitigating factors in the Caribbean*

An estimated 30 million children out of primary school in Commonwealth countries (2004), e.g. 35% of the world's total. (57% of these are girls): *Need to meet MDG and country targets, by getting them into schools.*
Poverty and societal issues relating to gender, class and ethnicity all contribute to the current numbers out of school: *Notion that education eliminates poverty.*
Education excellence seen as the epitome of personal, family and national success – *need to maintain this ethos in all circumstance.*
Poverty and livelihood constraints keep girls (and boys) in varied labour environments in order to help their families subsist: *Economic advancement seen as a solution to this barrier via education.*
Despite access, boys' underachieve with a high level of drop-out rates, prior to and at secondary level: *Need to fight to keep all children in schools.*

However, the main reason for making a comparison between the two environments regarding the issue of Exclusion, is to highlight reasons why parents of Caribbean heritage backgrounds react against exclusions as a behaviour sanction, in general. Their expectation of an education system is to sustain education at all costs, and to find ways to deal with difficulties on a day-to-day basis in schools. In the Caribbean they would never have been called to collect a child from school, and a child would certainly not have been 'rejected' from school as a behaviour sanction.

Caribbean heritage parents therefore find this issue harder to accept than most, are ready to challenge and tend to interpret the 'exclusion' culturally, with deeper complex meanings. For example, among other racially interpreted reasons, it is associated with family shame, suggesting an inability to bring up children properly and a failure to uphold other Caribbean Life Principles as related in Chapter 2. This explains why Caribbean schools' behaviour management of a pupil, is never taken beyond the school.

Whilst this book offers some approaches to managing behaviour deviance, these are not definitive, since there are multitudes of good, workable methods that are meritorious and are applied routinely in dealing with challenging behaviour. What is important for parents to understand, is that within the various approaches that schools take in managing pupils' behaviour, there are legal and government-directed forms of sanctions which they must familiarise themselves with, in order to understand the actions taken by schools, as well as their Rights and Responsibilities as parents, in adhering to those behaviour sanctions in general. The benefit in investing in good education management at all levels, far outweighs the cost investment of remedial and other interventions as outlined above.

SELECTED REFERENCES

Fleetham M., (2006) :Multiple Intelligences in Practice: Enhancing Self-esteem and Learning in the Classroom: **Network Educational Press Ltd.**

Coard B., (1971): How the West Indian Child is Made Educationally Sub-Normal in the British School System:The Scandal of the Black Child in Schools in Britain: **New Beacon Books.**

Preventing Social Exclusion:The Social Exclusion Unit's report presented to Parliament, March 2001 and May 1998.

See also   Breadline Europe:The Measurement of Poverty, (Studies in Poverty, Inequality & Social Exclusion):(2001), Policy Press.

Hayden C., & Dunne S., (1998)::Violence,Truancy and School Exclusion in Britain and France, DfEE.

Guidance on the Use of Restrictive Physical Interventions for Pupils with Severe Behavioural Difficulties. Date of Issue: September 2003. Ref. LEA/0264/2003.

Tony Sewell & Lee Jasper – guardian.co.uk – *"Look Beyond the Street"* 19th July 2003

UNESCO's *Millennium Development Goals* (MDGs).

Dakar Framework (2000): *Education for All.*

5 | Competing Philosophies

Introduction

This chapter looks at the education systems in the Caribbean Region and Britain, and details the philosophies that underpin behaviours in both regions; that of the individual, society and which have resonance in a shared global environment. It argues that migrants who have moved from one setting to another have philosophies that may be viewed as paradoxical in a host society. Outlining the different philosophies supports an understanding of Caribbean people's ideological thinking, discourse, and behaviours. These, the chapter shows, have wider implications for Britain in a global environment.

Philosophy, in this chapter refers to the beliefs espoused by individuals and institutions that guide their decision-making and actions. In this context, it is defined as a coherent body of knowledge and values, applied to a plan that helps to facilitate a process of decision-making, designed for curriculum implementation. The outcome is to enable equal access for the development of the person *(individual)*, who will in turn, contribute to the development of his/her country *(societal),* thus creating the possibility to share and participate in a universal or *(global)* environment. The beliefs which are reflected in an individual's or institution's philosophy usually embody the following:

Current and planned socio-economic, political and other realities that the education should prepare their emerging generations to cope with

1. Feature of an attractive or ideal society to be developed;

2. Knowledge of how the above is to be achieved;

3. Principles or codes of acceptable moral and ethical behaviours; and

4.   Samples or models of the "best" that can be attained or enjoyed by some over others.

Caribbean Regional Philosophy

It is important to understand the controlling philosophy of migrants who have moved from one environment to another. Reasons for this are that they will be guided by principles and ethos which may have an impact on the new environment. That their expectations and realities may, as a result be at odds with one another, and consequently create paradoxes thwart their development. For Caribbean migrants, the (Organization of the educational philosophy of the Eastern Caribbean States) OECS, is being reflected here firstly, because since the early part of the early 20th century, migrant Caribbean families have come to Britain from this sub-region. It is important therefore, to detail the prevailing education principles which many British Caribbean parents were instructed in, and which would have an impact on them and their children in a British context. The OECS represents the sub-region of the Eastern Caribbean territories, and one of its philosophies is to develop a strategy for education that engenders a regional outlook and foster a spirit of co-operation, as the basis of the national development of each Caribbean island. **(Figure 5.1)**.

The focus of such a philosophy lies within the tenets that emphasize regional co-operation and harmony (see *Foundations for the Future: OECS Educational Reform Strategy* – 1991). The reform of education it envisages, suggests that education in the region should take account of the wider Caribbean perspective of which the OECS is part.

Figure 5.1 – Caribbean Educational Philosophy

That reform of education must seek to devise a framework for inspiring noble visions of a Caribbean society and the Caribbean person within the context of a global vision of human civilization and humanity.
That education must be a civilizing force and reforms in education must seek to position the region to contribute to advancing civilization.
That efforts to reform must aim to achieve the harmonization of the education systems of the OECS and promote functional co-operation within the sub-region.
The pooling of resources within the sub-region should enable the countries of the OECS to overcome some of the limitations of their small size and strengthen their capacity to negotiate with external funding agencies.

The benefits of linking as a group to satisfy the criteria of scale, which each country, bargaining separately, will be too small to meet.
The harmonization of the educational systems of Member States and the pooling of education resources to help ensure that reform efforts are sustained.
The principle of consultation and participation in decision-making will provide a good foundation for the reform efforts in the region; and
Harmonizing the education systems of the OECS will lead to significant improvements in the quality of education delivered.

In addition, the OECS view on philosophy for primary and secondary education is that **Primary Education** should be designed to meet essential learning needs and skills, literacy, oral expression, numeracy, problem-solving and basic learning content. These essential learning skills and basic content are required to enable human beings to survive, develop capacities, live and work in dignity, participate fully in initiatives to improve the quality of life, and make informed decisions as well as continue learning p.78.

For the **Secondary Sector,** it directs that such education should cater to the personal development of adolescents and assumes the mastery of some basic functional standards in preparation for learning at this level. It regards Secondary education as intermediary, with its main function as preparing for Further Education and not just for the world of work. That Secondary education must be of a general nature in a wide range of fields, while catering for specialization in a particular field based on aptitude, achievement, interest and aspiration. Above all, it directs that Secondary schooling should not be terminal but should be the instrument for directing the new social order.

For example, in Grenada's case, a document entitled *Pillars for Partnership and Progress (2000),* reiterates the philosophical stance taken in the policy document *Foundations for the Future*, with regard to harmonizing the sub-region's school systems and co-operation. Responding to directives on the Secondary sector development, the government, via its *Grenada OECS Education Development Program* (2002), implemented a comprehensive programme of secondary education development, funded by the World Bank in 2002. Grenada's Education Policy (1999) stated that:

> *Education is one of the main vehicles through which a country attains national development. It is a necessity condition for genuine personal, economic and social development. As such it is the Government's belief that *all citizens of Grenada should have a right to education so that*

> *they could become productive members of the society and develop the*
> *competence and ethos that will enable them to manage change effectively*
> *in an ever-changing world" p.2 (1999): *(my underlining for emphasis).*

One important expectation for these small island-states is that of fostering an outlook of belonging to a larger political entity. This is projected in the preservation and acceptance of *individual national identity* as well as strong solidarity and conscientious allegiance to a *larger regional identity*.   A major benefit for the grouping of these small islands, is the sharing of human and other resources among them.   It enables them to redress the imbalance caused by limited resources and lack of a competitive advantages based on size, among larger, neighbouring countries.   It also means that Grenada is able to pool resources with other member states, in order to provide good quality services in education.

The Ideal Caribbean Beneficiary

The view taken by this author is that ALL CITIZENS must also include ALL RANGES OF ABILITIES. Necessary for the formation of an ideal society is the notion that it must develop an ideal person. Therefore, this means that for curriculum-planners, (and those responsible for education development within the society), there is the notion that a particular person needs to be modeled **(Figure 5.2)**. The image of that ideal therefore becomes part of the goal that must input into education policy as a desired outcome. Here are some of the characteristics of the ideal Caribbean person regarded as an outcome of education development in the Caribbean.

Figure 5.2: Ideal Caribbean Citizen

A person who is aware of the importance of living in harmony with his/her environment
Is respectful of his/her culture, and displays a positive attitude towards work, religious and other ethnic cultures as a strength not divisive
Is self-confident and emotionally secure, and has a healthy respect for human life.
Has a high regard for the family and kinship matters as well as good moral rectitude
Projects culture and the creative imagination as integral to the development of economic and enterprising areas of life
Promotes and contributes to the welfare, health, beliefs, and traditional practices of the country but at the same time, embrace technical and global innovations as part of the global community, for individual and societal advancement.

Develops the capacity to create and take advantage of opportunities to improve, maintain, promote and control physical, mental, social and spiritual well being of the community and the nation.

Fostering a spirit of gender equality, the development of a person's full potential and embracing cultural and other differences on all levels of society, as a source of strength

(**Source:** *Creative and Productive Citizens for the Twenty-First Century; Georgetown, Guyana:
Caribbean Community Secretariat (1989) The Secretariat)*

Is the above vision so different from the strategic vision of 21st century education ideal in Britain? There is no doubt that the political party of the day in any country projects the type of society it wishes to be developed. In fact, its manifesto informs society of the total education delivery, within which are curriculum and other policies it intends to develop. In other words, it is this vision that it articulates that influences the electorate's decision on choice of political parties. Construction of the English education system has followed complex paths, engendered mainly by social and economic concerns within society.

Principles of the English Education System

Perhaps the most important piece of legislation, in the history of English education, of the twentieth century in Britain, was the Education Act of 1944, also known as the "Butler Act". This act replaced all previous legislation. Up to this period Education had become a sensitive social, economic and political issue in most European countries, and it. The tenets of the Act reflected the conviction that education was vital to the nation, the individual and political tendencies as well as social and economic issues of the day.

> *"It shall be the duty of the local education authority for every area, so
> far as their powers extend, to continue towards the spiritual, mental and
> physical developments of the community", (1944 Education Act Part II,7).*

This underscored the fact that the individual's education needs were not only to do with communicating academic information but also involved a holistic approach to developing the person. Looking at a history of education in England highlights the importance of religion and spiritual values, exemplified by instruction on how the school day should begin:

> *"The school day in every county school and in every voluntary school shall
> begin with collective worship on the part of all pupils in attendance".*

The same principle was also reiterated in the Education Reform Act 1988, that education should,*"promote the spiritual, moral, cultural, mental and physical development of pupils at the school and of society":* a view shared by all social classes and political parties. What gave the impetus for this type of legislation is the fact that there were only Elementary Schools for children between the ages of 5 and 13 and places were limited. The world of work for a primary child was the only way forward with little or no possibility of an academic career.

The general nature of education changed when it became possible for a restricted number of pupils to gain free places in a Grammar School if they passed an examination at the age of 11. Elementary Schools began to consider preparing for the examination as one of their main functions. The entrance examination tested the ability of the children in English and Arithmetic, neglecting other subjects. Emphasis was placed on the reputation of the school which was judged mainly on its success rate at this examination.

The examination formed the basis of what is known as the 11plus (11+) examination. It led to divisions in schools (streaming), in the country (social class distinctions) and also led to irreconcilable political attitudes (Labour v. Conservative). The general view is that Conservatives favour this type of selection process whilst Labour is supposed to be against it. This dichotomy between the main political parties, the 11+ exam and the selection process has led to the development of the modern Comprehensive School system.

The fact that some Grammar schools still exist today, indicate that despite the various arguments for and against 11+ examinations as entry to such schools, it was (and is still true), that the future life of a child was decided at about 11. Pupils who didn't sit or who failed the 11+ examination could only gain access to a Secondary Modern School and later perhaps to a Technical School. This gave rise to a tripartite system of education made up as follows:

- *Grammar Schools*
- *Secondary Modern Schools*
- *Secondary Technical Schools*

Grammar Schools

Grammar schools catered for those who were interested in pursuing their studies beyond the O-level GCE stage. It provided an academic education for pupils between the ages of 12 and 19. Their pupils came through the selective process of the 11+ examination and therefore these schools had the most academically gifted children. Most of the pupils entered university after school. These schools were therefore regarded as middle class institutions.

Secondary Modern Schools

Pupils normally attended a four year course leading to the School Leaving Certificate. The course offered instruction in English, at least one other language, geography, history, mathematics, science, drawing, manual instruction or domestic subjects, and physical exercise. When pupils left these schools, they normally went to work.

The choice of curriculum was not influenced by future academic achievement but was child centered. It developed out of the interests, needs and ability of the children. There was no external examination at the end of the course. However, changes occurred in the 1950's when the possibility of staying on in school for a further year. It means that those who stayed on into the 5th year, could sit the General Certificate of Education (GCE). An increase in the number of pupils staying on and taking the GCE led to examination adapted to Secondary Modern Schools, and in 1963, a new type of external examination, the Certificate of Secondary Education (CSE) was introduced for fifth year pupils.

Secondary Technical Schools

These schools, though less popular, provided an alternative to the Secondary Modern School. Pupils who failed the 11+ went to a Secondary Modern School but at the age of 12 or 13 could gain a place at a Secondary Technical School. The benefit to this type of school is that it was linked to industry and commerce and therefore provided vocational education, with its emphasis on technical subjects and preparing pupils for a trade in the world of work.

However, these schools were not successful. One reason is that there was a lack of qualified teachers, which would have had a corresponding impact of failure or lack of success on pupils. Another reason for this could be attributed to the fact that psychologically scared pupils who had failed at 11+ stage, were put off by the experience of failure and therefore were less inclined to try harder to succeed.

The present education structure

Today, the tripartite system of secondary education has been replaced by the Comprehensive School. Between the ages of 5 and 11 children attend a primary school and are then expected to progress to a secondary school, which normally means entry into a Comprehensive School. Among the Comprehensive Schools are also the Voluntary denominational schools (or faith based schools), a dominant denomination being Roman Catholic Comprehensive Schools, private or independent schools and special schools.

Comprehensive Schools

Officially, Comprehensive schools are "intended to provide all the secondary education of all the children in a given area without an organization in three sides". .These schools admit all pupils, regardless of ability. An exception would be children with a Statement of Special Education Needs (SEN), who would attend a Special School, if his/her needs cannot be accommodated in a State Comprehensive School.   Comprehensives admit children from a variety of social backgrounds, with a variety of abilities, and needs, hence the name "comprehensive". There is no examination or any other selection process for entry. Comprehensive Schools, have no entrance exam or selection criteria but at the same time, have within their classroom structures distinctions based on "streaming" and "setting". In other words, groups of pupils arranged according to their learning ability. Approximately 93% of English school children attend such schools, (See Table below).

Since 1998, there have been 4 main types of maintained school in England:

1.   **Community schools** (formerly county schools), in which the Local Education Authority (LEA), employs the schools' staff, owns the schools' lands and buildings and has primary responsibility for admissions.

2.   **Voluntary controlled schools**, which are almost always church schools, with the lands and buildings often owned by a charitable foundation. However, the LEA employs the schools' staff and has primary responsibility for admissions.

3.   **Voluntary aided schools**, linked to a variety of organisations. They can be faith schools (often the Church of England or the Roman

Catholic Church), or be non-denominational schools, often linked to London Livery Companies such as the Worshipful Companies of Haberdashers, Skinners and Drapers. The governing body contributes towards the capital costs of running the school, employs the staff and decides admission arrangements. The school's lands and buildings are normally owned by the charitable foundation, **(Table 5.1)**.

Table 5.1: Structure of State (mainstream) Schools in England

Age on 1st Sept	Year	Curriculum stage	Schools		
3	Nursery	Foundation Stage	Nursery school		
4	Reception		Infant school		First school
5	Year 1	Key Stage 1	Infant school		First school
6	Year 2	Key Stage 1		Primary school	First school
7	Year 3	Key Stage 2	Junior school	Primary school	
8	Year 4	Key Stage 2	Junior school	Primary school	
9	Year 5	Key Stage 2	Junior school	Primary school	
10	Year 6	Key Stage 2	Junior school	Primary school	Middle school
11	Year 7	Key Stage 3	Secondary school		Middle school
12	Year 8	Key Stage 3	Secondary school	Secondary school with Sixth Form	
13	Year 9	Key Stage 3	Secondary school	Secondary school with Sixth Form	Upper school
14	Year 10	Key Stage 4 / GCSE	Secondary school	Secondary school with Sixth Form	Upper school
15	Year 11	Key Stage 4 / GCSE	Secondary school	Secondary school with Sixth Form	Upper school
16	Year 12	Sixth Form / A-level	Sixth form college	Secondary school with Sixth Form	Upper school
17	Year 13	Sixth Form / A-level	Sixth form college	Secondary school with Sixth Form	Upper school

4. **Foundation Schools,** in which the governing body employs the staff and has primary responsibility for admissions. The school land and buildings are owned by the governing body or by a charitable foundation. The Foundation appoints the majority of governors. Many of these schools were formerly **grant maintained schools.** In 2005 the Labour Government proposed allowing all schools to become Foundation schools if they wished.

There are also a smaller number of **City Technology Colleges** and **academies,** which are funded and monitored directly by the Department for Children, Schools and Families. Approximately 7% of English schoolchildren attend privately run independent schools.

A fee is charged for education at independent schools. Such schools, some of which are **boarding schools,** cover primary and secondary education, with fees charged at between £3000 to £30,000 per year. Some schools offer scholarships for those with particular skills or aptitudes or bursaries to allow less well-off students to attend.

Other forms of Education

The Education Act requires parents to ensure their children are educated either by attending school or otherwise. This style of education is often referred to as *Elective Home Education.* The education can take many different forms- from home schooling, where a school-style curriculum is followed at home, to schooling where a structure of educational provision is relaxed. Parents do not need permission to educate their own children. There is no requirement to follow the National Curriculum or to give formal lessons. Parents do not need to be qualified teachers, or to follow school hours or terms. Parents who choose to educate their children otherwise than at school have to finance the education provision themselves.

Britain's Vision for Education in the 21st Century

Despite the many changes that have taken place in Britain's education system, succeeding Education Reforms continue to be underpinned by the founding tenets of the 1944 and 1988 Education acts that education must :

> *"Promote the spiritual, moral, cultural, mental and physical development of pupils at the school and of society".*

It is therefore, imperative that the government of the day must have knowledge and understanding of the characteristics of the society it intends to develop, when creating its various policies. The case for Britain's education provision; and examining the philosophy of the present government is therefore premised on the following characteristics:

- The need to operate democratically, with freedom, justice, prosperity and equality for all. Within these characteristics is also the necessity to project trust, based on honesty and integrity, as well as a society that can be adjudicated independently, in inculcating the fairness principle.

- Other areas included are to do with economic development such as the right to ownership of property, full employment, sustainable growth (for both the individual and the UK), accountability and efficient management of the nation, satisfaction of the basic, social, economic and other needs of Grenadians and sovereignty of the country within the European Community.

In addition, there is the *Every Child Matter : Change for Children*, a National framework for changes underpinned by the Children's Act 2004, which is the legislative spine on which the present government want to build our reforms of children's services. In attempting to do so, it has established for England:

1. A Children's Commissioner to champion the views and interests of children and young people;

2. A duty on Local Authorities to make arrangements to promote co-operation between agencies and other appropriate bodies (such as voluntary and community organisations) in order to improve children's well-being (where well-being is defined by reference to the five outcomes), and a duty on key partners to take part in the co-operation arrangements;

3. A duty on key agencies to safeguard and promote the welfare of children;

4. A duty on Local Authorities to set up Local Safeguarding Children Boards and on key partners to take part;

5. A provision for indexes or databases containing basic information about children and young people to enable better sharing of information;

6. A requirement for a single Children and Young People's Plan to be drawn up by each Local Authority;

7. A requirement on Local Authorities to appoint a Director of Children's Services and designate a Lead Member;

8.   The creation of an integrated inspection framework and the conduct
      of Joint Area Reviews to assess local areas' progress in improving
      outcomes; and

9.   Provisions relating to foster care, private fostering and the education
      of children in care.

Focus on local change

The Children Act 2004 gives a clear focus and a new status to children's services but, in itself, it is not enough. Its implementation is part of a wider process of change, focused on outcomes and taken forward by local change programmes in 150 Local Authority areas set within a national framework. The *National Service Framework for Children, Young People and Maternity Services* (NSF) is integral to this. It sets out a ten-year programme to stimulate long-term and sustained improvement in children's health and well-being. As it is implemented by Primary Care Trusts (PCTs), Local Authorities and other partners including other health organisations, it will contribute to the achievement of the five outcomes.

What the outcomes mean

1.   **BE HEALTHY**

      • Physically healthy

      • Mentally and emotionally healthy

      • Sexually healthy

      • Healthy lifestyles

      • Choose not to take illegal drugs

      • Parents, carers and families promote healthy choices

2.   **STAY SAFE**

      • Safe from maltreatment, neglect, violence and sexual
        exploitation

      • Safe from accidental injury and death

      • Safe from bullying and discrimination

      • Safe from crime and anti-social behaviour in and out of school

- Have security, stability and are cared for
- Parents, carers and families provide safe homes and stability

3. ENJOY AND ACHIEVE

- Ready for school
- Attend and enjoy school
- Achieve stretching national educational standards at primary school
- Achieve personal and social development and enjoy recreation
- Achieve stretching national educational standards at secondary school
- Parents, carers and families support learning

4. MAKE A POSITIVE CONTRIBUTION

- Engage in decision-making and support the community and environment
- Engage in law-abiding and positive behaviour in and out of school
- Develop positive relationships and choose not to bully and discriminate
- Develop self-confidence and successfully deal with significant life changes and challenges
- Develop enterprising behaviour
- Parents, carers and families promote positive behaviour

5. ACHIEVE ECONOMIC WELL-BEING

- Engage in further education, employment or training on leaving school
- Ready for employment
- Live in decent homes and sustainable communities
- Access to transport and material goods

- Live in households free from low income
- Parents, carers and families are supported to be economically active
- Every Child Matters: Change for Children

These outcomes embody *"spiritual, cultural, moral, intellectual, physical and social development"*, of individuals, who in turn, will be empowered to develop their society. The Framework makes it clear that equality of participation by all regardless of *race, age, gender, creed, political persuasion* is a most desirable outcome. Furthermore, to do so, the Framework provides for various bodies and a wide cross-section of stakeholders and service providers to participate in education development.

There are expectations also for both private and public sectors in the creation of a strong and diversified economy, which depicts a British society within a macro-policy implementation as follows, **(Figure: 5. 3)**.

Figure: 5. 3 Societal Expectations

One that is transformed and diversified economically;
That has evidence of sound social and infrastructural development, equitable distribution of the proceeds from growth and development;
An environment conducive to private, domestic and foreign investment;
Political and industrial relations that are stable and peaceful, conducive to the pursuit of high ideals for its citizens;
The provision of a safety net for the vulnerable and poverty stricken, and
The socialized acceptance and promotion of gender balance, especially that of women, as equal partners

Expectations of a 21st century school system

The Governments vision of a 21st century school system (2008), was set out in **The Children's Plan,** to make England the best place in the world for children and young people to grow up. Its central ambition is to produce world -class schools and world-class standards for every community. The vision, outlined by Ed Balls, Secretary of State for Children, Families and Schools, projects the following ambition that:

- Provides excellent teaching, personalized education and development in an environment of good behavior;

- Enables schools to identify and help to address additional needs;

- Provides a range of activities and opportunities to enrich the lives of children, families and the wider community; and

- If characterized by schools working more extensively and effectively with parents, other providers and wider children's services.

- Within the vision is supporting infrastructure which includes:

- A revised accountability framework and school improvement strategies which focus on all outcomes to which schools contribute, underpinned by the new School Report Card;

- A highly skilled and motivated children's workforce in schools, that is well led and effectively deployed; and

- Resources in the system deployed to the best effect to improve outcomes for children and young people.

The Plan lays emphasis on delivery of the five *Every Child Matters* outcomes, as outlined above, for children (age 5-18 years), in England. It provides linkages between the social background, deprivation and low educational achievement. Key areas are on standards, progress, wider personal skills, identifying and addressing additional needs (including SEN), parental engagement, support of a highly expert workforce, collective determination that will provide excellent teaching, an environment of good behavior a range of activities and opportunities to enrich the lives of children, young people, families and the wider community.

However, as far as the *Antoine Behaviour Excellence Model* and its strategic approaches to education is concerned. the characteristic elements of the Government's 21st century Plan are not new. For the past 15 years, (during the 20th century), The *Antoine Behaviour Excellence Model* has been persistently interrogating and delivering education (now presented by this 21st century Vision), which is evidence based on its workability and success ratio.   What Ed Balls envisages for children and young people who attend a 21st century school, and their families, are characteristic approaches to education and behavior management of the *Antoine Behaviour Excellence Model,* as outlined in Chapter 8.   The government outlines what it expects the **benefits would be to children, young people and their families** are that the school:

- *Addresses the needs of each child or young person* better, offering a personalized and tailored approach: (includes teaching and learning that is highly responsive and engaging to children's own learning, stretching children to do their best to attain well, focusing on the personal and social development, provision of a personal tutor for each child, extra support for those with additional needs).

- *Engages and consults pupils in the school,* not just on their own learning and additional needs but also on issues related to the school as a whole;

- *Is a resource for the whole community*, building on the provision of access to extended services (including childcare), opening up its facilities for community use, providing wider opportunities for children, young people and their families to take part in sporting, play, recreational, cultural and learning activities, and offering easier access to other children's services within the local area; and;

- *Engages parents and Carers* in the child's learning and development and facilitates access to support to help parents and carers do this more effectively.

We already know that where there is real commitment to raising standards for ALL pupils, and tackling barriers to learning, goes beyond the school building. We also know that omitting to respond to the major part that a child's cultural and social circumstances and the many elements that have a really damaging impact on their learning, would render the 21st Century Vision as impotent; making it a *vision* only. The core mission of a school can only be achieved if it has the strong linkages that the *Antoine Behaviour Excellence Model* outlines, as being integral to achieving real success for EVERY child.

The Government's 21ˢᵗ century **vision for schools** is that they will:

- *Place an even stronger emphasis on working in partnership:* (with parents and carers – focusing on learning but also additional needs, e.g. those of parents and carers also in supporting their child's learning and development; with other schools, early years education providers, Connexions, employers, Further Education colleges and Sixth Form colleges, Higher Education institutions and other education and training providers, to broaden curricular offer. Added to the list of partnership are also those delivering other children's services in the local area, whether statutory, third or independent sector – under the umbrella of the Children's Trust).

- *Take responsibility for improving outcomes for children and young people* in the wider community as well as those on their own roll. Meaning, working with the local community to improve pupils outcomes and help raise standards across the community.

Whilst I welcome the fact that the Government has finally caught up with my own vision, which was projected some 15 years ago, I am more elated that the *Antoine Behaviour Excellence Model* can now act as a catalyst and an exemplar of the potential outcomes envisioned, if real commitment at grassroots level, is able to match the political will.

The *Antoine Behaviour Excellence Model* has been successful for all the children and families it provides services for, because of its strong leadership, strong and supportive local partnership with the community and parents, high expectations, recognition and celebration of achievement, accountability to all its service providers and clients, its focus on child-centered learning that takes into account a holistic approach (i.e. including culture, socio-economic and historic), to education development and success outcomes. **(See also Chapter 8).**

At present, Britain is at the bottom of the ladder in terms of literacy development in the world. It is a sad indictment of educational standards on a country that has always prided itself, for generations, on educational excellence and the envy of the rest of the Developed or First World countries. The Government's vision then, in removing itself from the bottom of the ladder on equal par with countries like Romania, to the world-class vision it envisages is ambitious and calls for more than expressions of expectations. "Putting schools in the driving seat and giving them the influence and help they need to get the very best for all their pupils" (**Ed Balls July 2008**), will be a challenge to the government and all those working within the supportive national framework, and a test of their ability to raise the stakes of education development beyond various societal stigmas.

Were it the case that everyone in society had the same privilege without class differences and the resulting advantages/disadvantages, then the speed of delivery and excellent standards expected would, I believe, be easy to implement across the geographical divide of Britain. But one has to take into consideration possible drag-anchors such as the stigmas that may thwart the outcomes which are envisioned.

There are stigmas attached to the different education providers (e.g. mainstream, vs independent sector partnership). Other disadvantages include affordability to buy in extra educational support by some and class divisions; stereotyping and a lack of recognition or acceptance that culturally sensitive and socio-economically approaches are integral to educational planning and attainment in our multi-cultural society. Within the partnership framework should be the support of the media, (a tool which shapes and can re-shape how society views children and young people). Without a plan of action to incorporate or tackle these potential barriers, the Vision of 21st century schools in Britain is likely to fall short of its expectations and projected outcomes.

Areas that an ideal Curriculum should target

But how are these goals translated in practice? An ideal Curriculum should demonstrate sensitivity to the needs of persons *(including those with disabilities),* their Rights, and provide intervention at various stages of growth (from pre-school to working life), for its delivery. Where any of the above elements is absent, an approach should firstly prepare society, specifically Care-givers, to work with children who have "specific" learning needs throughout their lives. Specific needs may not necessarily fall within the present definition of "Special Needs". One such example is a *culturally sensitive and socially specific* learning approach. Such curricula will need to include:

    i.   Additional needs in Development – understanding those with additional needs that are culturally and socially based and how management of this is to be developed;

    ii.   The roles of parents, community workers and teachers in learning and teaching about such groups;

iii. Rehabilitation in the community (working with media and other local organizations),with regard to changing existing views about those in need;

iv. Understanding factors that influence the development and learning processes as well as associated behaviours, of those from different cultural backgrounds

v. Establishment of a community empowerment service – participatory development for an inclusive service delivery approach;

vi. A curriculum that reflects respect for the rights and dignity of all, irrespective of their cultural and social backgrounds;

vii. Developing self-worth and an openness to new experiences/ cultures, to cope with change, especially with reference to critical thinking, creativity and problem-solving

viii. The provision of numeracy, literacy and communication skills and with aesthetic qualities for the child with socially specific and culturally sensitive learning needs;

ix. Creating learning objectives that supports an understanding of the child (cultural background and socio-economic circumstances). This will guide his development and changing needs throughout the various phases of his life;

x. Understanding the basics of child-development in the context of social and cultural development;

xi. Assessing the child with special learning needs for pre-school intervention in the social and cultural context of its natural settings;

xii. Developing an understanding of the important aspects of home-based early care, and cultural /family-centric service by the caregivers, in helping children develop their abilities;

xiii. Providing a framework that addresses the social, economic, historic an cultural needs of pupil as well as their learning needs;

xiv. Development of their cultural assets that impacts on their ability to work towards and prepare for the world of work, as well as the opportunity to pursue economic independence; and

xv.   Creation of a tolerant and respectful atmosphere in all schools for all abilities, thereby creating values and behaviours that are commensurate the ethos of Every Child Matters.

Some Weaknesses in the Education System

Despite there being a National Curriculum, that includes Special Education Needs (SEN), provision via a SEN Code of Practice, and a strategy for 100% inclusion, there is still the sense that gaps exist which account for a good deal of our current problems in schools. This means that there is much work to be done in making the British government's **Vision** for each citizen, applicable to **everyone** in its society. There have been efforts by individuals, local organizations and social groups to address additional learning needs, evidenced by the existence of extra provisions outside the mainstream school and the State control, e.g. Supplementary Schools, Saturday Schools or Mother Tongue Schools throughout Britain.

However, situation analyses have shown that huge gaps occur in mainstream provision, and that account for the level s of poor performance and underachievement among some sections of the community. The "supplement" or "complement" provision or extra education by culturally diverse groups, who experience educational difficulties in the classroom, point to the need for mainstreaming education provision and approaches that deliver a culturally sensitive and socially specific approach to education provision within the National Curriculum. This has been the focus of my own research on the ground with schools, principals and parents; as well as examining various documents on general education provision in the country. It is important to say that there is NO curriculum or policy for inclusion of a culturally sensitive or socially specific approach to developing, which I would call, **Additional Special Educational Needs** provision in Britain.   There is, of course the **English as an Additional Language**(EAL), and English for Speakers of Other languages (ESOL) provision, but what happens to those sections of the community who have "English" as their first language but whose needs are more culturally based, than linguistically derived?

Though the levels of underachievement and the underperformance in schools and the labour market compared with the initiatives taken by individual groups and associations in society, attest to their necessity in dealing with inclusion, raising attainment levels and achievement and developing self-esteem that eventually leads to follow on success. Documentation which highlighted needs that impact also on curricula needs development are among the following:

The Scarman Report

In April 1981 Brixton, South London and other impoverished inner-city areas of Britain, (such as Toxteth, in Liverpool and Moss Side in Manchester). Youths took to the street in an unprecedented scale of riots across the cities. These cities were in economic and social decline. Brixton had a housing shortage, despite a falling population; many low income households, one-parent families and high incidences of disability and mental illness. At a time of national recession, unemployment in Brixton stood at 13% and 25.4% for ethnic minorities. Unemployment among black youths was estimated at 55%. Following the riot, Lord Leslie Scarman was appointed *"to inquire urgently into the serious disorder in Brixton on 10-12 April 1981 and to report, with the power to make recommendations"*.

He said that, "complex political, social and economic factors" created a "disposition towards violent protest". He found several factors had contributed to the disorder. Firstly, the riots were not planned, but were spontaneous outbursts of built-up resentment sparked by particular incidents with the police. Lord Scarmann, also reported loss of confidence and mistrust in the police and their methods of policing. Liason arrangements between police, community and local authority had already collapsed before the disturbances. Lord Scarman recommended that concerted efforts should be made, to recruit more ethnic minorities into the police force, and changes in training and law enforcement. He highlighted the problems of racial disadvantage and inner city decline and a more concerted and co-ordinated approach to tackling them.

"Institutional racism" did not exist, he said, pointing instead to "racial disadvantage" and *"racial discrimination"*. Lord Scarman called for *"Urgent action"*, to prevent racial disadvantage becoming an *"endemic, ineradicable disease threatening the very survival of our society"*. He concluded that positive discrimination to tackle racial disadvantage was *"a price worth paying"*. Swann's *Education For All.*

Approximately 4 years after the Scarman Report, Lord Swann's report (1985), pointed to the need for changes in behaviour and attitudes throughout Britain. Although he recognized that *"the education system must not be expected to carry the whole burden of that change, schools in particular are uniquely well placed to take a lead role. Britain has evolved, over many centuries, institutions and traditions which, whatever their shortcomings, have been taken as models by many nations, and were indeed an important part of the attraction of this country to the ethnic minorities who are the essential concern of our report."* Lord Swann defined change in the context of *"the pluralism which is now a marked feature of British life"*. The Swann Report stressed the urgency of the need for "change where attitudes to the ethnic minorities are concerned," within his, Education for All philosophy. The call for changes as expressed by Lord Swann some twenty eight years ago, is as relevant to Britain as it was in the 20th century, as its needed in our 21st century.

Low achievement Levels – The Rampton Report

Low achievement levels among African and Caribbean children, especially at secondary level. The results of Factors which contribute to this is an imbalance in the curriculum, which is insufficient to meet the needs of this group of pupils. Slightly earlier than The Swann Report (1977) but completed in 1981, Lord Rampton's report on 'The West Indian Community' , the Select Committee on Race Relations and Immigration highlighted the widespread concern about the poor performance of West Indian children in schools. The Committee therefore recommended, amongst other measures, that *'as a matter of urgency the government (should) institute a high level and independent inquiry into the causes of the underachievement of children of West Indian origin in maintained schools and the remedial action required'.* However, 32 years have passed, (the time span of a generation) and today there is still the need for *"urgency"* that Lord Swann had expressed. Furthermore, the levels of underachievement that Lord Rampton highlighted, also 32 years ago, is still prevalent in our society.

Poverty & Children of Ethnic Minorities

According to a report, *Parallel Lives? Poverty among Ethnic Minority Groups"* published in 2003, three out of four British children of Pakistani and Bangladeshi descent, are growing up in poverty-stricken households. A study by the University of Essex found that 73 per cent of Pakistani and Bangladeshi households in Britain were living on less than 60 per cent of the UK average income, a level widely recognised as the "poverty line".

The report also found that only 35 per cent of adult Bangladeshis were employed and that the economic activity rates of Pakistani women were half those of the rest of Britain's female population. The research underlined significant differences in the economic achievements of ethnic minority groups in Britain. The proportion of people living below the poverty line was 25 per cent among the population as a whole, and about 33 per cent in Indian communities. This increased to 40 per cent among Caribbean families and 50 per cent of black African households.

The unemployment rate among young Caribbean men was twice that of the sector as a whole, the report said. Martin Barnes, director of the CPA, said the levels of poverty among children from ethnic minority groups were "staggering". Despite government efforts to improve the living conditions of poor children, the UK still has one of the highest rates of child poverty in the developed world, according to UNICEF (2005). Approximately one in seven children grow up in poverty in the UK, defined by Unicef as households with income below 50% of the national average. With 15.4% of British children falling into that category, the UK ranked seventh from bottom of a list of 24 industrialized nations studied by Unicef. (*By Daily Mail Reporter The Mail On Line :Last updated at 12:32 AM on 08th December 2008*).

There is a need for an integrated approach to behaviour management. However, it is my view that attending CPD on behaviour management alone is not enough, there needs to be a commitment to contextualise it for relevance and benefit. Ultimately, as with the *Antoine Behaviour Excellence Model,* it is a process that necessitates an integrated plan of action, creativity and determination. In *Chapter 9* details are given on how to create your own Adverse Behaviour Reduction Plan. **(See Fig: 5. 4 below).**

Socio-cultural Factors

There is a gender issue present in Britain among Caribbean children, whereby males are being outperformed academically by females. Males also have lower participation in secondary education. This is an issue being addressed by *The Antoine Behaviour Excellence Model* over the past 15 years, with a very high percentages of both behavior and academic success at TCS Tutorial College.

Cultural Imperialism and Globalization

The need to operate within a globalized environment has implications for Caribbean children's cultural/traditional identity. The high rates of crime; student behavioural problems, (among both boys and girls); the speed and freedom of regional and global movement; and a lack of structured parent-centered education to help sensitize them of their roles in a global economy; present challenges that require widespread parents' participation in children's education , (as exemplified by the *Antoine Behaviour Excellence Model)*, at both the school and their wider levels of involvement.

The Professional Standards for Teachers in Britain have a specific focus on behaviour management. Within a Core of Standards, the following, in particular, relate to behavior. These do not include cultural sensitivity as an approach to behavior management.

Figure: 5.4: Behaviour Management: Teachers Professional Standards

C1: Have high expectations of children and young people, including a commitment to ensuring that they can achieve their full educational potential and to establishing fair, respectful, trusting, supportive and constructive relationships with them
C2: Hold positive values and attitudes and adopt high standards of behaviour in their professional role.
C10: Have a good, up-to-date working knowledge and understanding of a range of teaching, learning and behaviour management strategies and know how to use and adapt them, including how to personalise learning to provide opportunities for all learners to achieve their potential.
C16: Know and understand the relevant statutory and non-statutory curricula and frameworks, including those provided through the National Strategies, for their subjects/curriculum areas and other relevant initiatives across the age and ability range they teach.

(Source:www.tda.gov.uk/standards)

Conclusion

This chapter began by examining the philosophies of the Caribbean, and a comparative analysis with Britain, from an educational standpoint. Outlining the differences of the two educational environments, gives rise to an understanding of Caribbean people's ideological thinking, discourse and behavior patterns. It explains the Caribbean-heritage person's understanding of educational expectations, life principles which guide parents codes of behaviour and attitudes to educational processes and outcomes. In the main, the aims, objectives and benefits of educating young people in both the Caribbean and Britain are similar – each geared towards attaining national development, producing knowledgeable young people who will create a productive workforce, and who would be able to develop competences necessary to manage change in a constantly changing world.   Differences highlighted were the harmonizing philosophy of the Caribbean region compared with the fragmented nature of Britain's plural environment; the cultural underpinning of educational development as being integral the development of economic and enterprising areas of life - these are very high on the Caribbean's education agenda.

Therefore, what happens to people immersed in such ways of thinking in a developing environment, who have to adjust to a denial of the aspirations and high ideals they expected of life in Britain? The next chapter looks at the realities of Caribbean people's existence in Britain from the 1950's to 2008. It charts the complexities that their social and historical sojourn in Britain have produced to date. It reveals a community that has greatly transformed from their Motherland ideal, to one that is affected by a number of institutional and social causations. It also presents the various factors that created psychological dilemmas for British Caribbeans, in the changing face of Britain.

SELECTED CHAPTER REFERENCES

Annex A: Total Departmental Spending, 7391 Departmental report 2008, Department for Children, Schools and Families. £43 billion total spending on schools.

Action Group: *Parallel Lives? Poverty Among Ethnic Minorities* (2003), Issue No. 5, University of Essex.

Table 1 Total Departmental spending, Departmental report 2008, Department for Innovation, Universities and Skills. £14.3 billion spending on HE, £4.9 billion on FE.

Estimate for the United Kingdom, from United Kingdom, CIA World Factbook

Table 1.2: Full-time and Part-time pupils by age, gender and school type, Education and Training Statistics for the United Kingdom: 2008, Department for Children, Schools and Families. Enrolment at independent schools is not partitioned by stages in the source, and has been estimated using an equal division. The error is within the precision of these figures.

"Higher Education Enrolments, and Qualifications Obtained, at Higher Education Institutions in the UK in the Academic Year 2006/07". Higher Education Statistics Agency (2008-01-10). "The total number of HE enrolments at English HEIs stood at 1,957,195 in 2006/07."

"Further Education, Work-Based Learning, Train to Gain and Adult Safeguarded Learning - Learner Numbers in England: October 2007". Learning and Skills Council (2008-04-10). "There were 1.75 million learners in LSC-funded FE on 1 October 2007."

"School attendance and absence: the law". Directgov.

"School leaving age set to be 18". *BBC News* (2007-01-12). Retrieved on 2008-12-07.

"Categories of Schools – Overview". *GovernorNet*. Department for Children, Schools and Families (2003-09-05). Retrieved on 2008-12-10.

"What are Academies?". *Standards Site*. Department for Children, Schools and Families. Retrieved on 2008-12-10.

Richard Garner (2002-01-28). "Rising number of parents decide they can do a better job than the education system", *The Independent*. Retrieved on 9 December 2008.

Mathew Charles (2005-03-18). "Growth market in home education". *BBC News*. Retrieved on 2008-12-09.

Katie Razzall; Lewis Hannam (2007-09-26). "UK home-school cases soar". *Channel 4 News*. Retrieved on 2008-12-09.

"Elective Home Education: Guidelines for Local Authorities". Department for Children, Schools and Families (2007). Retrieved on 2008-12-10.

Terri Dowty (editor) (2000). *Free Range Education: How Home Education Works*. Hawthorn Press. ISBN 1903458072.

Grenada Government: *Foundations for the Future:* OECS Educational Reform Strategy (1991)

Grenada *OECS Education Development Programme* (2002)

"Educating your child at home".*Directgov*. Retrieved on 2008-12-09.

"Teacher training providers". Office for Standards in Education (2008-12-05).www. dcsf.gov.uk

Chapter Notes

The Swann Report (1985): *Education for all:* Report of the Committee of Enquiry into the Education of Children from Ethnic Minority Groups: Chairman: Lord Swann:Cmnd. 9453 London: Her Majesty's Stationery Office 1985 © Crown copyright material.

The Rampton Report (1981): *West Indian children in our schools*.Interim report of the Committee of Inquiry into the education of children from ethnic minority groups Chairman: Anthony Rampton OBE

Presented to Parliament by the Secretary of State for Education and Science by Command of Her Majesty June 1981.

For information on a history of education in England, please see: Gillard D (2007) *Education in England: a brief history* www.dg.dial.pipex.com/history/

*"Poverty Grips the children of ethnic minoritie*s", The Independent Newspaper, reporter Ian Burrell, Home Affairs Correspondent, *Thursday, 23 January 2003*.

You can download the Professional Standards for Teachers from the **Training and Development Agency for Schools' website:**Teachers Standards:www.tda.gov.uk/ standards

6 | The Dichotomy of the Black Presence in Britain

*"It can be legal justice or
Street justice, I don't really
care anymore!"*

Introduction

This chapter illustrates profoundly, the historic and present generational attitudes and lifestyle responses reflected in the behaviours of British Caribbean people; including families and young people in general. It also looks at the types of influences affecting the conduct of young people in a variety of settings and presents anecdotal evidence to explain specific behavioural forms. Some of these are psychological in origin, having been affected by migrants' aspirations, a legacy of trauma, a developing black consciousness in Britain, and community approaches to problem-solving.

If the word *Caribbean* is problematic to some who now claim to be *Black British* of Caribbean heritage, the psychological dilemma is more profound for those who were brought up during the period of colonization in the region. Firstly, one has to remember that these early migrants were identified as West Indians, who encountered (for the first time in their lives), racist, extremist behaviours which highlighted their blackness. The majority of them experienced derogatory forms of "identification"; for example, being called "*blacks*", "*coloureds*", "*nig-nogs*", "*golliwogs*" and would have witnessed "*Paki-bashing*" and other forms of racial violence in England. What is interesting are the strategies they employed to deal with these psychologically, confusing state of affairs.

"Mother" Country Aspirations

It is important to remember that some of these early migrants, especially those who arrived in Britain in the late 1950's and early 1960 have, arrived in England before their islands became independent from Britain. They had lived all their lives up to this point as British citizens, with an imposed British (colonial) education system and structure of political governance. Consequently, they displayed a fierce allegiance to Britain, seen as the `*Mother Country*' with pride and conviction that they had come to a land that was `paved with gold' and would receive a welcome that would naturally accept them as "children" of the "Mother", or as **equal citizens** of Britain and the Empire. For them, the Empire was as a real as the Britain they were now living in, having celebrated throughout their lives all that it stood for, with marked periods in the annual calendar, that received Royal personages and representatives in celebrations that reinforced their allegiance and linkage.

Despite the movements toward Self-government, and pending Political Independence from Britain, by politicians and the governments of the day, for these early migrants, the heart of their educational and psychological development was a system of British upbringing that firmly etched in their psyches, an indelible identification with Britain so that their thought processes, (based on their colonial upbringing), and responses to the *rejection* they now faced in Britain, created a complexity of psychological and emotional responses. Today, this is still being displayed on complex levels of behaviours discussed below.

It is not widely known that Caribbean people had, via their system of British education management, had their exam papers sent to the region from the UK and was also marked in Britain, (as was customary up until the 1970's). They received an imposed English curriculum, with resources and texts that were solely related to things English (being British citizens in British colonial territories). In many of their cultural practices, it can be seen that they "thought" and "behaved" as British people, having imbued the British ways of life they were bred on. They are the migrants who arrived in Britain, qualified in various fields, with British Certificates, evidencing their qualifications, but who found they could not be employed in the professions they were qualified and certified to do. Instead, the majority had to do menial jobs in various sectors of British society.

It is important to remember that they were the people who zealously responded to British politicians' plea for them to come to Britain, to firstly help fight war and then to help "rebuild the Motherland". However, in return for their service, Caribbean migrants were abused, violated, ostracized, rejected, to the extent where employment in the health service, catering, transport, and hospitality industry did not reflect migrants' levels of intellect or professionalism. Today, many parents talk nostalgically about high expectations of life in Britain, counteracted by rejection that told them as far as housing needs were concerned that "**No Blacks, no Irish and no dogs**" were welcomed. What is interesting and would need further research is an exploration of their survival strategies in Britain.

These migrants would have become ex-colonials overnight, because the change of political status from colony to Self-government or Political Independence in their "back-homes", would have taken place without their participation and therefore would be more of an intellectual exercise than a reality to them. They had carried within them, the full conviction that the Britain they had admired and were now living in is, and would always be, their "**Motherland**". Many of the early parents, who now have second and third generation families in Britain today, would readily discuss how in the early days, they behaved as "service-minded" men and women, intent on defending Queen and country, as they and British soldiers did. In fact, some of the former conscripts of the two World Wars experienced a psychological blow, which contradicted their high expectations of being treated as British subjects, rather than `aliens' or `convenient British outsiders'.

In the Caribbean, they would have revered the iconoclastic English Great House in their communities, which housed Colonial masters – the progenitors of the Plantocracy regime; songs that dictated Caribbean nationals' allegiance to Britain and all things **British** . These are, educational systems; the English language; forms of dress; music and dancing; religion, especially Catholicism; food and festivities; the outrage of "attack" on Britain in the WWI and WWII, and their defiance in defending the Realm; forms of speech conventions (evidencing some of the best Orators of our time, demonstrated by Caribbean Political leaders, as well as those in society who were daubed "**man of words**". In this context, the use of "words" denotes the dignity and mastery of the English language, which demonstrates heights of educational /intellectual superiority: in fact, a total culture immersed in the British way of life. That was the pride of the early West Indian migrants to Britain.

It is important to understand the impact that an opposite experience in the "**Motherland"** would have, on a person believing he has a life-long identity which he considers to be intact, contradicted by life-changing experiences which reflected the opposite of all that he had come to know and understand as his identity. The result is a complex web of behavioural responses and strategies for survival, in what was, and to some extent still is, an extremely harsh, and "violent" society. *Violence* is used here in a relative sense because what transpired, further explains the complexity which is being experienced today, and which has meaning in understanding the general behavioural responses affecting British Caribbean children especially.

Perhaps one of the most severe forms of violence experienced by Caribbean migrant children in Britain took place in some of the schools they attended, and which have impacted on the way they view the education system, as well as educational responses to them. It is important to note that some of the early migrants and their children experienced a form of "branding" that represented ostensibly, a cruel form of psychological damage exacted on a child. Bernard Coard, a West Indian teacher in 1971, highlighted the extent of the damage experienced by West Indian migrant children in his book, *How the British School system made the West Indian child educationally subnormal* (1971). The reality of children being branded as "*educationally subnormal*" and being transported over long distances from home to schools that were referred to "Educationally Sub-Normal" (ESN Schools), is a form of violence that many of the early parents today, are still grappling with. In fact, many of those "ESN" pupils are our current parents, who view the educational system as having failed them, and who attribute their experiences of unfulfilled ambitions and underperformance to the levels of rejection and "hurt" they experienced in the early days. For some, the experiences are as real to them now, as it was thirty years ago. Their views of the educational, social, economic and political systems are, understandably, "coloured" by what they see as a continuum of adverse experiences for them and their children in Britain today. **(Figure 6.1)**

On one hand, the grandparents of those children, who now represent the early migrants to Britain, alluded to above, by virtue of their own educational, socio-economic, political, historical and cultural experiences, have different views, of the strategies that should be employed for survival in Britain. It can be seen in their various responses to behavior management of their grandchildren, how this conflicts with their (first generation).

Figure 6.1: British Caribbean Migrants' Journey

FAMILY LEAVING CARIBBEAN WITH HIGH EXPECTATIONS

- *Culture intact*
- *Social interaction good*
- *Invited to take up jobs*
- *Varying degrees of qualifications*
- *Experiences rejection*

FAMILY ARRIVAL IN BRITAIN

- *Shattered illusions*
- *Culture shock*
- *Poor Social housing*
- *Low-paid (menial) jobs*
- *Education `branding' of children*
- *(discriminatory) Immigration Laws*

FAMILY LEAVING CARIBBEAN WITH HIGH EXPECTATIONS

- *Experience with Educationally Sub-Normal (ESN) Schools and "branding"*
- *Low attainment levels*
- *Low teacher expectations*

FAMILY LEAVING CARIBBEAN WITH HIGH EXPECTATIONS

- *Confrontations with law enforcement personnel*
- *Increase in Black Mental Health*
- *Low participation rate in employment*
- *Underachievement*
- *Gang and Gun crime*
- *Parents Looking back at the Caribbean as a bridge-builder for solutions*

children's views. The levels of responses therefore to behaviour management becomes complicated, and can be viewed as generational in character. The complexity of responses can be viewed thus:

1. **EARLY MIGRANTS RESPONSE** – at times quiet submission to conflicts and attitudes that suggest pacifying (to the point of neutralisation), rather than confrontation. The double allegiance factor, (that of old psyche of colonial affectation and the reality of protecting and instructing their flesh and blood, collude to produce a confusion of emotional responses that can seem illogical in conclusion at times).

2. **FIRST GENERATION CARIBBEANS IN BRITAIN** - would probably have entered Britain, having personally witnessed and experienced several changes in their Caribbean systems of governance. In fact, many of them would have arrived in Britain, having experienced changes to their education system, (the change from the British examination and exam paper marking in Britain, to the Caribbean Examinations Council (CXC), which was founded in 1981, control as well as changes in their country's social and economic systems. Most importantly, their experiences of change from British to Caribbean allegiance, as opposed to their parents' colonial experience, would have brought about changes in their perspectives on life, as people inheriting a dual nationality – a Caribbean and a British one. These changes were brought about by a change in consciousness, which favored Caribbeanness, over a long history of struggle for self-determination and independence from Britain. This would ultimately impact on their behavioural responses to aspects of life as it affects them in Britain.

Therefore, the reality of the complex web of behavioural responses from different members of whole families has to do with their individual experiences, at different times and on different levels in Britain. Evidently, both children and early migrant parents, now living in Britain, have a path of convergence of different experiences and historical backgrounds, to which a third dimension has been added. This third dimension is that offsprings of second generation "British" Caribbeans which reflect life experiences that are predominately British in character, with an absence of Caribbean culture per se.

3. **THE THIRD GENERATION OR BLACK BRITISH CITIZENS -**
   are the interesting element in this dichotomy of behavior in Britain today. It would be true to say, that despite not experiencing real life in the Caribbean environment, their Black British cultural make-up is an amalgam of different inputs – from colonial Caribbean, early migrant or grand-parent perspectives, ESN parents' views and their own experiences which are at times, reflective of a continuum of warring perspectives, ideals and realities. A history of migrant Caribbean communities in Britain is a testimony of the many socio-economic and political changes which they have undergone on different levels in society (see Fig. 6.1). It is these varying perspectives that impact on young British Caribbeans, and which also, should be the subject of greater policy analysis, if the educational and social welfare issues of this section of British society are to be better understood by all. **(Table 6.1)**

Table 6.1: Generational responses by British Caribbeans

TYPE	RESPONSE
• Early migrants	Quiet submission to conflicts and attitudes
• First generation migrants	Witnessed changes to Caribbean systems of governance
• Third generation	An amalgam of the colonial Caribbean and migrant experiences

Changes highlighting development of a Black British consciousness

Changes in Immigration laws that legally changed their status and "former rights" as British citizens have affected their nationality at different times in Britain. Some of the feelings and sentiments have been captured in textual forms e.g. Linton Kwesi Johnson's *Englan is a Bitch* (1979) and Benjamin Zephaniah's *Dis Policeman* (1995), connote the realities of experiences. He reports in his poem, "Dis policeman keeps kicking me to death"!

The continual struggle between law-enforcement representatives and the black community have been translated by Dub Poets and Oral Performance Poets as living in *Babylon* or in a state of continual war, at grassroots level. These poets, and many others, who articulated the experiences of the Black Briton, (during the 1980's) became part of what can be interpreted as a developing protest movement, in which the community participates in instructions and a sharing of experiences on the ground. Such experiences as highlighted so far, can be seen to have led to alienation, rather than integration in society and an awakening of black consciousness and racial pride.

Evidence of this is seen in the characteristics of the literature: that of styles (oral performance), African heritage rhythms, black language (Creolised patterns of speech), Song techniques (reggae musical framework) and the black experience. In other words, the movement towards *blackness* became a means of breaking down the dividing walls of mainstream standards, values, cultural theories, social, economic and political organizations, as well as mainstream culture and ethos. In retrospect, it can be said that the early poets were creating a distinctive culture, vastly different from "their oppressors", as a means of dealing with the community's struggles. Consequently, there was a sense that politics, a developing black consciousness, black aesthetics and black art, went hand-in-hand, with reshaping Caribbean or black consciousness in Britain. This had its correlative in the kind of reggae protest songs of Bob Marley, Burning Spear and Peter Tosh on Jamaican society.

It is important to note that the style of delivery (use of Creole language as opposed to Standard English), infused within a Dub Reggae musical framework and sharing of experiences, took the form of 'ritualistic' oral performance. It also signaled a return to the African and Caribbean traditional expressive oral art-form or a turning away from values that were considered British; in as much as the daily British experience were abhorrent. Black Power Movement artists of the 1970's in the USA, had made earlier pleas for black literature to free blackness as a distinctive cultural roots from the influence of the white racist cultural values. LeRoi Jones, a black American poet, called on poets to:

"Learn to sing and dance and chant their words, tearing into the substance of their individual and collective experiences. We must make literature move people to a deeper understanding of what this thing is all about, a kind of quest, a black magician, working ju-ju with the world on the world."

In other words, the role of the artist in society is that of liberator, reporting and reflecting the nature of society, decrying what is negative, abhorrent and destructive and instead promoting black images as a means of fostering black consciousness, nationhood and culture. These views have implications for British Black artists, (like Linton Kwesi Johnson and Benjamin Zephaniah), whom it can be said, became the 'people's mouthpiece' and were instrumental in directing/re-directing the consciousness of those who were struggling at grassroots level. A history of Black British literature confirms that the Black art-form helped to shaped the lives of the people and became a refining of experience that is characteristic of Black poetry. Therefore, culturally, these early artists were able to review black art in ways which showed allegiance to the sentiments expressed by Black American artist, Amiri Baraka:

"We want poems that kill
Assasin poems that shoot guns
Poems that wrestle with cops and take their weapons leaving them
Dead, with tongues pulled out".

Amiri's views were that black art must have social and political dimensions of life as it is being experienced by the oppressed. Consequently, Linton Kwesi Johnson view of the British dimension, claims in his text that, ***Englan is a Bitch!*** Therefore having adopted the text as a kind of creative and influential medium, Caribbean writers in the Diaspora were able to question their heritage via artistic forms — some highlighted the African heritage input (Edward Kamau Brathwaite), in favour of Western cultural values; some acknowledge both heritages — African and Western (Derek Walcott), while others looked towards the Caribbean region (Samuel Selvon); in a revision of historic experiences, (modification approach), which showed their reaction to philosophy, psychology, culture and the politics of colonialism, imperialism and Eurocentric identities. It is noteworthy that earlier views had been expressed in the 1960's in the pre-independence struggles against British education in the Caribbean.

Sparrow (Dr. Francisco Slinger), had questioned in his unique oral art-form, the calypso, the relevance of a British education in the Caribbean, the fact that a colonial education made Caribbeans dysfunctional:

> *The lessons and the poems they write and send from England impress me*
> *they were trying to cultivate comedians.*
> *Comic-books make more sense.*
> *You now it is fictions without pretence*
> *J O Cutteridge wanted to keep me in ignorance."*

Twenty years later, differences in choice of allegiance became more apparent.   Grace Nichols in, *I is a long memoried woman* (1985), and Edward k Brathwaite in his **Arrivants Trilogy** (1973), have produced poetic sequences which explore the physical and psychological consequences of the Middle Passage crossing (experiences of slavery), in considerable depth, as counter-discursive approaches in the Caribbean region's canon. This kind of ideology reflects a revolutionary change in black perspectives in ways which generate interest in the **collective** rather than the **individual**. In other words, issues which assume importance and centrality to Black literature, are inextricably linked to a sense of place or national identity, (**where do I belong?**), and consciousness (**who am I?**). Answers to these questions depend on the levels of consciousness and experiences of Blacks in Britain today, and is based on their psychological levels of thinking and discourse.

There is therefore a sense that the Black British community is made up of as many of the views shared by the various artists, as are individuals who do not have a particular perspective. The fact is, there are those who may not be able to articulate their reality or have any knowledge of the sum total of where they have come from, where they want to go or what they think of the future of their existence in Britain. Theirs is the daily struggle to survive, based on their individual experiences in their environment.   However, as often as the above questions are posed, individual responses to them are affected by greater controlling forces in society, evidenced by the various laws passed in Britain since the 1914, which determine a person's status, **despite** his personal preferences,

Changes on a national/authoritative level

Laws which further dislocated the Caribbean-heritage person's sense of self and allegiances are enshrined in the history of the English legal system. These continue to affect the views and perspectives of who a person thinks he/she is, and impact on behavioural responses within the environment, are as follows:

1. Early English and British nationality law

2. British Nationality and Status of Aliens Act 1914

3. British Nationality Act 1948

4. Acquisition of Citizenship of the UK & Colonies
    *   Requirements for Naturalisation or Registration
    *   Citizenship by Descent
    *   Citizenship by Declaration
    *   Citizenship by Marriage
    *   Citizenship by Adoption

5. Independence Acts

6. British Nationality Acts of 1958, 1964 and 1965

7. Commonwealth Immigrants Acts

8. Immigration Act 1971

9. British Nationality Act 1981

10. British Subject and British Protected Person

11. British National (Overseas) & British Overseas Territories Act 2002

12. Nationality, Immigration & Asylum Act 2002
    *   British Nationals with no other citizenship
    *   Overseas born children of British mothers
    *   Deprivation of British nationality
    *   Citizenship ceremonies
    *   English language requirements
    *   Life in the United Kingdom test
    *   Children of unmarried British fathers

13. Immigration, Asylum and Nationality Act 2006

14. Laws concerning immigration and naturalisation

In examining these, there is a sense that Britain has had to come to terms with how *she* views her "scattered children", whose fate is decided by either ownership, or conditions attached to their linkages with the *Motherland.* The various laws referred to above therefore legitimizes the actions taken to bring about the changes on the ground. However, each new change would generate certain responses from migrants in ways that altered their initial perceptions and beliefs of a British *ideal*, compared with their prevailing conditions and experiences.

From the Black community's point of view, perhaps the most notable form of "legal" and unacceptable intrusion comes from their experiences with the police in Britain. Many saw and still do, some police action as displaying brutality and harassment; some of which have led to constant and unnecessary *"stop and search"* procedures. Many migrants are convinced that the police have used these procedures to provoke responses from them that have been construed as "violent" and defiant against adherence to the law. Their intolerance of these ongoing situations climaxed in a series of civil disturbances (dubbed as `riots' by the authorities) as early as 1958 (in Nottingham), the 1980s in other English inner-city areas; namely Brixton, Leicester, Toxteth, Handsworth, Nottingham and Moss Side, and more recently, in Handsworth (Birmingham late 2005) involving Asian and Caribbean youths and the police. **(Figure 6. 2)**

Figure 6.2: Time line of Race Riots in Britain

YEAR	DETAILS	DATES
1950's		
	Race Riots in Notting Hill (London)	
	and Nottingham –	September 1958
1960's		
	Violence flares at right-wing rally –	July 1962
	Cvil rights protesters defiant –	January 1969
1970's		
	Man dies in race rally clashes –	June 1974
	Notting Hill Carnival ends in riot –	August 1976
	Teacher dies in Southall race riots –	April 1979
1980's		
	Liverpool riots –	May 1980
	Brixton, London, riots –	November 1981

	Brixton, London riots –	September 1985
	Toxteth, Liverpool and Peckham riots -	October 1985
	Tottenham, London riots –	October 1985
1990's		
	Brixton, London riots –	December 1995
2000's		
	Oldham, Lancashire riots –	May 2001
	Race violence erupts in Burnley –	June 2001
	Bradford race riots over stabling –	July 2001
	Handsworth, Birmingham	October 2005

NOTES: The Police and Criminal Evidence Act which was implemented in January 1986, gave the police certain powers covering stop and searches of people or vehicles, road checks, detention of people and intimate searches of people.   Stop and search in England and Wales rose from 118,000 in 1987 to a peak of nearly 1.1 million in 1998/1999. Three quarters of people who were stopped and searched in 2003/4 in England and Wales were White. Bearing in mind the White population made up 91% of the population in 2001 census. In 2003-4 the main reason sor searching ethnic groups was drugs, followed by stolen property. Almost a quarter of people searched for firearms and just under a fifth of people searched for offensive weapons were Black. Overall Black people accounted for 15% of those stopped and searched. In 2001, only 2% of the population was Black.

Source: **Home Office: National Statistics: 6ᵗʰ March 2006: Social Trends No. 36-2006 edition**

LAW ENFORCEMENT: On the personal level, many Black men and women relate the multiple, unwarranted police raids on their parties, under the pretext of searches for drugs and other (minor) offences. Black drivers have countless testimonies of being stopped and insulted by police officers, especially if they were driving sports and other prestige cars (including the popular BMW). Families experienced raids on their homes too, and in some cases, where there was clearly no evidence of what they were looking for, "*planted*" drugs conveniently "*appeared*", so that their children were criminalized at will. Studies which confirm this type of practice confirm drug-related police corruption. **(Table 6.2)**

Table 6.2: *Ethnic composition of stop and searches, 2003/2004

	Drugs	Stolen property	Going equipped	Offensive weapons	Firearms	Other reasons	Total
White	69	79	83	67	65	84	74
Black	18	13	10	19	23	5	15
Asian	10	5	4	9	8	4	7
Other	1	1	1	2	2	2	1
Not recorded	2	2	2	2	3	5	2
Total (x 100%) (thousands)	322.8	214.4	87.8	59.3	10.6	43.1	738.0

Ethnicity of the person stopped and searched as perceived by the police officer concerned

Findings of law enforcement corruption have indicated that there are two distinct types of drug corruption. "Type 1, characterized as a "Search for Illegitimate Goals". is the traditionally conceptualized corruption involving bribery, theft, and similar activities. It is characterized by two behavioral motivations, defined as a "user-driven cycle" and a "profit-driven cycle". Type 2 is labeled "In Search of Legitimate Goals" and involves corruption of the criminal justice process, in which officers violate criminal procedure, perjure themselves, and plant evidence as means to facilitate drug-law enforcement". *(Journal of Criminal Justice, 1990).*

In addition, arresting police officers whose methods of managing a black person 'under arrest', resulted in extreme force and violence, at times resulted in brutally and in extreme cases, some have died in police custody. Those who were not associated with criminal behavior or activity, were branded **criminals**, when, after an allegation of crime, they could not coherently account for their whereabouts. What followed were abuse of their Rights as well as abuse of the legal procedures of arrest, charges and acceptance of Statements made in the absence of legal representatives.

There have been approximately 1,000 deaths in police custody in the past 30 years - and not one officer has been convicted as a result confirms the persistent institutional racism at the heart of government law enforcement institutions. The stories of Shiji Lapite, Brian Douglas, Ibrahima Sey and Joy Gardner, four innocents who died at the hands of police brutality, highlight the plights of families and their thwarted struggle for justice in Britain.

Shiji Lapite was stopped by two police officers for "acting suspiciously" on 16 December 1994 . Half an hour later he was dead. The cause of death was asphyxia from compression of the neck consistent with the application of a neckhold. Four months after Shiji Lapite's death, on May 3 1995, 33-year-old Brian Douglas was on his way home when he was stopped by two police officers, PC Tuffy and PC Harrison. Brian was with a friend when he was stopped. The officers ordered them out of the car and, apparently unprovoked, hit Brian on the head with a new US-style baton. In contrast to this thwarted brutality, the police profiles of this victim projected by the mainstream press described him (not as a father of two or an asylum seeker), but a drug-dealer, with claims from an undercover officer that he had found crack cocaine at the incident. One officer told the inquest that Shiji, only five foot ten was, "the biggest, strongest, most violent black man" he'd ever seen. PC McCullum admitted kicking him twice in the head as hard as he could, and said he was using "reasonable force" to subdue a "violent prisoner".

In December 1995, Wayne Douglas was arrested for suspected burglary. He collapsed and died while detained at Brixton police station. Also, in March 1996, another asylum seeker, the Ghambian born, Ibrahima Sey, was forced to the ground, sprayed repeatedly with CS gas, and then held face down for 15 minutes. When he went totally limp and stopped breathing, an ambulance was called. He was dead by the time they reached the hospital.

The anger and resentment which has built up in the black community has been the blatant but common denominator with all the deaths in custody – no apologies for the wrongdoings; instead, almost as a justification for the actions, the victims' characters are publicly sullied. Another example of this is Joy Gardner, who died after police stuck 13 feet of tape round her face while trying to restrain her. She was always shown in a photograph as wild and uncontrollable. The poignancy expressed in Joy's mother's grief, "I didn't believe human beings could be so cruel to each other. You don't know how much I cry. My tears will catch them," is also the depth of feelings which constantly circulates among the Black community in Britain and constantly serve as a reminder when each child or black person is arrested. There is a history of fear and mistrust of the system which, to all intents and purposes, is supposed to administer justice, but which behind the institutional framework, breaks the law at will, in the name of justice. Myna Simpson, Joy Gardner's mother states *"It's important for people to fight for justice and don't stop because there is no other way to get justice but to fight for it, and I am still fighting for justice for Joy and not only for Joy, as I say always but for all. I am fighting for justice for everyone that has been unjustly killed."*

Today, the young children who are arrested by policemen are angry, uncooperative, uncaring of the consequences and are resolute to do battle with the System. Students readily say "I don't care!" and mean it. My 25 year experience has shown that no amount of sessions on *"Consequences of Crime", "Weapons and Drug related Crimes", "Stop and Search procedures"* or *"The law and You",* seem to generate respect for law enforcement. They are keen to listen to the information presented at an open Forum where they can ask questions but those who are already involved can be seen to accept whatever outcomes and are interested in the lengths of sentences for individual crimes and the likelihood of punishments for different kinds of crimes. One reason for this is that young people's own experiences and that of others known to them, e.g friends, families, associates and their families, as well as historical community information; present overwhelming evidence of the reality of their own situations.

The prevailing paradox of perspectives is that there is an Establishment belief that the British police are the best in the world and that to acknowledge they are capable of, and sometimes guilty of, crimes would undermine the system. This perspective squared against the community's views of what it means to be Black and under the "protective" eye of law enforcement in Britain is a contradiction in terms. One must not be mistaken that such histories are inconsequential to the Black community. Instead, consideration should be given to how they regard the concept of justice. They are convinced that those responsible for the deaths of their loved ones will be punished. However, time has shown that they have lost faith. Summed up by Brenda Weinberg, Brian Douglas's sister, "The only thing that does happen is that as the time gets longer it's any justice; it can be legal justice or street justice. I don't really care any more." If this is representative of the community's feeling, the reality of the progression of gang culture smacks in the face of British justice.

In other instances, those who happened to be, legitimately, in the vicinity of a crime, would be deemed guilty of the crime especially if their description was "made to fit " the description of the perpetrators.. This has happened with frequency, over the years, and across the generations, causing a build up of anger and resentment among whole families, in a vicious cycle of hatred and mistrust for what they see as scape-goating and victimization by "the system". Furthermore, culturally-determined responses by young men and women whose language and behavior were interpreted as "violent", "inappropriate" or extreme, resulted in many migrants' incarceration in mental hospitals and sectioned under the 1969 Mental Health Act.

Image of the "Mad" woman

The image of the "strong" Caribbean woman has often been expressed with admiration and seen as a positive attribute for decades. This traditional matriarch was created in an environment where she has been the main pillar in the socialization process of the Caribbean region. For example, in terms of keeping the family together, rearing and caring for children, a strong disciplinarian, her responsibility of passing on traditional wisdom; have been seen in the storytelling traditions of the region as an important leader within the community. A senior mother *(the grandmother)*, is the holder of cultural wisdom, the one to whom referrals are made, in terms of disputes in the home - a peacemaker. This means she will attempt to pacify quarrels and upsets and if they remain unresolved , they are passed on to the final arbiter - the male, *(father, grandfather, priest, or a male' figurehead' of good repute)*.

As the parent who remained at home whilst men were out working, mothers made decisions, functioned as administrators of legal matters, (e.g. managing land and other legal and financial responsibilities to do with the home and family assets). Decisions about children's development i.e. schooling, payments and choices, correspondence, and the whole process of education, are her responsibilities.   In terms of influencing children's future progress, the Caribbean woman figures greatly, as she is instrumental in helping to direct choices that children make, and are often involved in cultural activities and events that enable an understanding of educational and cultural development. This promotes the *"learning by doing"* ethos in Caribbean children. Therefore, children who have been left in the Caribbean with aunts and uncles and grandparents, whilst their parents migrated to Britain, have had an upbringing which is all-embracing, not seen as abandonment, abuse or rejection.   It is for these reasons the bringing-up of children by extended members of the Caribbean family, is seen as a natural or traditional process of family development.

What then happens to the same Caribbean woman in Britain? How does the socialization process in the British environment affect her traditional role? Without the social networking and structure she is accustomed to, she is on her own.   In an environment of harsh realities – changed perceptions of a woman's role in British society; the struggles for gender equality(within the host society); the perceptions of women as being the "weaker sex"; the image of the single mother parenting as dysfunctional; the "invisibility" of her culture; the lack of a *voice* (as both black and female); in some cases her social status of dependency on State help; her lack of knowledge of the system she is operating in; for some, their experiences of having been branded as "**Educationally Subnormal**"; in receipt of very low wages; working in menial jobs; experiencing racism and discrimination and relating these experiences daily in the home; having little support from some male counterparts (at times, by virtue of their own experiences of similar circumstances and a inability to remedy the situation); situated in very poor housing conditions with large families and all embodied in a social class level that accords her very little credibility as a member of society in Britain.

Faced with these disenabling situations, that characterize "strength" is called on to do battle with a system that is unable to understand or interpret her actions. It is inevitable that she will draw on the qualities which make her the "strong" woman that she is. The qualities of that "strength" as related above, can become counter-productive in an environment which prefers to brand her as a "**mad**" woman. The Caribbean woman faced with adversity will rapidly begin to put matters right, so she demonstrates her forcefulness in demanding her right to be heard. She makes it her duty to defend her children's rights and this is often done vocally, in an attitude which is interpreted as aggressive and violent at times. She questions and demands answers in actions which are seen as troublesome; therefore she is a **troublemaker** and is shunned. Her insistence for justice and her persistence on seeking that right, causes her mentality to be questioned, and she may be pathologically described as "**mad**" because she dares to challenge "**the system**". Here "the system" means any established or institutional arena (e.g.,housing, education, legal, social, law enforcement), where she will be severely dealt with. Her former or once admired "strength" becomes a target to be broken down, eliminated, so she ultimately becomes a "**targeted**" person, is branded and is **at risk** of grave harm and possible injustice.

What is interesting is that those who view her mad or a troublemaker, are in fact afraid of her "strength", a natural weapon at her disposal, because evidently she has nothing else to fight with. Alienated from immediate family and other community support, she will become aggressively persistent on understanding her Rights, justice or lack of it. The result could be catastrophic, as at times the attempts to silence her becomes greater than her physical and emotional strength could bare without support; and a new form of branding ensues – she is seen as someone who rants and raves - **she is mad!**

Consequently, if she is not in a position to pay for justice, and that is often the case; she will get **rough** justice, and so will members of her family. There is no doubt that the legal Aid system in Britain will not be able to support the quality of legal assistance she needs and therefore she is short-changed. In other words, procedures and processes (e.g. the legal system) will be masked as "help", for many which is too little and some cases too late! In extreme cases, she will be criminalized. If the intention is to get to other members of her family, she will operate as a *fierce defender* of her territory, for which she may be systematically broken down until she capitulates.

This may be through **loss** of many kinds – *respect, health, emotional well being, finance, housing, constantly being brought before courts or incarcerated, lose the support of friends and community confidence, conflicts in the family who may become confused by her actions, the will to fight and loss of continued support.* (Figure 6.3) In other words, her "strength" has become her greatest enemy in the battle of wits and to control her. The 'fight' gets more intense against her when Inter-agencies collaborate to add weight to strategies used to complete the label and eliminate the "threat" seen as the "mad woman". The danger is, where she fails to get equal rights and justice, the 'fight' is taken up by those who have been witnessing her plight and a vicious circle ensues. Consequently, other members of family are forced to do battle on hers and the family's behalf, in a cycle of conflicts that ensures the stereotypical image of the Caribbean woman in Britain.

Figure: 6.3 Behaviours and Institutional Practices

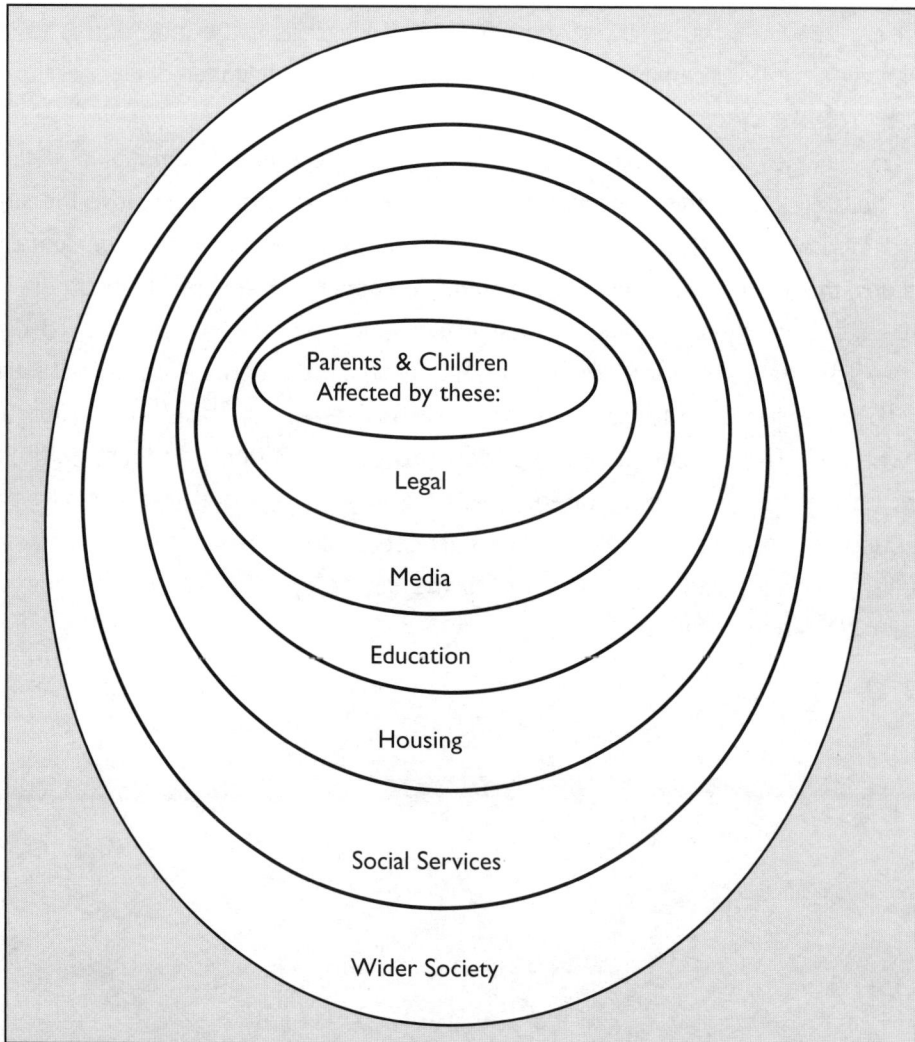

Parents & Children
Affected by these:

Legal

Media

Education

Housing

Social Services

Wider Society

NOTE: *This figure shows levels of institutional influences which affect general behaviour . Each sphere of influence, helps to generate a variety of behaviours, that are impacted on depending on the quality of interaction experienced by both children and their parents. There is a cyclical pattern of behaviour where negative experiences create negative expectations, with each institution. The result is combative mistrust, and the creation of stereotypes (by both the institutions' representatives and members of the community), due to misplaced perceptions.*

Case Study 1: Institutional racism

The case of *Madam X*, a self motivated, determined and successful, black Caribbean woman, who runs a 16 year old educational institution, she founded in the early 1990's, is a classic case of institutional racism at its best. The fifty year old, has shown that self-reliance, a passion and a mission to create developmental changes within the Black community is an achievable goal, using a community participatory approach and working within a framework of excellence. Leading on many initiatives which responded to the community's needs for a period of 15 years, with a good deal of success; having transformed thousands of lives and communities in Britain, has brought her national recognition and acclaim. She demonstrated through her role modeling, that whole families can achieve success, via her numerous initiatives aimed at reaching every sector of community life in Britain. A hard worker, maximizing 12 hours a day shift, 6 days a week, and working tirelessly to support those who have been rejected by various sectors of society, has branded her a *Wonder Woman*. The humble and unassuming small figure, who delights in the success outcomes of young people and the positive changes they are able to make in their lives; faced her "Waterloo" when she was unceremoniously branded *a criminal, bogus, in denial of her guilt and fraudster* by three government departments.

To do this, these departments were helped by vulnerable and desperate black illegal immigrants to eradicate the educational institution and Madam X, by false accusations, lies and use of the media, with gross fabrications, to discredit the community initiative and its Leader.

The extreme forms of institutional racism, demonstrated by members of the three government departments, showed use of tactics which, to all superficial intents and purposes, presented *Madam X's* institution and illegal immigrants at war, whilst they instigated all the strategic moves from behind the scenes. However, in essence, it transpired that the illegal immigrants had no real grouse with the institution but it was the racist Officers, hiding behind the structure of a government department, and misusing their positions within the organizations to carry out wanton, and illegal destruction to the point where they influenced local media, instigated erroneous information, under the pretext that their positions in local government, is to be believed above any other information, especially black counter-arguments.

The psychology of this level of racism is that it operates within a stereotypical and existing framework in society, where it brands one section of society as the inferior, underdog, lacking humanity, therefore needing no sympathy; justifies its bestial treatment of the victims. At the same time, it projects the white racist attitudes, (even among the most respected in society), as supreme and justified in whatever treatment it metes out to the underdog. However, it is illogical, irrational, operates in denial that it is happening because it is blinded by its own innate arrogance of what logic and justice is. Therefore, its characteristics have wide-reaching effects among like-minded sectors of the population, where it has no problem finding collaborators among the good, the great, the titled, even the *white* underdog and outcasts in society.

When we talk of institutional racism, it goes beyond the physical structure or institution (the building, bricks and mortar or structure) as being racist! Not so! Commonsense has shown that It is **the people** who operate within those institutions who are racist. One has to remember that outside of their government jobs, many of these employees are to be found within racist Right-wing organizations, have traditional hatred of the "other" and "differences" which they see as inferior. Among them also are to be found those who are Right-Wing in their politics, hiding behind their desks and positions and operating in stealthily and subtly destructive ways; almost imperceptibly at times.

The counter-balance to this is a degree of naivety among those who believe that the 21st century has changed or eradicated those long-standing personal traits, because they themselves have a yearning for the mistakes of the past to be absolved and lessons learnt to override the continual existence of racist attitudes in society. Therefore, when racism is discovered among Judges, Lawyers, Policemen, Probation officers, Teachers, Priests, and among housing, health, social services and other government sector occupations; there is a shock and horror response. This is because there is an "expectation", almost as if the very job position probably absolves them from covert and overt forms of racism in their daily duties. There is also the "expectation" that given such positions of "power", racist practices will not flourish in our present time. However, *Madam X* discovered that this kind of thinking could not be further from the truth!

In a battle to defame and denigrate the work of 25 years service to the local and national community, the government representatives bent on "extermination", sought to exact a kind of revenge for the good that was being done by *Madam X* and the difference that the work was making to the community. There was scant regard for the benefactors (society's "misfits", those discarded by government sectors as socially and educationally excluded); as the institutional machinery went into top gear to achieve its aims. *Madam X* experienced legal collusion between the government prosecutors and her own racist representatives. In her own words, she was "bamboozled" with trite and erroneous explanations aimed at orchestrating her downfall, in the hope that she would accept the "impeccable advice" given. It transpired that *Madam X* was bullied to accept the "legal advice" given, with the hope that she would quietly capitulate unquestioningly. In fact there was arrogance on the part of her legal representatives, as well as the prosecutors, to believe that *Madam X* would not object or fight back. It was not surprising therefore, that without the good and just legal defence, *Madam X* persisted in her own investigation and defence, despite her legal representatives bullying, that she discovered that the case against her had no legal basis, since she and her institution were *"Exempted" (as were all other UK education institutions),* from such prosecution. The fact that she was branded "a criminal", "fraudster", "bogus", and their own integrity and *reson d'etre,* highly questionable, action and attitudes was irrelevant to them.

The assurance of the institutional racist support and the help of society's prevailing stereotypes, these government officers continued with their assault, irrespective of the law which existed in her defence. This showed the strength of their conviction that their power to orchestrate a black person's downfall would find favour among the general populace unquestionably. However, finding their own expectation of ease and swift outcome thwarted by the challenging *Madam X* who "dared" to fight her corner and appeared to show resistance to their plans, they called on the help of the media, (print and online newspapers). This is a weapon which society knows only too well, (based on its tradition of unquestionable acceptance to the print media, and a play on the ignorance of the general population), would help to defeat *Madam X*, by finding favour among White extremists who would object to the resistance and challenges from this one black "criminal and obviously guilty" woman.

Using their job titles as bona fide employees, and parading as workers in service to Her Majesty's government they extract information from sources to taint character and plant seeds of doubt and destruction in people's minds. The defamation was represented by a flurry of activities in letter writing emailing and telephone calls to various *other* government departments, by pretending to do their jobs whilst covertly in pretence that to help them achieve their destructive aims. When this method appeared too slow or not as inflammatory in achieving mass support, their next strategic move was going back to the illegal immigrants to instigate media coverage from their end, so that cross-racial reporting of erroneous and inflammatory and defamatory information would cause public outrage and eventual destruction from public opinion.

What ensued in *Madam X's* case is a collaborative effort of legal representatives, government departments, probation service, the judge and news media, all hastening the downfall of *Madam X,* whilst she continued to challenge and persist in claiming her innocence. The prevailing racism and the stereotype of the *"mad"* black woman, the expectation that *black* is synonymous with, fraud, illegalities, crime, questionable integrity, and a refusal to accept that advancement and success could be got via legitimate and hard-working means. The visual dynamics, the lone, black, female figure, silent (since legal representatives have to speak on her behalf), against the towering, psychologically and in actuality more "powerful" white prosecutors, administrators of justice, probation service, white legal representatives, the white media, all shrouded in the mystique and misplaced arrogance and superiority, that they cant all be wrong – after all, they are "white" and she is "black". In the scheme of things, the opposite can never be considered in such circumstances – therefore, she must be brought down and eradicated for her "guilt" of being who society's stereotype says she is, and what she must, (at all cost, via their conspiratorial actions), accept as her fate! Appearing to fight against such dilemmas brands her as a "manipulator!", "that woman who causes stress!" in other words, she is obstructing the status quo, shifting the power balance in ways that are not normally associated with her kind – how dare she!

The fact is Madam X had a case brought against her that was, in fact, illegal in content, approach, and procedure, by people who society says represent the law!

She suffered for 2 years at their hands, whilst they hide in government institutions that society says, are not racist because of Equality and Anti-Discrimination laws and 20th century advancement in terms of social and community relations in Britain. However, the Rampton, Swan, and more specifically, McPherson Reports had already unearthed this kind of malaise in society with recommendations for its eradication. The fact is, ten years on in 2009, have proved that institutional racism is just as rampant and extreme in our 21st century, as it was in 1999.

The psychology of racism

Analysing the psychology of racism in **Case Study 1,** highlights the struggles of an individual, (who represents a social group – black, minority), and is contesting, ideologically, to win the argument against her and the 'criminal' branding labeled against her character. This racism is supported by an existing belief system and perpetuated in society, that her race is always associated with criminality and adverse behaviours. Against this societal image, she must engage in power relations that involve a contest of knowledge, power and truth.

Firstly, the right to absolute and uncontestable power is displayed by those in society who help to maintain the stereotype at all cost, (e.g. the media, law enforcers), by their attitudes and actions and an expectation of unchallenged acceptance of the status quo by all they come into contact with. For these sections of the population, where racism is inherently entrenched in their belief system, as well as thought and action; they exercise a right to wield such power in a repressive, brutal, subtle and sometimes in an open and direct manner. A consequence of this practice in society is its linkage with the quest for knowledge and truth by the victim of such adverse behaviours to the point where persistence and determination are regarded as negative, challenging and sometimes labeled as aggressive actions. Again, the word *aggression,* because it fulfils the characteristics of the stereotype which are associated with such minority groups.

What creates an imbalance in the minds of those who are faced with such "resistance", is their persistence in believing that power in general, is inextricably tied up with their automatic rights to **knowledge and truth**. In other words, by virtue of the powerful position they hold in society, their **knowledge,** (measured in any proportion), is also Divinely granted to them, to the exclusion of all others in society. Over a period of time, this prevailing thought then becomes a belief system of the masses which they later present as **truth/fact,** against the minority group, (seen as society's 'underdog'). Consequently, when the minority seeks justice, it is inevitable that they will encounter great resistance to shifting the negative stereotypes and status quo. Additionally, instead of presenting the truth, this group depends greatly on stretching the truth or sensationalizing information in order to win hearts, minds and mass support from the majority group.

Institutional Power and its Implications in the UK

It is often said that the injudicious use of power or the abuse/misuse of it can have implications for both the facilitator and the facilitated (the recipient) of that power. Like most Western democracies, the UK's power is both effusive and diffusive; that is, it can be self-authorised as well as delegated by institutions representing diverse interests: government, the legislature, legal, military and civil society in general. The exercise of power is therefore both mandatory and discretionary depending on who, and what instrument of the State or other, is responsible for the utility or execution of power.

British monarchical rule has created the patronage system – this involves informal/unwritten Constitution. The absence of a formal Constitution has effectively corrupted law-making and given rise to the Peerage view of an `elective dictatorship'. So that any political party that accedes power can use both Houses of Parliament to dictate legislative agendas which the average electorate know little of, or even appear to care about. Many have been schooled to merely regurgitate uncritically, opinions and views that are media-inspired, rather than constructive and sensible debates from representative segments of British society. As a result, issues to do with ideological and political thought ignore the views of `Citizen Kane' and confine these to so-called `opinion leaders' and `view-moulders' whose `contrived' expertise carry far more weight than that of the masses.

One example of the effusion of power is the way new laws are passed in Parliament and the manner in which law enforcement agencies conduct their affairs, especially when dealing with minorities, (the persistent use of `hard' power to enforce their brand of `justice'). Another instance of this type of power is best seen through the institutional apparatus of power-brokers – lobbyists, (`Big') business and other power-brokers. Stakeholders are those who facilitate the use of power while `lay' facilitators are those with grassroots influence, who are capable of altering the balance of power due to their activism and knowledge of the system. For power to be understood however, it is vital to pose a few searching questions.

What is Power?

For instance, how is power conceptualised? How is it defined? How is it developed? What are the instruments of its execution? And how is that power sustained? There are many definitional forms of power; namely, coercive force (legislative and military), persuasive power (subtle threats or 'peace offerings') and 'soft' power (diplomacy via dialogue and discussion using intermediaries). The latter has distinct advantage – a 'win-win' situation, which means that there is a mutual benefit for all. Each party offers a combination of views – some common, others divergent. Generally, parties agree to disagree, especially if issues to do with their mutual interests, are at stake.

The proper use of power is vital if we are to eradicate the potential for organised chaos and social disorder in the name of the law, in the UK. When majorities and minorities have to co-exist in an environment where prejudice and discrimination are institutionalised, the scales are tipped in favour of the majority; because this group carries the preserve of *'might is right'*. Their legitimacy of power is vested in both governmental-legislative and civic/communitarian structures. Institutional prejudices and subtle forms of racism against the minority, continue to thwart the course of justice in British society. There is a range of well-documented miscarriages of justice in support of this claim, that continue to put Britain behind by some 20 years, compared with the structural and legal processes of the United States of America.

The myth that is often peddled is that a few modifications in law-making can do the trick, to resolve inherent human prejudices. In fact, it is a rather 'neat trick' to suggest that piecemeal legislation or policy-making 'on the hoof' can miraculously sweep aside all (historic) vestiges of race discrimination in Britain today. In fact, legislative bungling has an iodine effect on the system of governance to such an extent, that both perpetrators of prejudice and the 'victims' suffer simultaneously. One is the arbiter of power and the other is a passive or neutral recipient of the power-abuser.

Diffusive Power

It is common to find the diffusion of power largely executed through a variety of institutional bureaucracies involving both high and low-ranking officials in state bodies. These officials claim that in their sometimes over-zealousness and indecent haste to carry out their legitimate functions, tend to make gross errors of judgement, by misusing or abusing their authority in dealing with legal, civic and other cases involving minorities involved in business, industry and local government politics. These people tend to be singled out for constant attacks even where issues may be trivial or bear no resemblance to public duty. The pressures on public officials to meet targets, mean that their interest in ensuring justice and fair-play, is probably the least of all priorities.

The notion that some minorities should be singled out because of their skin colour and their aspiring ambitions, has become somewhat of a `siege mentality' by senior officials responsible for trading standards, local government agencies, the police and a range of enforcement bodies such as bailiffs, collection agencies, etc. The punitive nature of their administration of justice beggars belief, as to whether these public servants are, in fact the `final arbiters of judge, jury and executioner' of State laws. Quite often when members from the majority community flout the law or commit other misdemeanours, the media is ready to conduct `forgiveness-type- campaigns, a public defence of their errant ways, ensuring that most of the `good side' of that person or persons is given `full' public mention. In the case of minorities, the opposite is true.

In fact, sections of the media take delight in not only exposing minorities' human frailty, but engage in unstoppable character assassination campaigns to such an extent that by the time minorities are exonerated or found to be innocent of alleged "charges", the `die is already cast' – their reputations are already in tatters. This type of collusive power, involving both the media and institutions of democratic governance is today responsible for wholesale miscarriages of justice and persistent acts of prejudicial forms of discrimination, all in the name of British Law or Justice. What then of the British `moral high ground', in terms of its way of life; that is, decorum and respect for the `right of the individual' and the Race Relations Amendment Act of 2000 and its successor the Equalities Act of 2007?

Another distinctive utility of governance in the UK is that of **Moral Power,** often used in favour of the majority. It is here that the `kernel' of ethics is publicly exemplified through civil and legal forms of institutionalism. This can be seen in the treatment of animals and children and the amount and quality of column inches and air-time they receive from a very biased media empire that `preys' on the propagandistic sympathies of mainstream society to evoke selected forms of morality and social `cringe'. Yet this sense of humanism is not appropriated for minorities. Again, the media is complicit in this affair. Most editors have no real experience of race discrimination in their lives. Far from living 'open' lifestyles, they are protected by a system that is incestuous and glorifies in utter patronage. So in cases where *minorities* become the affected *majorities*, there is likely to be cover-ups, misinformation or disinformation, repeated denials by the majorities and classic finger-pointing or blame cultural obfuscations, with the hope that 'Joe-Public' will become tried and accept a `verdict' based on the endorsement of the majority. In effect, the majorities are buttressed by a system of racial and prejudicial hierarchies, all of which safeguard the status quo, risking the exposure of corruption even when its blatantly obvious.

What is even more petrifying, is that the very media machinery is obsessed by kleptocracy, (corrupt government), in 'Developing' countries, but is happy to mask its own lack of assault on serious deficits in its internal and 'democratic' systems of governance, especially as they relate to minorities. The searing contradiction in treatment between majorities and minorities in British society today, is not only cause for concern, but it also begs the question further, what has British justice become when an experienced Judge can ignore the erroneous Administration of Justice in a case, and instead insult a Black female Defendant, for having been brave and audacious enough to unearth the line of corrupt penal practices, (involving two government departments, and legal firms represented by white 'legal' representatives)? How has this come about, she had been proven right in her lengthy and unswerving insistence of innocence, in a criminal case that had, for two years, been heavily stacked against her? The revelation of her innocence revealed, not only a long list of gross inaccuracies and maladministration by all those concerned, (including the Plaintiffs and her own white Defence lawyers), in forcing make a **guilty plea,** by that her evidence and submissions were totally ignored.

Instead, in his summary of this revelation, the Judge attacked the Defendant as "**that woman there**!" labeling her a "**manipulator, who has, at this last 12ᵗʰ hour, caused stress**." In fact, rather than apologise to the Defendant for the fact that she had sustained 2 years of a miscarriage of justice, defamation, emotional and financial loss; or indeed reprimand those before him, for their malpractice which led to the revelation, the Judge apologised to the perpetrators instead. He became so incensed and enraged that he wielded his "power" by commanding the Defendant to "**stand**" and for the first time addressed her by her surname, instead of her title, demanding that she accept that she was to, "**Admit it, you are a manipulator**"! The psychology of this type of racism underscores behaviours that evidence collective and culpable forms of sexism, racism, classism, and experience of a threat or imbalance in the power relations; because a 'minion', a minority, a Black Woman, had dared to question the **seat of power**. In other words, there is an expectation that, in knowing 'one's place in society', one must accept whatever is meted out by virtue of your social and racial status.

BLACK MENTAL HEALTH: A major concern among the Black community in Britain is their experience of mental health issues, practices and the law relating to this. The express view of the Black Mental Health UK, a well-known organization championing equality issues of Black mental health, is that "the UK experience reveals that it is in the field of forensic psychiatry that racial injustices and cultural oppression are felt most acutely by African Caribbean service users. People from Black and minority ethnic (BME) groups suffer poorer health, have reduced life expectancy and have greater problems with access to health care than the majority White population. The work of the BMH UK has been highlighted here to show the level of concern, especially as it relates to behavioral issues concerning the black community in Britain. There is no doubt that behaviour-wise, whole families are involved and this has implications for pupils at school as well as how they are assessed and managed generally.

Inequality in mental health services between Black people and the majority White population has been the subject of ongoing debate and study for decades. It is well documented that people from BME communities and African Caribbean's in particular fare worse under the British mental health system. **(Figure 6.4)** There is a history of misunderstanding and discrimination when it comes to the use of compulsory powers against African Caribbean's. Black people mistrust and often fear services, and staff is often wary of the Black community, fearing criticism and not knowing how to respond."

Mental Health Law

BMH UK believes that mental health law should be framed within both human right and race relations legislation and geared towards reducing discriminatory practices and increase the protection of the rights of both patients and Carers engaged with mental health services. In the BMH UK's analysis of mental health services experienced by African Caribbean peoples shows the following:

Figure 6.4: Analysis of Mental Health Services

Rates of admission into hospital are three or more times higher for black and white-black mixed groups compared with the average.
Black groups are up to 44% more likely to be detained under the Mental Health Act compared to the average. 4% of patients were referred.
The risk of being referred to mental health services by police or by the courts is almost double for Black Caribbean and Black African groups.
Men from the Black Caribbean, Black African, Other Black and Indian groups were about 50% more likely than average to be secluded. 8% of inpatients had experienced one or more incidents of control and restraint. The rate was 29% higher than the average for Black Caribbean men.

Source: All figures taken from the (MHAC Mental Health and Ethnicity Census 2005

The 2007 Mental Health Act fails on all of these points, BMH UK believes this Bill is unethical and unworkable and has thrown away the opportunity of updating the 1983 Mental Health Act so that it meets the demands of a 21st Century multicultural society. In "Mental Health services within the UK: The African Caribbean Mental Experience"

The David Bennett Inquiry report made the crisis in BME (Black and Minority Ethnic) mental health a national issue and has brought to light the discrimination in mental health services that has led to black people being excessively diagnosed as 'schizophrenic', over-represented among people who are 'sectioned' (involuntary committed to hospital) and apprehended in excessive numbers by the police as 'mentally ill', despite having similar rates of mental ill health as other ethnic groups.

Culturally appropriate and acceptable behaviour has also been wrongly construed as symptoms of abnormality or aggression. The recourse to advocacy, tribunals and appropriate care packages has been slow to positively impact this group. A recent social exclusion report on mental health acknowledged that Black people have higher levels of dissatisfaction with statutory (mental health) services and are twice as likely to disagree with their diagnosis.

Academics and professionals in this field purport that psychiatric power and race working together in combination, in collusion, is a deadly mixture. This was tragically highlighted by the death of David Bennett an African Caribbean inpatient in a mental health unit in Norwich, England. Bennett was racially abused on the night of his death by a fellow patient after a dispute over access to the phone on the ward.

He was subsequently forcibly restrained by five nurses for almost half an hour. They only released him after they realised he had stopped breathing. No attempt was made to resuscitate him. A subsequent Public Inquiry into his treatment and care and circumstances surrounding his death concluded that Mental Health Services within the UK are institutionally racist. Findings in this report typify the African Caribbean experience of mental health services. **(Figure 6.5)**

Figure 6.5:   Statistics on Black Mental Health in the UK

• 10% of mental health inpatients
• 3% of the general population, according to the 2001 census
• 50% more likely to be placed in seclusion
• 29% more likely to be subject to control and restraint
• 44% more likely to be sectioned under the 1983 Mental Health Act
• 50% more likely to be referred through the criminal justice system
• 14% more refused treatment than white people when asking for help from MH services
• Referral to psychiatric services by the Police is almost double for black people in general
• Referral through the courts is almost double in the Black African and Caribbeans.

Source: *Commission for Healthcare Audit and Inspection (2005) Count Me In, Results of a national census of inpatients in mental health hospitals and facilities in England and Wales.*

There are other 'ethnic' issues in mental health services which signal increasing concerns among the black community. These show that black and ethnic minorities are more often:

1.   Diagnosed as schizophrenic
2.   Compulsorily detained under the Mental Health Act
3.   Admitted as 'offender patients'
4.   Held by police under Section 136 of the Mental Health Act
5.   Transferred to locked wards from open wards
6.   Not referred for psychotherapy
7.   Given high doses of medication

8.   Sent to psychiatrists by courts

9.   Have unmet needs

(Source : S. Fernando (2003) Cultural Diversity, Mental Health and Psychiatry:
The Struggle Against Racism)

Achievement and Employment

In charting the journey of the Caribbean migrant to Britain, the development of a Black British community and their interlocking dichotomies and paradoxes of existence in Britain, show a trend that is no longer based on the initial admiration for a former "Motherland". More concerns have been voiced over the educational underachievement among Black Caribbean or Black British chidren who are at the bottom of the ethnic attainment ladder. Such statistics do not inspire promises for a positive future. Over the last decade all ethnic groups have seen rising attainment levels among the younger generations.

However, whilst there are slight improvement in the attainment of five or more GCSE grades A to C or equivalent by ethnic groups overall, Black Caribbean children are still at the bottom of the ladder. The figures for 2004 showed 15 year olds in England had the highest GCSE attainment among Indian and Chinese pupils, with grades Higher than those from the White British pupils and ethnic groups. Three quarters (74%) of Chinese pupils and 67% of Indian pupils gained five or more grades A* to C at GCSE or equivalent in 2004. White Irish (58%) and White British (52%) pupils attained the next highest results. Bangladeshi (46%) pupils had similar attainment levels to White British pupils, followed by Pakistani (45%) and Black African (43%). The lowest grades were achieved by Black Caribbean pupils (36%), which is an overall increase on previous figures. **(Figure 6.6)**

Figure 6.6: GCSE achievement among racial groups

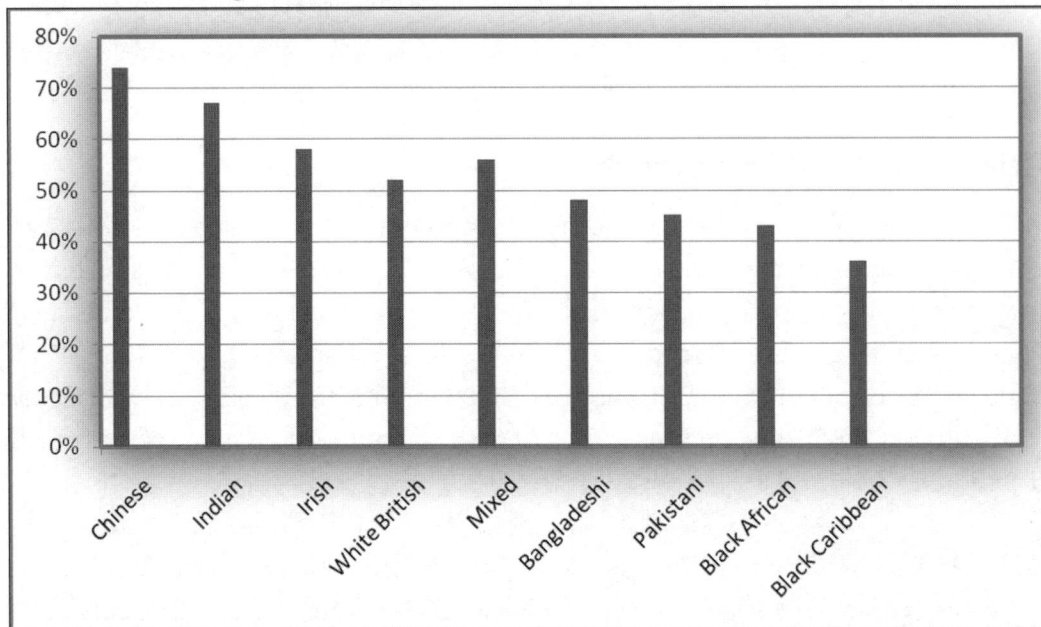

Causes of this level of underachievement, has been attributed to socio-economic positions of many Black children. The corresponding effect of such poor achievement levels is the equally low participation rates in the labour market, where unemployment among Black Caribbeans also stands at a very high percentage. Other factors which contribute to the lack of performance in schools have been attributed to Emotional and Social Behavioural Difficulties (ESBD or EBD) which impact on a pupil's ability to access the curriculum. Behavioural difficulties at school have been linked to gang culture and the rising rates of crime and criminal activities among Black youths.

Conclusion

We have already discussed the role that fixed and permanent exclusions play in the life of youths who are affected by this dominating force in their lives. From experience, many parents who seek a Head Teacher's advice and support for their children's involvement are not able to identify the signs of gang involvement and are not informed on the workings of gang culture. Many are oblivious of the very threats that their children's involvement in gangs, pose to the entire family members' lives. The above chapter shows the complexity of factors which impact on young people's behavior; stemming from both the micro environment (home) and the macro environment (society). Where injustices are experienced by families at the hand of authority figures or "the system", rather like a perpetual feud, this has implications for generations, and given the small size of the Caribbean community in Britain, feelings about issues that affect the community are spread much faster and embody a larger proportion of the community in general.

The next chapter will discuss the psychology of gang formation and the government and the community's coping strategies aimed at dealing with the phenomena of gross disorder and life-threatening behavior.

SELECTED CHAPTER REFERENCE

Coard B.(1971): *How the British School System made West Indian children educationally subnormal*, New Beacon Books, London.

Nichols Grace: (1985): *I is a long-memoried woman,* Caribbean Cultural International 1983.

Brathwaite E. K., (1973): *The Arrivants*, Oxford University Press, London.

The Journal of Criminal Justice, December 1 1990, Volume 6, No. 4

7 | Coping Strategies

Introduction

Why do our youths join gangs? What is the psychology behind the structure of gang formation that makes it attractive to young people? Despite the wide variations in the types of gangs, (irrespective of the racial grouping), they are predominately males in their teens to early twenties, whilst females are in the minority, usually as followers, without becoming as heavily engaged in activity as their male counterparts. The basic unit in a gang, whatever its origin or larger structure, is a group of youths who are about the same age. These groups are also called posses or sets and may consist entirely of one set or it may be allied with similar groups as part of a larger gang. This chapter explores the various strategies employed by members of the community and the government in coping with social disorder. The chapter looks at various viewpoints and methods employed by individuals and groups to deal with aggressive, violent and persistent trouble-making youth.

The Psychology of Gangs

A gang is made up of a group of people, whose members recognize themselves as a distinct entity and are recognized as such by their community. They are usually involved antisocial, rebellious, and illegal activities which results in negative responses from the community. Distinctive characteristics of gangs include:

- a recognized leader who organizes and plans strategies
- does not get involved in activities on the ground

- formal membership of gang members who are caught up in the carrying out of the business of the gang, with initiation requirements

- rules for its members involved in committing offences;

- its own territory, or turf identified by postcode areas;

- standard clothing or tattoos;

- private slang;

- a group name.

Gang-related violence has risen sharply, involving very young children (11yrs), who are increasingly ready to use deadly force to perpetuate rivalries or carry out drug activities. In addition, the scope of gang activities has increased, often involving links to drug suppliers. Gangs can be categorised into several types.

Territorial ("turf" or "hood") gangs are concerned with controlling a specific geographical area. Organized, or corporate, gangs are mainly involved in illegal activities such as drug dealing. *Scavenger gangs* are more loosely organized than the other two types and are identified primarily by common group behavior – *"wannabies"* and *"look-outs"*. Gangs are found among all races, whether migrant or not. British black gangs, whose members have vast descriptions of names have long been active in inner-city areas of London but gangs are found in all parts of the UK. (Strickland & Cengage 2001).

Whereas the early form of white gangs were the skinheads (named for their close-shaven heads), who typically embrace a racist, anti-Semitic, and anti-foreigner philosophy, the resentment also involved displays of neo-Nazi symbolism and beliefs. There are thought to belong to political parties such as the British National Party (BNP) for which there were 130,000 London voters and the gain of one seat in the London Assembly in May 2008.

Factors for Gang involvement

A variety of factors have been cited as causes for involvement in gangs. Social problems associated with gang activity include poverty, racism, and the disintegration of the nuclear family. Some critics claim that gangs are glamorized in the media and by the entertainment industry. On checking children's behaviour during break times, when they are able to access computer labs and the internet, it can be guaranteed that 90%

of pupils access and can be seen chanting, gang-related songs, comparing web pages and reveling in the information.

On a personal level, adolescents whose families are not meeting their emotional needs turn to gangs as substitute families where they can find acceptance, intimacy, and approval and that all important word RESPECT. This accounts for the reason behind the violent reaction to "dis-ing" an individual. In other words, to DIS-RESPECTED him, a like committing a cardinal sin! On the grassroots level, disrespect is what he experiences at the hands of the law, in school, especially to do with his identity, ability, expectations of him, racial stereotyping and in some instances may have experienced bullying or other forms of violence. Psychologically the gang acts as a barrier or healing with affords him possibilities of elevation from the dull-drums and his life of contradictions and in most cases hurt. Gangs can also provide the sense of identity that young people crave as they confront the dislocations of adolescence, and lack of an acceptable transition to manhood or rites of passage.

Teenagers also join gangs because of social pressure from friends. Others feel physically unsafe in their neighborhoods if they do not join a gang. Our school lost a very promising young student at the cusp of taking his GCSE's because he had made a change in his attitude to his future and had begun to project "education" in his language, behaviour and attitude. He had chosen to do 6 GCSE's and all predictions for exam results suggested an A/B pupil. This change was not popular with his associates, who terrorised him daily, making it difficult for him to leave his house. Despite the fact that his mother intervened the knife threats on the street where they lived, she feared for his safety beyond the home and requested of the school, alteration to his school timetable, so that he arrived later in the morning and left for him earlier within the school day. A modified timetable was agreed with the Local Education Authority but just before examinations this pupil had to flee London for another part of the country for fear for his long-term safety and that of his family. For some people, the connection to a gang is through family members who belong- sometimes even several generations of a single family. In this boy's case there was no back-up family member and personal choice was obviously not an option for him!

Yet another incentive for joining is money from the gangs' lucrative drug trade. Drug profits can be so exorbitant as to dwarf the income from any legitimate job: one sixteen year old, on preparing to leave school told me, "Miss can you see me in a college? I have everything I want, why do I need to go to college, if I can get £2,000 a week without having to blow my brains out with study". Only less than a year, after stating this remark, he is currently incarcerated in Feltham Young People's prison, for committing drug related crimes.

There is an obvious attraction and admiration for the notorious American Crips and Bloods gangs (who provide the examples for gangs in Britain). These well-known gangs consist of many sets, with names such as the Playboy Gangster Crips, the Bounty Hunters, and the Piru Bloods. It is to their clique or set that members feel the greatest loyalty. These neighborhood groups have leaders, who may command as many as 200 followers. In groups affiliated with larger gangs, these local leaders are accountable to chiefs higher up in the gang hierarchy.

The lowest level on which a young person may be associated with a gang is as *"a lookout"* -the person who watches for the police during drug deals or other criminal activities. Lookouts, who are commonly between seven and twelve years old, can be paid as much as three hundred dollars a week.

At the next level are *"wannabes,"* or *foot-soldiers* who are older children or pre-teens who identify themselves with a gang although they are still too young for membership. They may wear clothing resembling that of the gang they aspire to and try to ingratiate themselves with its members. Sometimes they cause trouble in or out of school as a way of drawing the gang's attention. They are the visible layer of a gang and it is this group that are most at risk of becoming a victim of violent crimes.

Once *wannabes* are being considered for entrance into a gang they undergo some form of initiation. This often includes committing a specified crime as a way of "proving themselves." Certain initiation rituals are practiced also, such as "walking the line," in which initiates have to pass between two lines of members who beat them.

One thirteen year old boy related his initiation at the age of 11 years, where he had to survive the beatings otherwise, the whole process would be repeated. He related the experience which took place in a disused warehouse, with a gang leader of 22 years old, with nostalgia. At present, he is currently serving a 5 year prison sentence for sexual assault and grievous bodily harm; having been caught on CCTV camera. In other cases, initiation brutalities follow a less orderly course, with a succession of gang members randomly perpetrating surprise beatings that initiates have to withstand without attempting to defend themselves. Other rituals, such as cutting initiates or "branding" and mixing their blood with that of older members, are also practiced. Tell-talesigns f this activity is the covering up of the wounded area with gloves. Pupils arc often seen wearing gloves in scorching weather conditions accompanied by the hooded top, also in sweltering weather conditions, **(Figure 7.1)**.

Other difficulties associated with control are linked to 50 Cent's philosophy of *'Get Rich or Die Tryin'*. Additionally, the maximum sentence for someone caught in possession of a knife has just been doubled from two years to four years. However, this evidently does not deter thugs. In fact, many even see a *prison sentence as a badge of honour,* an inevitable consequence of their street life. Many have counteracted the difficulty single-handed by *purchasing stab-proof vests,* costing £120 with clients as young as 10years old, who fear they're going to be knifed at school or on the street.

Figure 7.1: `Pull-and-push' factors of the Gang Culture

• Social problems; namely, poverty, racism and the disintegration of nuclear families
• Adolescents deprived of emotional support from traditional-type families
• Lack of respect from elders and authority figures in society
• The longing for a sense of identify, protection and trust
• Social pressures from friends, rivals and others in similar age-groups.
• The desire for material goods – money derived from drug trade.
• The fad and notoriety associated with the `gangster' culture
• Status symbol associated with the gang culture hierarchy.

Community Solutions

Criminologist Simon Hallsworth thinks Britain's political parties are fuelling a "moral panic". He claims in a BBC News interview, that attitudes to young people - particularly those from poor or ethnic minority backgrounds - had been negatively affected. His view is that despite there being lower levels of crime politicians who were attempting to out-do each other to appear "tough on crime", were involved in creating crime waves.

Mr. Hallsworth, director of London Metropolitan University's centre for social evaluation and research stated, "Even where there are gangs, such as in parts of south Manchester, members tend not to join until they are 18 to 21." Notwithstanding Mr. Hallsworth's research, the fact remains that a child is stabbed to death in Britain every two weeks and knife killings outnumber gun homicides three to one, said Norman Brennan, a police officer and director of the Victims of Crime Trust. *'Knife crime is out of control and kids carry them like fashion accessories,'* Brennan said. The youngest child to be suspended from school for brandishing a blade was just five. Some 42 per cent of boys aged between

11 and 16 in state-funded schools admit to having carried a knife. Students have brought machetes, combat knives, swords and sharpened screwdrivers to school, police say. Girls have been caught with blades hidden in lipstick and mascara tubes.

Despite this information, Hallsworth's research in deprived parts of Hackney, east London, revealed that although young people hung around together, this did not automatically amount to a gang. He said, "Standing with trousers down to your crutch and your hood on does not make you a member of a gang. Some of the poor kids I spoke to were excluded from everything. They were living in homes they shouldn't have to live in and were being called anti-social. Police were moving them on." *(itzcaribbean. com Caribbean London).* However, it would seem that although we cannot ignore the fact that young people need to group together, as part of their basic human need, at the same time we cannot ignore the fact that increasing levels of must be combated with voracity. Hallsworth's comment on our approach to young people is noteworthy, "Maybe we should understand *(them)* more and condemn less." [my addition]. *(itzcaribbean.com Caribbean London)*

This view has been long held by this author, as a strategy for engaging our future generations. For this reason, in a film commissioned by **The Roselle Antoine Foundation** (2008), young people around cities in Britain, (London, Wolverhampton, Northampton, Leicester, Birmingham), were invited to expressed the localized difficulties they faced and to suggest solutions to what they were experiencing. The outcome was a frank, articulate and coherent analysis of a wide cross-section of British youths discussing what they see as a nationwide malaise. Their evaluation in the film entitled, **A Voice of Their Own (October 2008)**, pointed to social and economic deprivation, problems with housing, transport, health facilities and lack of opportunities for young people, as contributing to their difficulties in Britain.

Interestingly, the filmed youngsters, who related their present problems, were optimistic of a good future, barring the rising statistics of gun, knife and gang crime. It is now also an offence to use someone to mind a weapon on your behalf. Teachers have recently been given the power to search pupils who are feared to be carrying weapons **(The Independent 28 May 2008.** From October the age of a person allowed legally to buy a knife will increase from 16 to 18. Last year 90,000 knives were taken out of circulation during a national knife amnesty November 2008, crime statistics showed a reduction in knife crimes by 17%. The new measures follow the introduction of the Violent Crime Reduction Act Perhaps emerging optimism have come from changes in crime management and punishment, and could possibly account for this. **(Figure .1).**

Strategies for Scotland

Looking at a UK wide spectrum of the growing problems associated with gangs, Justice Secretary Kenny MacAskill says, "The Scottish Government is determined to take action to help those who are involved in gangs. To help them break out of the cycle of drink, drugs, deprivation and crime and to help their communities recover from the problems and become safer and stronger. "I hope we can persuade more of these youngsters involved in gangs and the crimes and antisocial behaviour associated with them - or on the cusp of gang membership - to think again about whether gang life is really the way they want to go." That the problem is widespread is evident, as endorsed by Superintendent Michelle Martin who said, "Tackling disorder and violence has been core police business in and around Shettleston, Baillieston and Greater Easterhouse for far too long now, and while we have been fortunate enough to receive funding which enabled us to get more officers, more regularly on to the streets, we know only too well that enforcement alone is not the answer.

"The introduction of some fairly innovative ideas and facilities to channel youngsters' energies into recreation, including the Outdoor Gym at Sandaig Park, Barlanark and the Phoenix Community Youth Bus, with parents also seeing a difference and endorsing the message that antisocial behaviour is unacceptable and will not be tolerated. (**The Scottish Government news- 15.10.08**).   Additionally, The Centre for Social Justice (CSJ) in February 2008, think-tank has revealed that there are 170 teenage gangs in Glasgow.

Strategies for Wales

Barbara Wilding, the Chief Constable of South Wales, says family ties have been abandoned in place of "tribal loyalty" among young gang members, who have become "almost feral". Ms Wilding, the longest-serving female chief constable, said that social breakdown means violence and drugs have become a way of life in deprived parts of many larger English cities. She claims that custody could only provide a short-term solution, she said, with policies based primarily on enforcement "set on sand". Ms Wilding attributes the causes to "many of our larger cities, in areas of extreme deprivation, [where] there are almost feral groups of very angry young people. Many have experienced family breakdown, and in place of parental and family role models, the gang culture is now established. Tribal loyalty has replaced family loyalty and gang culture based on violence and drugs is a way of life." It is said that her remarks could be seen as indirect criticism of government policy and the criminal justice system,

reflect wider concern about the spread of gang culture. Local authorities, police and magistrates are being urged to use acceptable behaviour contracts, parenting orders and individual support orders to encourage better behaviour. Her remarks echo a speech by the Home Secretary Jacqui Smith, also in May 2008, in which she advocated a policy of early intervention to target unruly youths. (*Telegraph 2 July 2008*)

Figure 7.2: Gang-formation across the UK

GLASGOW	Dominated by the Barlanark Young Team and Calvay Boys. There are more than 170 gangs.
BRADFORD	Run by the Ointment Gang which allies itself with Bradford City - to the club's annoyance - and has been linked to Manningham Lane race riots. Mobs of Asians often clash over drug cash which is said to be laundered through a network of shops.
LIVERPOOL	Blighted by a string of turf wars between the Croxteth Crew, Nogga Dogz, Moss Edz and Dovey Edz. The rivalries - centred on Norris Green, Croxteth, Huyton and Dovercot, sparked nationwide outrage last year when innocent 11-year-old Rhys Jones died in his mum's arms in a pub car park after being shot in the neck.
MANCHESTER	Ruled by mobs like the Doddington Gang and the Gooch Boys, city has been dubbed "Gangchester".
NOTTINGHAM	Feuding mobs include the Meadows Posse, St Ann's Crew and the Radford Road Posse. Being on the drug route between London and Manchester has led to a huge increase in gang violence.
BIRMINGHAM	Race-HATE thugs e.g. the Johnson Crew and Burger Bar Boys plague the city. Clashes between Black and Asian gangs in the Lozells area in 2005 left three people dead. In 2002 Letisha Shakespeare, 17, and Charlene Ellis, 18, were shot dead after a party in a vendetta between rival black mobs - who later joined forced to fight Asians.
CARDIFF	Football thugs like Soul Crew have been sidelined by Canton Youth and other teenage gangs. Canton Youth specialises in intimidation and vandalism.
LONDON	Violent gangs include the Peel Dem Crew, Murder Dem Pussies, the Peckham boys, the Untouchables and the Tottenham Man Dem. It is believed that there are up to 400 mobs in London.

Strategies for England

In England, similar action was articulated by The Prime Minister, Gordon Brown *(August 2007),* who has promised that the Government will carry out "intensive work" to deal with the growing problem of teenage crime and gang culture. He told reporters in Downing Street that tougher enforcement of existing laws and the passing of new laws, if required, were high on the Government's agenda following a spate of recent stabbings and shootings involving young people. *"Where there is a need for new laws, we will pass them, where there is a need for tougher enforcement we will make sure that that happens."* *(No10.gov.uk – 15.10.08)*

In addition there are projects designed to tackle the problem head on, e.g. 'Leap Confronting Conflict' project, trialled in Glasgow and North London, works with rival gangs. This has been based on encouraging gangs to engage with one another and consider the consequences of their actions. This project has been successful in soothing gang relations enabling members of rival gangs to attend community events together.

Additionally, the Manchester Multi-Agency Gang Strategy (MMAGS) launched in 2001, was modelled on the Boston Gun Project in the US, which was a problem-orientated policing initiative to reduce gang violence. MMAGS tackles street gangs involved in firearm use in Manchester, aiming to reduce the impact of gun and gang related activity, rehabilitate those convicted of gun or gang related offences. It offers young people education and employment opportunities as alternatives to gun and gang crime. The project is voluntary, but some individuals are given court orders to work with MMAGS or it is a condition of their licence. The project has provided those who would not have been involved in education, the opportunity to gain qualifications. In addition, the project also does preventative work in schools and youth centres discussing issues such as gang culture, firearm legislation and peer pressure. (Table 7.1)

Table 7.1:   Summary of Major UK strategies related to Gang Culture

REGION	STRATEGY TYPE
Scotland	Innovative ideas to channel the creative energies of young people
Wales	Policy of early intervention to target unruly youths
England	'intensive work' dealing with problem of teenage crime and gang culture
Community	Role model, parental intervention, social perspective, community action

Gang intervention & the Black Community

Like the UK governments, many Caribbean parents who with their families, become victims of gang warfare and deaths among their families, are assiduously trying to find ways to eradicate this type of social ill. One drastic solution of protecting their loved ones is seen in the growing trend among Britain's Caribbean community, of sending wayward boys to the Caribbean to attend schools where discipline is stricter, violence less prevalent and teachers are generally more respected.

Spencer Fearon – Role model

Spencer Fearon is a successful boxing promoter and property investor. His disruptive nature as a child meant that at the age of nine he was sent from home in Kennington, South London, to live with family in rural Jamaica. I loved it because it was part of the Jamaican culture I didn't know. I was with family who loved me and cared about my development. I believe that the **best role models are parents, not footballers, entertainers or entrepreneurs**. Values come from the home and that's where black kids are being failed, by their parents. Black people who kill have a total disregard for each other.' *(itzcaribbean. com Caribbean London)*

Lee Jasper – Parent's view

Lee Jasper, (the former Senior Policy Advisor on Equalities for the past Mayor of Greater London 2007), grew up in Chase, a rough part of Manchester. He was a disruptive teenager himself who now has nine children, including five boys. His view is that *"all black boys in Britain should be sent to the Caribbean or Africa for a gap year to show them what poverty is really about, when they get to around 13 or 14 they seem to adopt this semi-gangster attitude and sending them to places like that helps them to get a better perspective on life.* Lee is convinced of this strategy of parental management because, *"my three eldest sons are grown up now. Two were sent to Jamaica and one to Ghana for a year against their wills around that age and they all came back with a far better attitude. They are all doing very well now. My two youngest sons are 15 and 11 and they'll be going too."* *(itzcaribbean.com Caribbean London)*

Henry Bonsu - Media Perspective

Former BBC radio presenter Henry Bonsu is now a director of Colourful Radio, an internet radio station. He said: 'Violence has been casualised from images youngsters get on TV, in films and rap music and that has manifested itself in these **gang killings.** A lot of it has to do with self-loathing too. African kids generally have a stronger family unit than Caribbean families. After all, they retain their languages, names and customs and are generally obsessed with education and still think of going home to Africa. Bonsu's cultural identity theory is one which my research during the past 14 years have revealed as being a key factor to the many problems that dog Caribbean youths. Bonsu states, *'Many teenagers from a Caribbean background have no strong sense of cultural identity. I think every school with a large Caribbean population should have an outside connection with a Caribbean organisation because they need to be more attached to their cultural background.'* *(itzcaribbean.com Caribbean London)*

Derek Amory – Social perspective

However, Derek Amory, a social worker in Birmingham, who specializes in working with juveniles, does not believe that sending wayward youngsters to the Caribbean will help. He feels education is the key. *'Using shock tactics by sending kids to the Caribbean won't work. They'll just treat it as a holiday."* Amory's answer lies in the fact that 'the world has become Americanised" He states that *"Street culture is universal"* but *"crime needs to be taught as part of the school curriculum just as much as maths and English"* *(itzcaribbean. com Caribbean London)*

Twlight Bey – Social Interventionist

Within the black community, much is being done among organizations in workshops and projects that see social intervention and change management strategies as key to bridging the gap between rival gang members. A proponent of this type of intervention is the well-know Twilight Bey who was a key figure in the initiation of the Peace Talks in 1988 between rival Los Angeles Street Gangs. This led to him becoming a key organiser of the Cease Fire Agreement between the Bloods & Crisps of Watts, California in 1992. He works among black youths in London Communities and Institutions, Contributing to local and international efforts in youth and community focused initiatives e.g. violence reduction strategies, capacity building, service learning, mentoring, community building and leadership development. There is certainly agreement with Derek's Amory's point on the universality of street culture and by implication the ease of gang formation.   It confirms the fact that gangs are not only Black youths. The following comment made by Ms Wilding, a former Deputy Assistant Commissioner at the Metropolitan Police, *said the focus [on solutions] should be on tackling the complex social and economic issues underlying criminal behaviour"* because *"in an age of cost-benefit analysis... there is no appetite for solutions that have no visible return and no patience for any which will not bear immediate political fruit."* This is indeed a sad indictment of the Britain that we live in, the fact that scoring political points and cost benefits, come before *real* human development.

Mothers and Sons as locum parents

A corresponding phenomena of external or environmental violence, is the internal violence meted out by sons to their mothers. This is the result of a complex relationship of the young men assuming the "authoritative" roles of their **absent** fathers (**locum parents** or surrogate parents), so that in the home environment, the young boys, are given carte blanche in decision-making (especially in relations to themselves and younger members of their families) at home. In her zealousness to invest in her son the status of young **man**, without the necessary transition rites of passage, she may at times, confuse the young person by allowing him to take charge of looking after siblings, reprimanding them in her absence, and assuming responsibilities in the home; may not realise how much she has contributed to the youngster's confused sense of self. **(Figure 7.3).**

The fact is, emotionally, he is a child who mother will admonish occasionally, using her adult and parental Rights. What ensues is a pattern of intermittent periods of child **powerfulness** (temporary parental invested power) and **powerlessness**, (temporary parental denial of power), so that he crosses "loosely" imposed boundaries with defiant outbursts, and may physically attack his mother; reflective of adult-male behavior, when things are not to his satisfaction. What then is the dynamics of this part-time, **power-struggle** in their relationship?

Prior to any relationship with Partners being brought to the home, the mother's form of unconscious off-loading burdens the child so that their method of communicating projects him as a "locum parent". It also results in the child feeling that he is equal to his mother – **equal**, in the sense that he can also make decisions and take actions single-handedly, whether negatively or positively. Invested with this power, many children readily adopt a form of adverse behaviour which they believe is "representative" of the absent adult i.e., cursing, swearing, and intimidating what they perceive as adult behaviour, and these become their assumed traits. A very poignant and personal comment made by President Elect of the USA, Barack Obama, (CNN, 2 Jan. 2009), when asked about the impact of his "absent" father on his life, suggested an approach that has worked for him: *"If kids know that you are the centre of their world, it makes up for a lot of instability".*

Figure 7.3: Parent-child relationship "in loco parentis"

Mother may have an absent partner and left with children to bring up by herself If the child is a teenage son, she may confide in him and relate daily issues to him in the same way that partners would relate the day's proceedings to each other.
The child realises he is treated as an adult and psychologically becomes protective of his one parent by accepting the listening role or active participant who is encouraged to respond, if not give advice, so that a "new" kind of relationship develops between. It is one that supersedes the mother-son relation to take on a "friendliness" that beaks down any barrier of parental hierarchy". In other words, the son has a double role – that of son and a kind of surrogate partner.
It is not uncommon to find that where mother has a Partner, who is unrelated to the child, or a "Visiting relationship" with another male, the son may react to this, especially if he feels this relationship will usurp the primary he has over all other males in the home so far.
The psychology is that he certainly does not want to take "orders" from another adult, least of all a mal. This defiance is more marked if there has been a total absence of a father figure in his life to date.
The likelihood of bonding is less also if the "present" father-figure takes the opportunity to assert his authority or shows evidence of staying longer than a visitor - in other words where the relationship begins to show signs of long-term development, it threatens the status quo.
Aggression and abject disrespect for the mother follows any form of physical confrontation by the male, whether justified or not. Many young boys have talked of the "hate" they have developed for their mothers in such instances.
So as not to "lose" her son, she allows him to continue as he has done up to the point of the "new" relationship. Consequently, this is a situation which creates a double indemnity for her – conflict with her Partner, if her son's behavior is blatantly unacceptable and conflict with her son if she is seen to "take sides" with the "outsider" male.

However, he warned that caution must be employed since it was not possible to *"measure absence."*

As a School Principal, many parents often report to me their helplessness in managing the child, who now hangs up the phone on his mother, curses her at will, tells her off and walks in and out of the home at all hours of the night, with no qualms about the response he would get from his mother. This is the child's ultimate and public blurring of all distinctions between what is acceptable in society, in the home, at school, as well as within the local environment.

Many mothers are unwilling to publicise the violence they suffer from their teenage sons, for reasons that they believe they cannot turn their own children over to the Justice System or make the information known to friends or members of their family, for fear of shame, embarrassment and blame. Other forms of compensation or over-compensation are, allowing the child to bring friends home, without rules or conditions attached. This may include the mother letting the child's friends sleep over in the home (both boys and girls); without restrictions. Again this signals to the child that he is on equal footing with his mother because at this point, he is able to make his own rules, to which his mother complies: how can she not!

Consequences of not agreeing to the child's demands are repetitions of adverse behaviour, (which can now be used as a form of blackmail or bullying), open defiance, 'loss' of a head sibling to mind the other children in her absence or his disappearance from the home for days on end. This is his way of demonstrating that he really CAN do what he likes. At this stage because mother needs the boy, (and he knows this), he expects her quiet submission or acceptance of this as a matter of course. My experience with parents is that some mothers go one step further – allowing the child to smoke whether in the home or not irrespective of the legal age restrictions. In some cases, the child bullies the mother to give and/or buy cigarettes. In return, and in order to placate the child, the mother unconsciously "buys" a quiet life by giving in to the demand.

Such children are often associated with truancy and slip through the net because by this time parents have very little control and become ineffective in their attempts to scold or reprimand them. Though not in all cases, they are often identified among parents who would not send in notes or letters regarding the child's absence, and do not turn up for meetings at school regarding behaviour and attendance issues. It is also not unusual to be at the receiving end of their verbal abuse, should you upbraid them, especially as adults, for not adhering to school rules.

The fact is, it is also commonplace that they would not be able to tell the school what time their child left home for school on any given day, whether the child wore school uniform or not, had lunch money for the day, or indeed whether the child even left the home at all! The police tend to agree that children who are out in the streets playing truant from school are responsible for a lot of minor crimes. Evidence was cited for 'a significant association between offending and poor attendance at school', *(Parsons, Hayden et al 2000).*

Figure 7.4: 'Styles of Parenting'

One example is that of a mother and her 12 year old son who was permanently excluded from mainstream school who came for an alternative placement at TCS Tutorial College. He had been problematic in both Primary and early Secondary schools and was labled as having Emotional and Behavioural Difficulties. His literacy level was low, well below average for his age. His level of anger and violence was intermittently uncontrollable, attacking both pupils and staff alike. He would smash windows, punch walls, leaving dents in wooden parts of the building and at one time coming close to violently and physically attacking a member of staff.

On one occasion, when mother was called in to discuss strategies for behaviour management, she was visibly afraid of her son (a strong, well built boy), whose language was dominated with "I don't care", threats of violence to everyone around him and visible physical displays of wanting to cause destruction. He refused to be part of the meeting which was called to discuss his behaviour and mother felt she had to follow his angry instructions. After they left, and were in the car park about to leave the school grounds, I was surprised to see that she had returned back into the school building, to tell off the teacher in question, as a way of giving satisfaction to her angry son. After this shocking display of "compensation", the boy smashed the glass inset to the entrance door and they drove off. As a form of mentoring and advising her, I was able to appeal to her sense of motherhood and she agreed that she could have handled the situation differently. However, it was not long before the boy was imprisoned for violently attacking a member of the public and is currently serving a 5 year prison sentence.

This type of relationship has serious implications for both parents and children because of the emotional ambivalence that develops among the young child. On the one hand, he is expected to behave as a "normal" child in all social settings, while on the other hand, he is expected to reflect an adult form of behaviour within the home setting. This situation blurs the distinction between appropriate parenting/parenthood and a child's ability to accept authority outside of the home.

Many boys, with *'absent'* fathers, project a kind of nostalgic imaginary relationship, which to them is an ideal. The fact that the lone mother has multiple roles tend to conspire against her in many instances. For example, she is mother, father, educator, friend, doctor, authority figure, someone who reprimands (with levels of severity), at times a strict disciplinarian or the one who "moans too much," and at other times she may project an emotionally "weak" or "strong" character - given her daily experiences, (as witnessed by the child), and jealously guarded from strangers by the child. In fact the lone parent (more often than not, is the mother who "knows everything" since her word cannot be contested by those outside the home as far as the child is concerned!

Therefore, while mothers enjoy this amalgam of complex characteristics, the father or male counterpart, also has an image attached to him. This is constructed from the child's longing or desperation for a sense of belonging and associating with males; the need to prove that he has not been abandoned; that the mother is not making up all the reasons why he cannot be associated with the father. At times his desperation could simply be the need to experience what he is being educated to accept as an ideal 'family unit' – mother, father, and children living together. Therefore in the absence of either parent, he knows that his world falls short of 'an ideal' and is in fact a reflection of "lack" or "a shortage", which he then experiences in nearly all areas of his life – educationally, emotionally, physically, economically, historically, morally, socially, and in some cases, spiritually.

My experience of working with children who have emotional and social behavioural difficulties has revealed, over a 20 year span, that young boys who are deeply scarred by the absence of their male parent, project behaviours they associate with the imaginary parent. On the one hand, this is often embodied in a complex web of constructed projection based on their social interactions, what they witness; (e.g. in the media, family, environment, with known associations, among fathers of friends, or internal resentment. built up by a constant barrage of negative, sometimes angry, portrayal of their fathers by their mothers).

On the other hand, the child then reacts adversely against what he begins to regard (by implication), as a negative association of biological linkage to the 'abhorrent' father. One father who has had to endure the negative play-off between his longing to honour his commitment to his children and his wife's unreasonable behavior and demands, is critical of the system that encourages gender-bias for parenthood in favour of mothers. **(Figure 7.5).**

This situation is prevalent among sections of the British-Caribbean population , especially those from fragmented family structures.   This means that in some cases, the problems related to lone parenting, underachievement and emotional and social behavioural difficulties, need to be understood by schools and educational authorities in general. In doing so, a culturally sensitive and a socially specific approach is more applicable to managing such children's behaviour. In fact, I would advocate that the government's vision for education in the 21st century, adopt this respectful interventionist approach to raising standards of educational achievement and behaviour management.

Many children in the school environment are burdened by a complexity of emotions based on their individual and collective experiences, that makes it difficult to understand their adverse behaviour. Being in the position of Heading an educational institution makes it easy, through our person-centered approach, to listen to young people articulate their various experiences. Understanding where their heightened emotions come from is imperative if one is to firstly offer approaches that enable them to understand themselves in the context of their personal surrounding, their locality, and the wider environment.

Figure 7.5: Consequences of 'Broken Families'

The stigma attached to broken Caribbean families in the UK, misses both historic and modern situations. As someone who was brought up in a nuclear family setting – both mother and father and grandparents including a great-grand mother. I have experienced firsthand the impact of parental negative behaviours on children from both a nuclear and single-parent families.

Educational underachievement among some Caribbean boys is mostly evidenced by the number of lone parent relationships and the absence of fathers either in the home or outside. The evidence is hardly ever interrogative regarding reasons for parental break-ups or for that matter, the singular issue relating to the `so-called' absent father. The fact is that in most couples' breakdown, children tend to suffer because either or both parents are unwilling (because of their own emotional turmoil) to engage in a constructive approach towards taking care of children in the aftermath of separation. In fact, children are sometimes the least consideration in a post-break-up situation. In the case of boys, they are either played off by mothers and/or father as an object of dispute or bargaining. Depending on who has custody of the child, that child can be a subject of manipulation involving both parents. A test of wills ensues to show which parent is better. In all this the children suffer emotionally, and psychologically. His ability to cope is not enhanced by parent's continual battle to control their own turf, forgetting that the most important part of their-post relationship is that of their children whose upbringing is far more important than their acts of trivial and oftentimes immature behaviour.

Ownership of children is a dual responsibility of both (biological) parents and is not sacrosanct or dependent on one parent. The all-round development of children into (eventual) adults rests with both parents asserting their duty and responsibility of love, care and attention to the child in question. Anecdotal evidence strongly suggests, that boys in particular who are deprived of `balanced' parenting, are often-times more likely to underachieve or under-perform in areas such as education, social interaction, group work, (formation of) relationships and other societal activities. This means that such deprivation has its genesis in the way children have been treated by either one or both parents and/ or the examples set by their parents in managing their own behaviours.

Source: Interview with Dr. C.A Johnson: Feb. 2009

For example, a child as young as 13 years old, who has experienced being persistently picked up by the police, arrested, who bears the shame of having his front door kicked down by arresting police officers, witness the shame of having his parent (in 99.9% cases), his mother, being verbally abused or made to feel ashamed or denigrated in front of him, is more than likely to develop hatred of the law and its representative authorities. He feels violated by the experience and loses respect for the "adult" world.

In addition, the child would be reprimanded repeatedly, constantly being reminded that the experience has brought shame on the family in their neighbourhood. Consequently, both child and parents become self-conscious that the stereotype of being branded as "trouble-makers or criminals", becomes a living reality, for the reason that the law is seen disrespecting them. In some cases these experiences create family tensions and in extreme cases family divisions. If it is regarding a serious matter, the child may subsequently be brought up before the court. In cases, where the matter may be treated more seriously than the family could explain, try as they may, it is possible that in the absence of their ability to articulate their position and the circumstances they find themselves in, could be found "guilty" unjustly. There is no doubt that this then results an indelible mistrust and hatred for the **"system"** that has treated them differently from others.

That child may know of other similar experiences that may be taking place among his peers or associates and resentment builds up on a large scale. The them- and- us scenario would ensue, and the need to defend themselves, or to exact revenge on the world that has caused them to become so, may be the path they choose to adopt. To do this the joining of forces or adopting the psychology of the gang, gives a sense that there is force behind their demanding Rights as they see them – Rights which give them power and inspires and instills fear in everyone.   This is the worst form of institutionalized racism as there is little one can do to "correct" that experience. In some cases the child becomes deviant because his emotions are in conflict with faceless figures he feels he must exact revenge or vent his feelings on.

Here the word *"system"* means *authority*; anything or anyone who exercises power and influence over them or dictates opinions downwards to them. It could be seen also as those who have the power to multiply or exacerbate their already adverse experience.. The consequences for children with the above experience, is that this forms a barrier to participation socially and educationally. This may present as a lack of interest in advancing, (the fact that all chances of progressing has been sullied by their young experiences), and there will certainly be little or no involvement with those they view as *"working for the system"*, meaning those among the community they must treat suspiciously because they appear to follow the status quo.

A worse scenario is where the young person witnesses a community leader or person held in high esteem in their society being treated with the same scorn or disdain as they themselves have experienced. At this point, there is a resultant recklessness and open deviance in the youth because they feel a sense of helplessness and view life as hopeless. This is because those he believe are able to prevent the level of discrimination that exists, are themselves undergoing similar attacks and denigration. What this reinforces, is a cycle of anger, hatred and resentment which becomes harder to unravel because the live experiences are stronger in "colouring" their judgements, than appeals to refrain from behaviour that reinforces stereotypes.

Conclusion

In conclusion, there is certainly a need for policy-makers to engage in open discussions about the negative consequences of families, where the child is a 'locum parent' which creates a confused view of the transition to manhood. Development programmes should explore ways in which "gender mainstreaming", is explored and should focus on the interaction between men, and the stereotypes of young men as aggressive, violent troublemakers; since this excludes them further from society.   Overall, questions of WHY children are aggressive need to be explored in depth, rather than minimized or viewed as flippant, stereotypical or as an adult expectation of their state as young people.

SELECTED CHAPTER REFERENCES

Drug-related corruption of police officers: A contemporary typology
by David L. Carte.r Journal of Criminal Justice, Volume 18, Issue 2, 1990, Pages 85-98.

Coard B., *(1971): How the British School system made the West Indian child educationally subnormal"* , New Beacon Books, London.

Mental Health and Ethnicity Census 2005.

Commission for Healthcare Audit and Inspection (2005): *Count Me In*, Results of a national census of inpatients in mental health hospitals and facilities in England and Wales.

Parsons, Hayden et al: *Research into the outcome, in secondary education for children excluded from primary school. Follow-up study commissioned by DfEE, 2000).*

Ed. Bonnie R. Strickland, Cengage, Gale *(2001): " Encyclopedia of Psychology.* 2nd ed..- eNotes.com. 2006.1 Jan, 2009 http://www.enotes.com/gale-psychology-encyclopedia/gangs.

Chapter Notes:

Black Mental Health UK is an online publisher providing independent news, features, comment and other internet based services including advertising and job vacancies for those who work in the mental health sector. BMH UK is community based and is independent of any professional body or society. www.blackmentalhealth.org.uk

8 | The Antoine Behaviour Excellence Model ©

Rationale

The Antoine Behaviour Excellence Model (ABEM)©, is a method of behaviour management which employs culturally sensitive and socially specific approaches to dealing with challenging behaviours. The model employs an ethnographic approach to schooling by focusing on the daily lives and meaning-making processes of pupils at school, in order to understand the origins of their behaviours, so that they develop on a scale which ranges from adverse displays to a model of excellence.

Generally, Ethnographers observe and participate in the routine activities of people they study. They explore the connection between locally based issues within a broader frame of reference and social organization. In other words, an ethnographical approach presents the potential to learn, encourage reflection, , critically engages with questions (in this case),what behaviour really is, how it is viewed, how it is assessed in society and among social and cultural groups There are four aspects to this approach and when questions are raised as to why use an ethnographic approach, answers are found in the following:

1. It studies real-world settings.

2. Its holistic, looking at the whole phenomenon or problem

3. It entails coming face-to-face with communities and groups

4. Draws on a variety of research techniques and as a result,

5. Produces a range of data via spoken and written; interviewing, observation, and participation techniques

6.   Facilitates the study of cultural practices with four aspects to its approach

7.   Allows the participant-observer to interpret the whole, collaboratively.

Traditionally, this approach has entailed becoming involved in unfamiliar settings over a long period of time – usually several years of fieldwork. Although this approach has been critiqued in recent years, such critical views have been in terms of questioning the relationship between claims that ethnographers can fully represent the perspectives of their informants. However, one way of overcoming this is by including all those involved in the decision-making processes of the work.. Therefore, the *Antoine Behaviour Excellence Model* is the collaborative effort (over 25 years), of producing outcomes by involving parents, pupils, the community at large, inter-agency personnel (education, housing, social services, legal, health), in documenting their own realities and allowing them to feedback information using their own words (e.g. via reply slips, confirmation/consent of data discussed and our interpretations of them. **(Figure 8.1)**

Figure 8.1: Ethnography as a main Approach

• Focus is on observation and assessment;
• Review of pupil's database, previous ethnography, file notes;
• Purpose of collaborative approach – individual education plan;
• This approach also delivers, tests, evaluates and make objective judgements;
• Reflect on reports, lack of/progress made and planning targets;
• Assesses *actual* vs. *projected* targets via a culturally sensitive/socially specific approach.
• Engenders flexibility and invites several viewpoints of all those involved;
• Provides the chance for further assessment and target-setting;
• Produces a shared sense of what is important to the school;
• The approach works in a tripartite way with pupils, their homes and the school;
• Promotes shared commitment among staff to involve students in the learning process;
• Promotes pupil mutual relationship/interaction (e.g. peer-group and team work);
• Encourages interpretation via a model of communication;

• Promotes teacher-student and student-student learning and development;
• Builds a culture of learning and leadership through observation;
• Builds collaboration, participation and shared reflection; and
• Used for professional development- opportunities for creativity/personal development.

The ABEM's perspective is that a person's attitude to the world, those around him, and his way of life, is tied up with his cultural upbringing. But based on the paradoxes presented in **Chapter 7,** it is possible to say that in a Black British setting, it is far more complex to say that behavioural difficulties are purely culturally directed. It is true that a person's culture is embodied in their way of life; their customs, dress, belief, the way they think and react, how they greet each other, prepare food and the way they express themselves – in other words, the structure of their social life.   However, this culture, whilst it identifies its people, over time it may undergo degrees of alteration, depending on various influences, geographically and politically, that impact on its survival.

The culture of Caribbean people is an example of this thought, from the point of view that from a common root, the individual, say from the Caribbean region, has various expressions of the same ideology (sometimes historically determined), and as a result, this makes Caribbean culture manifested among young Caribbeans in Britain, appear complex if not rather unique. This is just one cultural example.   However, a *socially specific approach* has more to do with approaches which acknowledge the differences between various social classes and the impact that these have on a child's academic and social skills development.

Theoretical underpinning of ABEM

ABEM is a form of behavioural intervention based on social learning principles *(Patterson 1982).* It aims to reduce risk factors associated with severe behavioural and emotional problems in pre-and post-adolescent children and at the same time enhances family knowledge, skills and competence. Families are able to self-regulate behaviours, thereby making one of ABEM's characteristics that of self-sufficiency. It promotes social and emotional, intellectual and behavioural competences through a positive, person-centred approach to educational and social development.

Social learning of parent-child interaction

The ABEM model promotes social learning of parent-child interaction that has a mutual benefit, or bidirectional nature of parent-child interactions *(Patterson 1982)*. The model identifies learning mechanisms which maintain coercive and dysfunctional patterns of family interaction, (including cultural factors), and predicts future anti-social behaviour in children (Patterson, Reid and Dishion 1992).

Research in child and family behaviour therapy

ABEM responds to research which focuses on rearranging antecedents of problem behaviour through designing more positive engaging environments for children as propounded by Risley, Clark & Cataldo, 1976; Saunders 1992, 1996).

Developmental research

ABEM targets children competencies in natural everyday settings, and draws on cultural social and intellectual competence to parent-child relationships (Hart & Risley 1995, White 1990). Consequently the risk of developing severe behavioural and emotional problems is reduced by teaching children and their parents to use naturally occurring interactions to teach children social skills and problem solving skills in an emotionally supportive environment. The ABEM model has recognized the fact that children are at greater risk of adverse developmental outcomes if they fail to develop core skills or control impulse during early childhood, (Hart & Risley 1995).

Developmental Psychopathology research

Research has identified specific risk and protective factors which are linked to adverse developmental outcomes in children (Emery 1982; Grych & Fincham 1990, Hart & Risley 1995; Rutter 1985). ABEM has recognised as have these developmental research that risk factors of poor parent management practices, marriage breakdowns, family conflict and family distress leading to emotional and other abuses, are targeted risk factors. We know that parental disharmony is the basis of many forms of risk factors in children and adolescents *(Grych & Finchamj* 1990; Rutter 1985); Saunders and Markie-Dadds 1997).

Background to the Model   1994 - 2009

The Antoine Behaviour Excellence Model is one that was developed as a result of managing pupils with a consistent pattern of emotional and behavioural difficulties which impacts on their ability to engage in the curriculum. This invariable led to disaffections, high levels of school exclusions and expulsions and an increasing engagement with the criminal justice system. The **Model** is based on an all-inclusive participation of the community in all areas of the curriculum.

The Antoine Behaviour Excellence Model although aimed at pupils at compulsory *school age,* also provides for those at post-compulsory education level. The principles are applicable to everyone, irrespective of race, class, gender, religion, political and other social persuasions. However, in general terms, the **Model** was developed over a period of 25 years, working with children of Caribbean and African Heritage and exemplifies that a culturally sensitive and socially specific approach to education excellence, especially with reference to managing difficult and challenging behaviour. It produces a high ratio of effective and successful behaviours and ultimately promotes engagement from Primary, Secondary, through to Further and Higher Education levels at 100%.success rate. **(Figure 8.2)**

Figure 8.2: Benefits of   the Antoine Behaviour Excellence Model

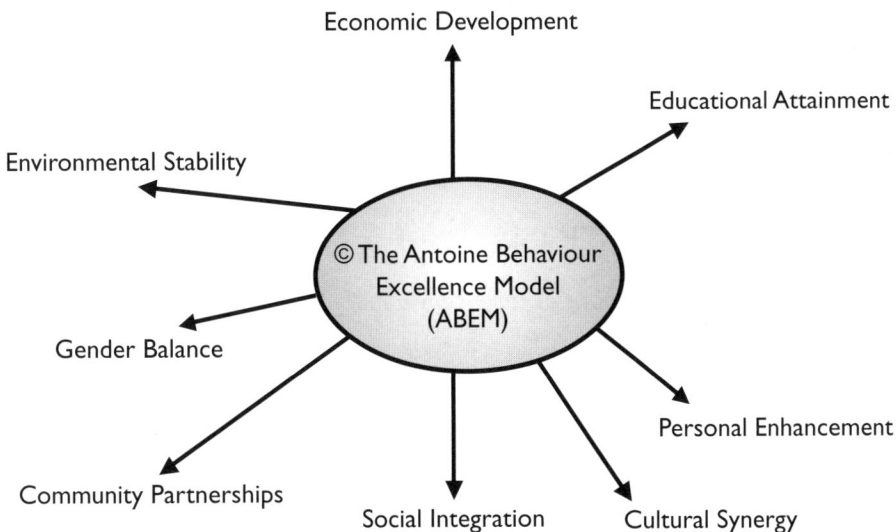

Economic Development

Educational Attainment

Environmental Stability

© The Antoine Behaviour Excellence Model (ABEM)

Gender Balance

Personal Enhancement

Community Partnerships

Social Integration

Cultural Synergy

The benchmark for the Antoine Behaviour Excellence Model is " Promotion of positive Behaviour by the community, for the community and within the community"

I.   HOW THE MODEL WORKS

The Model is underscored by five pillars: -

a.   Referrals supported SEN and supporting documents;

b.   Sessions with pupils/learners and families;

c.   Assessment of abilities and competencies over 4 weeks;

d.   Personal Action Plans and Individual Education Plans;

e.   Evaluation of record of achievement/underachievement; and

f.   Programme delivery based on a structured plan. **(Figure 8.3)**

The overall objective is to ensure that every person benefits from a practical programme of delivery based on his/her aptitude and potential. The **Model** contributes to a consistent pattern of educational and social success at a rate of 90%-100%.

Figure 8.3: Pillars of Execution

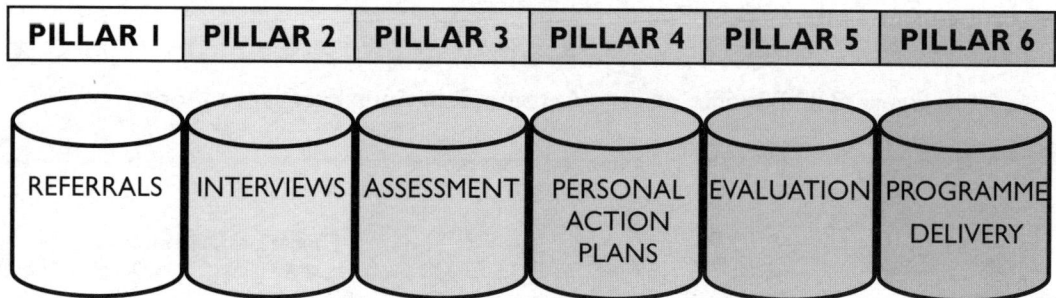

PILLAR I	PILLAR 2	PILLAR 3	PILLAR 4	PILLAR 5	PILLAR 6
REFERRALS	INTERVIEWS	ASSESSMENT	PERSONAL ACTION PLANS	EVALUATION	PROGRAMME DELIVERY

2.   GOALS AND ASPIRATIONS

Through the *Antoine Behaviour Excellence Model©,* a number of goals and aspirations have been reached, including: -

a.   To *capture/recapture* the confidence of pupils/students and other learners who benefit from education and training in an environment that seeks to enable them to take control of their actions;

b.   To *motivate* pupils to achieve their full potential in all areas of education and vocational attainment using their skills and talents and motivators to enhance overall curriculum development;

c. To *develop* a continuous devotion to learning and development amongst learners by using in and out of school activities, the community, ongoing opportunities for development via extra curricular programmes e.g. Leadership Development, Cultural Exchanges, Working within the community, Celebration of Achievement;

d. To *imbue* a sense of self-esteem and identity amongst all learners, in order for them to maximise their potential and maintain a sense of stability; and

e. To *inculcate* a commitment to participatory citizenship regarding positive behaviour management as necessary characteristics for development within the community and the wider society;

3. HOW THE MODEL LINKS

Working with *The Antoine Behaviour Excellence Model©* necessitates a tripartite movement involving families, communities and pupils/students. This is vital to towards achieving quality standards in education and training programmes, thereby reinforcing Best Practice. **(Figure 8.4)**

Figure 8.4: Model Linkages of ABEM

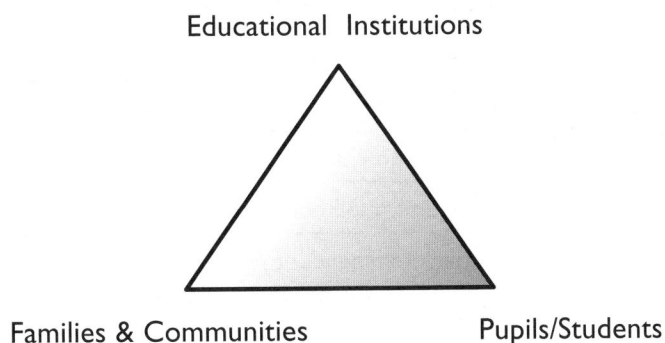

Educational Institutions

Families & Communities   Pupils/Students

4. VALIDATING THE MODEL

The Model is validated along the following lines: -

a. **Developing** profile of achievement by pupils over an extended period;

b. **Rewarding** achievement of both pupils and members of the adult community;

c. **Processing assessments,** reviews and reports;

d. **Involving parents** in curriculum development and general education programs;

e. **Consulting with stakeholders** in the wider community;

f. **Examining the role of religion, culture and traditional customs** in family development;

g. **Recognising culture** as a tool for education and social harmony;

h. **Researching trends** relating to Special Education Needs (SEN) for low achievers and high-achievers; and

i. **Designating each year** with particular *themes* to foster excellence at all levels. **(Figure 8.5 & 8.6)**

Figure 8.5: Vision of the Antoine Behaviour Excellence Model (ABEM)©

✓	ABEM was developed by this author, and implemented in the
✓	TCS Tutorial College School, where the author is both Founder and Principal.
✓	For the staff learning and teaching is a collaboration of commitment
✓	Experiences and ideas are shared and reflected
✓	Facilitates changes to both staff and pupil behaviour management
✓	*Reason* – teachers are able to think independently and creatively about the *"I Am Somebody Great!* Ethos, on which the model is founded, and which is also the School's motto.
✓	Using staff commitment of high expectations, irrespective of a child's background, to enthuse efforts through an exchange of understanding, educational experiences and development.

Figure 8.6: The Spirit of the Lesson Study based on ABEM©

✓	Collaborative activities
✓	Personalised/individualised approach to learning
✓	Sharing experiences
✓	Reflect on action and consequences
✓	Learning from each other
✓	Acquire knowledge/shaping historical experiences
✓	Continuous change which has implication for pupil, home and school

The spirit of the lesson is underpinned by principles, which promote the essentials of personal development within the tenets of the motto: *I am Somebody Great!* It necessitates an understanding of the pupil's problems, interpreting and creating strategies for their solution. Notwithstanding the presenting difficulties, there must be an expectation of high levels of outcome, based on the motto above. This begins to incentivise and affect the pupil's self-esteem and confidence, as psychologically and emotionally the pupil is engaged in a process of change and reparation. **(Figure 8.7)**

Figure 8.7: The Essentials of Personal Development

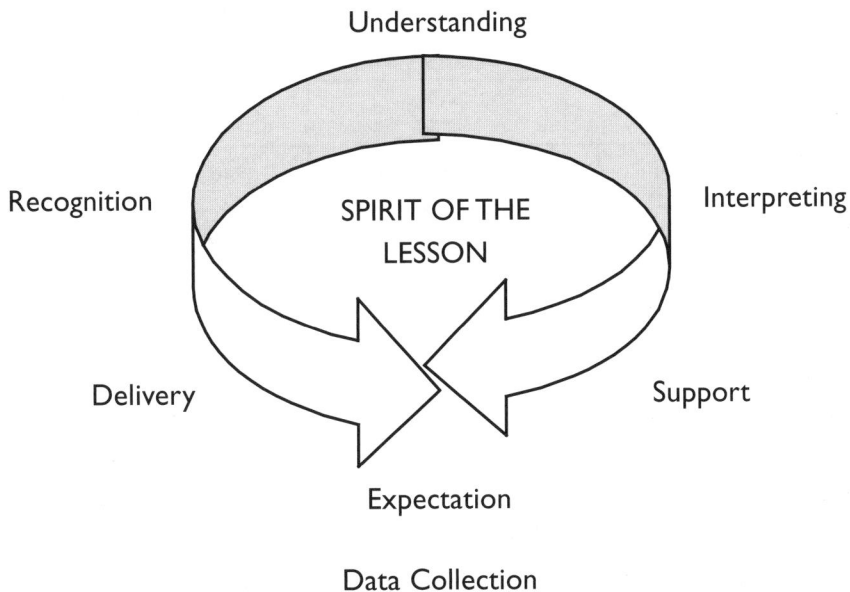

Understanding

Recognition

SPIRIT OF THE LESSON

Interpreting

Delivery

Support

Expectation

Data Collection

I employed several case studies for data collection and a qualitative approach for teaching analysis.

The school's method of using ethnography notes and participant observation enabled new and creative perspectives for research on classroom activities.

Teachers' reflective staff meetings, reflective papers, learning journal notes and school documents e.g. reports, behaviour management reports, mentoring programmes, Special Education Needs documents, parents' comments, staff and pupil self-evaluation.

A social and historical background of the pupils and their families and their structural arrangements as family units.

Teacher & Participant Observation

✓ Producing the lesson plan – *Plan* - person specific - more child centered

✓ Present Lesson – *Do, Check, Action* (individually and as a class/group)

✓ Revising curriculum as appropriate - *Plan – Do - Check – Action- Evaluate*

TEACHER AND PARTICIPANT-OBSERVATIONS VIA 5 STAGES:		
Stage 1	⇨	PLAN
Stage 2	⇨	DO
Stage 3	⇨	CHECK
Stage 4	⇨	ACTION
Stage 5	⇨	EVALUATE

Lesson Plans – Check points

✓ Paying attention to pupils' individual needs

✓ Assessing body language and physical appearance

✓ Evaluating pupils' moods and eliciting causes to minimise escalation of adverse conditions

✓ Choosing appropriate teaching strategies

✓ Examining how teachers adapt lessons to time allocated

Development

- Teachers acquire professional skills through participant observation

- Journal and ethnography filed notes

- Critical reflection on actions and collaborative work in each classroom activity.

- Lesson study is delivered based on a person-specific approach

- Data generated on student styles of learning and approaches/ attitudes to learning make database for student profile in school.

- Provides development of mutual relationships among students in classroom activities.

- Students are not forced to learn at the same pace, or within "year/ age appropriate" restrictions, where ability does not match that of their peers in the classroom.

- Creates less tension and rank pulling among peers and less need for avoidance techniques (e.g. distracting others deliberately, wanting to leave the room, making excuses or complaints or feigning sickness, need to use the toilet etc).

- Teachers and/or Assistants are able to interact between pupils on individual levels so everyone has a sense of producing and learning, thus minimizing need for unhealthy competition within the classroom.

- Promotes an atmosphere of composure and enables behaviour management.

The Antoine Behaviour Excellence Model© also necessitates a *high level of parental interaction,* as well as the high value placed on a tripartite working relationship, between parents, the school, the child and the relevant placing Education Authority). The underlying principles behind such an approach to education management are that pupils are not necessarily born with ESBD but that cultural, social and economic environmental factors contribute to character formation and behaviour patterns in ways which are both consciously and unconsciously imbued by those in their environment.

Common behaviour patterns include those which are regarded as anti-social, are widespread, but due to the complexity of factors that are involved, they are seen by their perpetrators as normative patterns of behaviour. At times such children can't understand why they are constantly being cautioned, reprimanded or sanctioned. In fact, their sense of outrage grows into developed feelings of being victimised, *their* world seen as unjust (the injustice perpetrated by adults), and eventually makes them defiant of authoritative figures.

Therefore, resulting behaviours in these circumstances are seen as inappropriate, and in everyday life, present as conflict, or in extreme cases, criminal and anti-social. For many, their behaviour manifests identity quests (as we see with gang and gun culture), since this provides an alternative sense of belonging in the face of adult/authoritative hostility. They stake out ownership of geographical areas also known as *turf or yard*. There is also dominance of certain types of dress and colours and boundaries identified as *no-go* areas. The result is the development of a sub-culture or gang warfare among interrelated groups, where crime and disorder are judged as yardsticks for inclusion. Often among these groupings are youngsters with ESBD; socially, are from *fragmented* families, deprived areas, economically are extremely poor (often pupils will have no money for lunch provision), with equally poor housing, and *absent* parents. In fact, some biological parents who do exist shirk their responsibilities, and instead frail grandparents do the "parenting". This then presents a sense of hopelessness and helplessness experienced by such families/pupils, who are at the bottom of the social class ladder and consequently may have a world view that will be vastly different from adults who want to "educate" them or lament the state of society with these uncontrollable youngsters!

Without being too dogmatic about labels and their stereotypes, these factors are characteristically to be found among those pupils labelled as having ESBD and consequently may or may not present with a Statement of Educational Needs (SEN), within an educational setting.

The *Antoine Behaviour Excellence Model* © also necessitates strong linkages and engagement with the community, in strengthening educational achievement, developing confidence among parents thereby eradicating barriers to participation in their children's learning. It provides community role models, as well as information and guidance to both pupils and parents. This model therefore demonstrates the life-long learning principle and projects an ethos of the "**education without walls**" (i.e., that education is not strictly contained within the school walls).

The Model works from a perspective of understanding legacies/experiences that may have impacted on present cultural groupings, within and without Britain, and consequently on the lives of pupils from such families. This approach creates a higher success rate of engagement with the pupils and their parents, instead of working from one conventional approach or the kind that produces high rates of exclusion, pupil underachievement and/ or teacher underperformance. It means that one has to take into consideration, societal changes and consequently changes needed in educational approaches that reflect Britain's multi-cultural environment in this 21st century. As a result the **Antoine Behaviour Excellence Model ©, generates** knowledge that would equips the educational establishment with valuable information which clarifies assessments and grading practices. In reducing unequal practices, it would provide answers to questions, for example on levels of **expectation,** (which, in some cases, may not match reality), but nevertheless, drive parental needs and wants, in an attempt to compensate for **lack** on many areas of their lives.

With such approaches in place, **the praxis on which the Model hinges** its workability, is the **absolute importance attached to Recognizing and Celebrating Achievement** with demonstrable short, medium, and long-term goals, as milestones which motivate and generate success. This particular characteristic of the **Antoine Behaviour Excellence Model ©,** is not only a vital element in educating and guiding young people on appropriate behaviour in Britain today, but provides experiences that would make future, progressive goals a reality.

Practical examples of ABEM at TCS Tutorial College

I have argued that the ethnographic approach is about self-reflection and observing everyday practices very closely within the educational environment (e.g. the school). It is from this setting that the world is viewed and the ABEM techniques for behaviour management, is creatively presented as learning, teaching and data provision (research). The above has been based on research on everyday practices but below will be seen how the TCS Tutorial College used the ABEM model via a community participatory approach, to extend learning "beyond walls" or outside of formal educational settings. The majority of pupils in this study over a 10 year period, had Emotional Behavioural Difficulties (EBD) and low attainment levels and were not rigidly observed. **(Figure 8.8)**

Figure 8.8: THE ANTOINE BEHAVIOUR EXCELLENCE MODEL

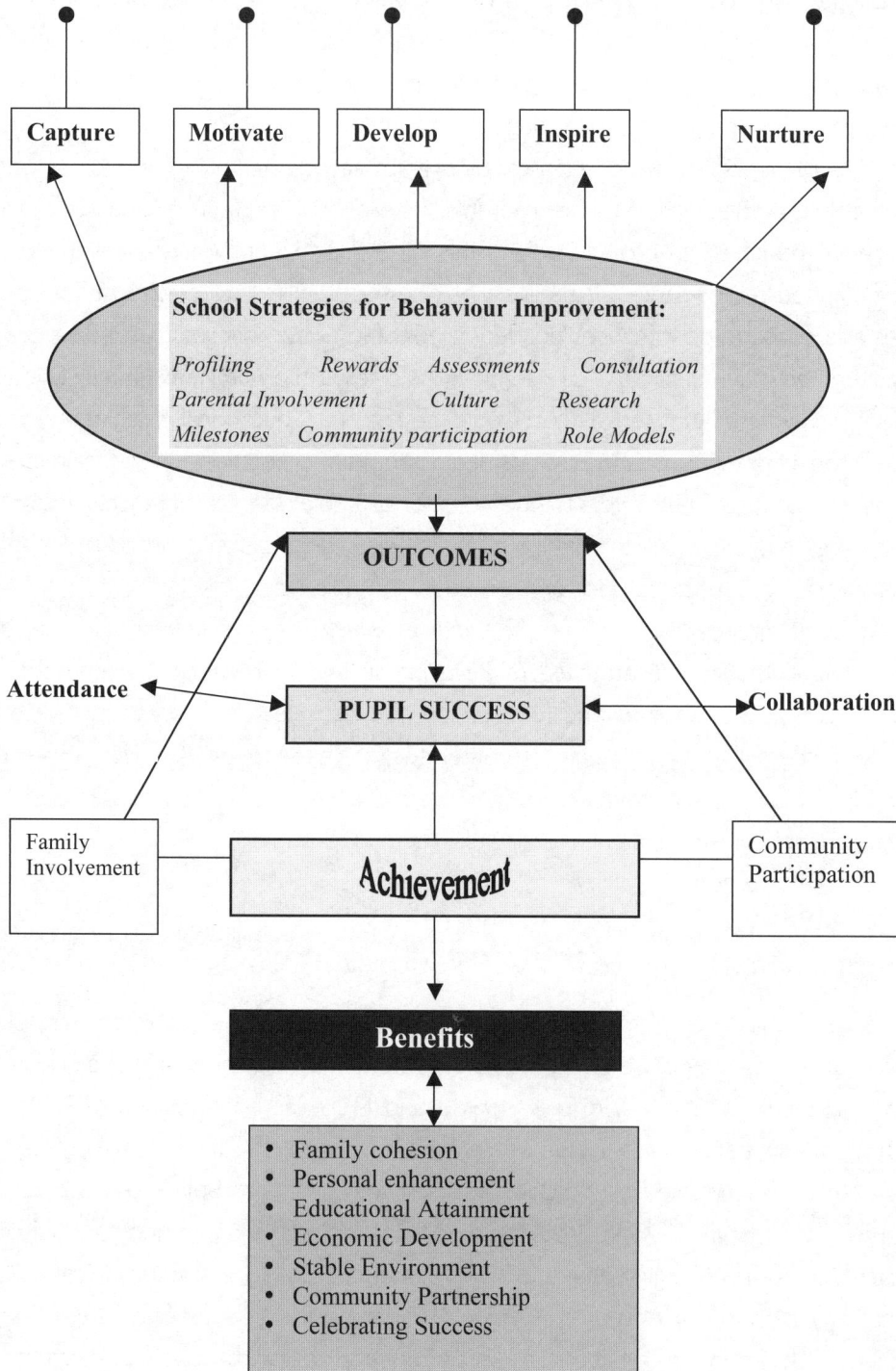

| Capture | Motivate | Develop | Inspire | Nurture |

School Strategies for Behaviour Improvement:

Profiling	*Rewards*	*Assessments*	*Consultation*
Parental Involvement		*Culture*	*Research*
Milestones	*Community participation*		*Role Models*

OUTCOMES

PUPIL SUCCESS

Attendance   Collaboration

| Family Involvement | *Achievement* | Community Participation |

Benefits

- Family cohesion
- Personal enhancement
- Educational Attainment
- Economic Development
- Stable Environment
- Community Partnership
- Celebrating Success

Therefore the data collected resulted from informal settings, learning among the local community (seen below), and within the institutional framework or the school. Working with the local community has been done to engender a sense of life-long learning and to promote the idea of learning beyond fixed boundaries or inside a classroom setting. This strategy has produced, within the School's Annual Graduation programme, actual examples of learning for life demonstrated by presentations made to recipients within the community e.g. **Annual Parents Awards** for support, service, and attendance throughout the year. Also a much coveted **Annual Community Award of Excellence,** is presented to members within the pan-London community, (the unsung heroes/heroines),for having given a minimum of 10 years of service to developing their local community, thereby promoting the ethos of "life-long" learning.

Developing Artistic and Creative abilities the ABEM way – to capitalise on the dramatic skills and talents of the pupils, TCS used Drama as an education enhancer in an approach to raising education levels of achievement. Interestingly, this strategy necessitated an approach to learning which was based on culture, because pupils who were not able to express themselves in the written format, displayed a greater understanding of, and were more expressive, using the oral form.

An example of this was demonstrated in 2002, at a time when many of the pupils in TCS Tutorial College School's After School and Saturday School were of Caribbean heritage. In order to make learning relevant to their lives, and to overcome some of the issues relating to underachievement, and low self-esteem, it was decided (based on previous experiences in West London schools),that they should develop a sense of self and confidence by performing a Caribbean Play – *Rufus and the Snake (2000).* This approach drew on teaching experiences in 1981 and 1982, in Primary schools, when I had discovered that such pupils' lack of literary development, stemmed from the fact that they were not relating their learning to themselves, and had adopted a kind of abstract association with their own backgrounds preferring to keep it out of the classroom or learning environment.

In fact, the conclusions of the 1980's were that the pupils had a sense of shame associated with cultural identification and instead adopted a stance that showed they were reluctant to identify themselves for various reasons e.g. shame, embarrassment and unsure as to whether accepting a Caribbean heritage background, instead of a "British" one, would alienate them from acceptance of the majority (British/English) which it would seem at the time was more important to acknowledge. But the many Workshop sessions among schools in West London, highlighted this cultural rejection in favour of an identification that blended with the majority or presented less questions and explanations of **Who am I?**. Twenty years later, though less marked, there were vestiges of the same cultural ambivalence but more associated with a lack of knowledge and an increased willingness to understand their backgrounds more.

So in 2002, the pupils had a 'working knowledge' of what Caribbean culture was but not much beyond identifying various foods and reggae music. As a result, they could not present a sustained Caribbean vernacular with accompanying performance that was reflective of life in the Caribbean, represented in the written text. They had a very limited knowledge of the nuances of cultural and traditional expressions and fluency of interpretive body language. Consequently, this presented a dilemma for the success of the planned performance. Notwithstanding this limitation, the pupils were adamant that they wanted to perform the play, for which the outcome was a planned public performance at an international conference, (**The Caribbean contribution to British society: 50 years of sustainable progress**), to mark The Queen's Golden Jubilee.

Strategies and Solutions

The strategies for producing a solution laid in the decision not to give pupils or character roles until they had a six- weeks' crash course in Caribbean Studies – i.e., culture and tradition, literature and history, (including their own family histories). The aim was to bring **meaning** and **life** to the text and **relevance** to their lives as 3rd generation Caribbeans, albeit British-born children in the UK. To support the initiative, the aims of the Lesson Plans were to assist the pupils' educational development, by focusing on **culture as an education enhancer and use of adults other than teachers in the classroom.**

One of the strategies employed included the use of parents who joined in the urgent "**passing on of the culture**" by taking performance roles themselves, albeit temporarily, so that both pupils and children were engaged in the sharing and learning process together. This proved an extremely worthwhile approach to learning, as it accelerated achievement of the objectives. Therefore by the end of the 6 weeks, the pupils had discovered their own strengths and weaknesses, in terms of what they could realistically do as individual performers. While a few felt the task was a great challenge than anticipated, most were now in a better position to confidently project themselves as performers, and better able to choose which parts they could perform.

This experience proved that a different kind of approach, inspired by ideas from a community/adult input in the school, enabled the narrowing of a generation gap, the documentation of both pupils and adult experiences, as well as a demonstration of how children's learning and development could be greatly enhanced when the school was able to draw on the resources of home and the local community as participants/learners in the education of children.

The success of the above experience meant that the school could now maintain the **community participatory approach** to pupils' learning. To capitalise on this idea, TCS Tutorial College School developed a **TCS Writers Guild.** Using a similar approach to dealing with the play above, it also drew on parents and adults' input. The Writers Guild existed to enhance literary development as well as to further bridge the generation gap among parents and children. However, the approach this time was aimed at developing the school's cultural mix and at the same time bringing cultures together. The success of this initiative resulted in the formation of TCS' **Harrow Black and Asian Writers Group (2002).**

The successful outcomes were measured and produced similar achievement levels to those experienced by the Caribbean play initiative. Pupils became less inhibited with parents and adults around them and were able to write poetry and prose together in workshops assisted by published writers in the community e.g. Courtier Newland and Alex Wheattle, guided the workshop sessions and this resulted in public performances showing parents and pupils together on stage (e.g. in local libraries, bookshops,), in a sharing of "live" experiences.

One of the highlights of the academic year is the **Annual Graduation and Celebration of Achievement(1994-2009),** presented within a "**togetherness**". This event as mentioned above, recognises the life-long learning principle, in an event which pupils, teachers, parents, and community members come together to celebrate the pupils' achievement for that year. In this event pupils are graduated and the ceremony, a colourful array of the school colours represented by the graduation gowns, a large audience of parents and the general community being presented by a very high profile guest, makes this a memorable and worthwhile event.

This represents the culmination of a thematic year e.g., **The Year of Personal Growth (2009),** when the school community works towards personal goals and projected successes, having achieved short-term goals on a weekly, termly and occasional basis. Goals are clearly defined and expectations are high, within a set of Consequences for performance (negative and positive). Motivated by the previous year's event and personal experience of public approval, our records have shown that the pupils' motivation levels and willingness to do well, increases by 50% each year, at the post-graduation stage. The value of recognizing and demonstrating appreciation and actually marking that success in a special way, has been proved to emotionally catapult pupils' self-esteem to great heights; generated by this personal, confidence-boosting experience. Psychologically, this works on several levels – the child experiences a moment of enhanced imagery witnessed by family members, his teacher and the whole school staff, his profile is raised among his peers and pupils in the whole school community.

USING STUDENT ROLE MODELLING or peer mentoring – TCS has created a structure of discipleship by enhancing the learning of younger pupils. To do this past students who had benefited from the teaching and learning at the school, were given opportunities to assist younger children in the Junior department, by assisting Class teachers, and at the same time, were able to give back to the school and their immediate community what they had learnt. As appropriate models, they were also recognised as employees on Saturdays and after-school on weekdays. Training enabled them to gain classroom and administrative experience. To do this benefit was gained on a number of levels e.g. by pupils being taught, teachers, the Student as mentor and the school. It sharpened the knowledge and skills of the Mentor in ways which gave them her greater insight into the process of education development as a whole. Consequently, it incentivised them to push ther own personal development further, and each of the mentors, have today, gone into Further and Higher Education with good results. They are now either employed in recognized professions.

PARENTS – *as advisors and facilitators for change* via our various *Fora.* Through the Women's Forum and the Men's Forum, initiatives conducted at TCS on behalf of *The Roselle Antoine Foundation,* (a UK registered charity). The Model was employed via a community participatory approach. The principle of **each one teach one,** ensured that men and women were able to come together to highlight problems affecting the community, in attempts to find solutions to them. Each Forum, was gender-specific, to enable frank and uninhibited discussions as they affected men or women.

READING IS FUNDAMENTAL – family reading activities (2000). This activity was the result of problems and needs highlighted in discussions within the individual forum. The initiative enabled development of literacy within whole families and promoted reading as a fundamental aspect of educational achievement and necessary tool for parents. **(Figure 8.9)**

Figure 8.9: Parents Evaluation

✓	Happy to have a culture sensitive environment
✓	It's an answer to prayer!
✓	I'm so happy - Culture will encourage good discipline
✓	This was the last school I was going to try
✓	I'm tired of trying, I was going to give up!
✓	Thanks for the help. You've given me a life.
✓	Lots of improvement since attending TCS
✓	I'm so used to being told after 20 minutes of dropping my child off to mainstream school –
✓	"Come and collect your so" -I got so used to it, but here it's different.
✓	Glad he is settling at last - improvement seen at home
✓	Only school she has stayed so long
✓	Impressed with progress being made
✓	She refused to go to school, before coming to TCS
✓	For the first time something is right in his life
✓	He likes coming to school
✓	Thank you for all the help – the boy is happy
✓	For the first time he doesn't have to be woken up for school
✓	He does it himself. I'm thinking of taking up studies or getting a job now
✓	The first school where you can have one to one regularly.

ENTERPRISE CULTURE – This initiative was created to give first hand experience to young boys who needed support in making decisions and choices for future careers. Working in partnership with businesses in the community, TCS was able to place young boys with business owners who took them under their wing and taught them a trade, out of school hours. This enabled a development of confidence and at the same time gave the boys the benefit of the authority of male companionship, leadership, discipleship, and role modelling. The disciplined approach required for the world of work and the incentives associated with this was an education enhancer. Consequently the pupils were able to use this form of development as a catalyst to further develop themselves (e.g. self employment choices), or to go into Further Education. These kinds of initiatives drew pupils and their families attention to the existence and contribution that local Caribbean businesses were making to the local economy and interest generation was reciprocal. The businesses themselves, many of whom have existed over a period of 30 years, showed an interest in and support for local Caribbean pupils, struggling to gain an entry into the job market or to gain the kinds of work experience that would reduce the barrier to their participation in the job market.

LOCAL EMPLOYER PARTNERSHIP – TCS was also able to work in partnership with the Brent Employer Partnership **(2004-2006),** who accepted young people on day release placements for longer periods of time than the formal Work Experience requirement for School Leavers. One such placement was extremely successful as he demonstrated excellence that resulted in an opportunity to meet HRH Prince Charles as a reward and a demonstration of the success of local work-based learning and education working in partnership to develop student's Life Skills. Such skills enhancement approaches have enabled students who would have completed their learning with compulsory school leaving age, to progress on to vocational and Further Education levels.

CELEBRATING MILESTONES – Caribbean contribution to British society (2002): During the last 14 years of research into the development of Caribbean culture, it was noticeable that the lack of cultural understanding and appreciation accounted for the low sense of self identity, and cultural heritage. Responding to this need the "I" of the motto was interrogated to re-emphasise the person making the statement, "*I am somebody Great!*" It also necessitated why there was a need to affirm greatness and questioned who had or provide role modelling to that effect. Providing answers to young people meant that they needed to acquaint themselves with the pioneers of progress, or Caribbean historical personages who would assist them in contextualising their own need to progress as part of their personal goals.

Due to the lack of available books and resource materials for this reality to be actualised, TCS School created a series of writings, entitled *Caribbean Greats.* These presented biographic profiles of Caribbean leaders in an attempt to pass on knowledge, enlighten and empower pupils to have a sense of belonging and to imbue a sense of *Greatness* as it related to their immediate heritage.   One such biography was T.A. Marryshow CBE , (*the Father of West Indian Federation*), from Grenada.

The express aim of the 2002 **Marryshow D**ay, was for London to observe its first-ever Marryshow day on the 115th anniversary of T.A. Marryshow's birth (Thursday November, 7th 2002). Underpinning this is the strategic aim of stemming the flow of underachievement among African-Caribbean children in Britain, seen as a direct incentive of the event. It was thought that by sharing knowledge of how greatness can and has been achieved, TCS Tutorial College, with their motto, "*I am Somebody Great*" was challenging the black community to be more aware of their history and identity and to foster a sense of pride and the building of self-esteem in themselves to inspire personal success, by emulating successful role models.

The A5 sized texts which accompanied their cultural learning provided evidence of facts they would not have come into contact with, since these were not in the public domain in libraries and bookshops in the UK. In other words, because the objective conditions were not available, these had to be created, in other to achieve the holistic aims of self development. It became clear that students who had been given the opportunity to participate in cultural learning, had developed a strong sense of self and purpose, with also a strength of character that have taken them beyond university levels. This has demonstrated the efficacy of the "*I am Somebody Great!*" ethos, applied in a holistic approach to self-development and purpose. One such milestone was the celebration of the first event in the UK, celebrating TA Marryshow, in an event known as *Marryshow Day.* **(Figure 8.10).**

As was attempted with creating the Caribbean literature for teaching and learning , Marryshow Day (a event which honoured the life of the Grenadian, T A Marryshow CBE), and a **Memorial Lecture,** celebrating the life of Trinidad & Tobago's Dr. Eric Williams**,** was aimed at instituting measures to educate via events. This brought alive the vast array of Caribbean pioneers, who contributed to an end to the Caribbean region's colonization by Britain, and the Movement to Federation or self-determination.

The converse of this approach is to allow the perpetual imitation of North American superstars, musical icons and habits that create behaviours that are associated with American Rap Artists, e.g. Fifty Cents and his sentiments of "get rich quick or die trying". The prevailing situation is that a Caribbean child is more likely to expound knowledge on American culture than on the Caribbean. Granted there is more exposure, technologically, to the glamour, glitz, and **bling-bling** world of American popular culture, and because of the ease of cross-cultural and cross-pollination of ideas and behaviour which globalisation has created, there is among the Black British youth, a kind of cultural imperialism, and little or no interest in the Caribbean, among young Caribbean heritage children, in preference for lifestyles associated with American street and gang culture.

Figure 8.10: Significance of `Marryshow Day'

As we celebrate Sir Theophilus Albert Marryshow's 114 birth anniversary and 43 years of his passing, we can take solace in the fact that he has a worthy successor to ensure that his incomparable achievements are not subsumed by complacency, pettiness, insularity and ignorance

Indeed, Dr. Antoine has seized the baton of leadership – she has shown us the way. This evening's memorial lecture therefore is more than just a symbolic gesture to the memory of T.A. Marryshow. It is instead, a representation of a series of constructive engagements with our people and the wider British society. It is a counter prevailing mechanism to relocate our history and culture in correct perspective. It is our small, but significant contribution to participative democracy in a land where one wonder's whether this principle is purely a real value or a smothering deficit.

Dr. Antoine's contribution to the architects of Caribbean Integration is therefore worthy of much pride and admiration in the context of the modern society (Dr. C.A. Johnson, November 2002).

Figure 8.11: Strategic Partnerships formed and Liaison with Schools

- Mail-outs to schools across the Primary and Secondary sectors, including Saturday Schools, Mother Tongue & Cultural Schools, as well as community organisations in Britain and Grenada in the Caribbean.

- Meetings and Consultations with Community groups and individuals in the UK.

- Special Reports and Feedback on progress in both UK and the Caribbean.

- Making a direct "*family*" link with Sir TA Marryshow.

- Inviting Brian Marryshow (grandson of Senator T A Marryshow CBE), in Grenada, to help concretize the information being presented and making the "live", heritage link, a real experience for students, families and the local community in Britain.

- Plan to unveil a memorial plaque in Britain at TCS Tutorial College to mark the historic event.

Some projects which were developed to assist in the development of Caribbean culture in Britain were based on knowledge sharing. An example was the Cultural Support Services (CSS) project which provided an advisory and information service for Caribbean artists/cultural producers in West London. It also offered technical support, training for unemployed and disadvantaged Caribbean communities involved in the cultural sector. **(Figure 8.11 above)**

CARIBBEAN STUDIES – Short Courses (2000): To widen the participation of Caribbean cultural development via the, *I am Somebody Great!* principle and raising awareness among the general community, TCS Tutorial College was able to offer Academic reinforcement and structured learning in the form of studies on the Caribbean region.

The courses were aimed at:

- Students who wish to learn about the Caribbean.

- Those who would like to go on to University courses which offered Caribbean studies as part of the combined Humanities Scheme.

- Those who want to widen their general knowledge of the Caribbean Region

This course introduced students to a series of studies on the Caribbean Region – its background, its peoples, where its located, why Caribbeans are in Britain and around the globe, and areas which are said to characterise the Caribbean and its people. The Course offered the following:

- Introduction to the Course

- Where is the Caribbean

- What do we mean by the Caribbean?

- History of the Caribbean Peoples

- The Caribbean Landscapes – Past & Present

- Living in the Caribbean – Environment as Resource, Hazards, Landscaper Changes

- Migration to and from the Caribbean

- Colonisation/Experiences of Revolts in the region and lessons learnt from them

- Literature and Popular Culture

- *'Welcome to Britain'* - Experiences of Caribbeans in Britain

In addition, to highlight the primacy of Caribbean cultural development, and as a counter-balance to British Caribbean youths cultural vacuum, TCS Tutorial College founded a voluntary organization entitled Caribbean Cultural Heritage Initiative. **(Figure 8.12)** Its objectives were to:

Black History Month – *'Essence of the Caribbean'*

Figure 8.12: Caribbean Cultural Heritage Initiative

To provide facilities for the development of Caribbean cultural education and the dissemination of information, good practice, and support to parents, teachers, children, and the wider community.

To promote forms of education that enable young people to engage positively with the growing complexity and diversity of social values and ways of life.

To raise self-esteem and confidence among Caribbean communities, and encourage a sense of responsibility for learning, goal-setting and good citizenship.

To develop an historical perspective by relating contemporary values to the processes of events that has shaped them.

To enable young people to understand culture's evolutionary nature and the potential for change.

To promote an understanding of cultural diversity by bringing young people into contact with the attitudes, values and traditions of other cultures, whilst exploring and understanding their own cultural assumptions and values.

To promote social care and support for the elderly in order to enhance their lifestyle and improve their welfare.

To encourage the elderly to be actively involved in community activities, using recreative therapy as a means of skills enhancement.

To promote health education via a range of activities and events for general well being.

To foster a sense of cultural cohesion and harmony among the youth and elderly in bridging the generation gap and promoting good citizenship.

Source: Constitution of TCS' Caribbean Cultural Heritage Initiative

Using the theme *"Essence of the Caribbean"* as a cultural bridge-builder, (2002 -2009), TCS was able to reflect a holistic nature of Caribbean heritage in the UK, in the form of a showcase of *Storytelling,* (demonstrating their impact on the curriculum, language, thought and survival of Caribbean peoples in Britain), *traditional and modern dance* forms (Quadrille, African, contemporary), *Music* (creative percussions and instrumentation),

Positive Role Models (via Careers and the professions of Caribbean personnel), *Caribbean businesses* (an introduction to their organization and performance), *Education - Youth Speak*, (participation of young people in community development, decision making, advice and future pathways), *Health* – Advice and presentation on health issues affecting the Caribbean community (sickle cell, Diabetes, High blood pressure), *Drama, Poetry*,(reflecting an intergenerational mix of the older members of the community with the youths), *Caribbean Food and Drinks* and a *Schools Pack for Primary and Secondary schools,* documenting aspects of the above.

In terms of need, this event was aimed at helping the Black community to develop citizenship through self-esteem, pride and the need to take part meaningfully in various processes of development and change in a multicultural Britain. The event represented one of TCS Tutorial College's methodologies aimed at solving problems of underachievement, especially among compulsory school-aged children.

Local and National Linkages

Having understood the urgency of the need to build the knowledge-base of the local community, TCS projected its services to the community, in order to meet the requirements of local and regional priorities. Some of these are:

LOCAL COMMUNITY FUND - improving the capacity and enhancing the community/ voluntary infrastructure of Black and Minority Ethnic residents in London.

DEPARTMENT OF MEDIA, CULTURE AND SPORT – developing cultural networks to encourage the building, production and distribution of facilities for creative communities in London's deprived areas.

UK DEVELOPMENT PLAN – enabling the disadvantage, the excluded and the unemployed to benefit from opportunities offered by cultural enterprises in the community.

NATIONAL STRATEGY FOR NEIGHBOURHOOD RENEWAL – providing community-based facilities which allow people to access new technology and support, whilst engaging more with Black and Minority Ethnic social enterprises, particularly cultural groups.

A Voice of Their Own – Antoine Behaviour Excellence Model's National imperative

There is recognition, as stated in Chapter 7, that the macro-environment of the pupil has much to do with his overall perspectives on life and the impact of this on his behavior in general. While there is an unprecedented focus on youth, crime and deaths among young people in Britain today, I believe there must also be equitable, if not more, attention paid to the process of change in the macro-environment. The *Antoine Behaviour Excellence Model* was researched using *individualized plans* for behavior improvement. However, using the empowerment approach for change to effect *group behavior change*, this author, via *The Roselle Antoine Foundation* charity, called on British society (2008), to engage young people in order to understand their vision for Britain's future, in a society where they will be the drivers for peace, democracy and tolerance.

Engagement was organized at the Queen Elizabeth II Conference Centre in London, when youth teams within various cities in Britain came together, to deliver a developmental vision for Britain *(October 2008)*. The aim was to support a constructive engagement, with the adult population, for greater understanding among the generations, sensitive to negative impacts of conflicts, and embrace initiatives to combat crime, violence and negative stereotyping.

Major objectives were to ensure that young people are actively involved in the process of change; articulate their views on upgrading, revitalising and improving youth services for them. The strategy showed how a creative and integrated approach to young people's participation, in designing and delivering plans for their future can bring about early intervention, real social, emotional, educational change, and improve their life chances.

The belief, based on the *Antoine Behaviour Excellence Model,* is that through a collaborative approach to development, there is mutual benefit, for the adult population, from the globalised minds of our 21st century youths, and vice versa. This strategic approach of macro (*society*) environmental changes impacting on micro (*individual*) environment is the key to overall change in young people's behavior in Britain. Findings showed that while young people were active and willing participants, the adult population (including the media, major inter-agency services and children are yet to show a national interest in the work of young people when it comes to constructive and positive pursuits

The Role of the Teacher

Engaging the *Antoine Behaviour Excellence Model (ABEM)* of effective behaviour management, is to be aware of the factors which lead to the child's adverse behaviour, (that means being aware of all the professional managers which have contributed to reports which make up the Statement of Educational Needs).

It is important that a teacher does not see the pupils with Special Education Needs as "bad, rude, disrespectful, mad, etc" The moment one retorts *"I didn't come here to be verbally abused and sworn at"* in the EBSD setting, it's at that very moment he/she should make speedy decisions to quit! This attitude shows that person to be in the wrong environment. It means that they have misunderstood the potential behaviours in environments where pupils with EBD are taught. Worse still, is the likelihood that they will mis-manage pupils by their level of criticism. In fact they are likely to be a potential underperformer as a teacher, rather than someone who can apply the level of support needed to impact on their behaviour positively. In fact, the critical retort above already signals that such an approach will be one which potentially promotes conflict rather than control

A most important element in the *Antoine Behaviour Excellence Model©* is knowledge and understanding of the cultural background of the child, for which a culturally sensitive approach forms the basis of supportive and corrective behaviour control/modification.

The key to this Model is knowledge of the family background. In other words, who in the family, is the one whose action on corrective behaviour is (especially from the child's point of view), seen as strong and unwavering, just, consistently and persistently applied, is responded to by the child and those around them for the majority of the times, and whom the child may want to please, not wish to learn of their adverse reports, who might reprimand at home, and apply sanctions which are adhered to.

A key element in *Antoine Behaviour Excellence Model©* is the constant and workable link with the child's home. When this is clearly understood, and the necessary parties meet to confirm the triangular relationship (home, school, pupil teamwork) then these factors will go some way to providing a supportive structure which enables the pupil to manage their own behaviour and consequently promote control of themselves. With this strategy, it is the pupil who learns to control himself and not the teacher taking control for him

It is important not to be dictatorial or lose one's control, as it demonstrates that you are opting for the "loudest and most challenging voice wins" attitude. An important point to make here is that a teacher of the same cultural background does not necessarily mean that such a teacher will readily be able to manage that child's behaviour. As with all cultures, individuals adopt various perspectives based on their personal experience, life principles, an understanding of what their culture is, their own sense of cultural values, experience in teaching, knowledge of their profession and most of all, their sincerity in wanting a child, through their supportive approach to take control and manage their own behaviour effectively.

The Antoine Behaviour Excellence Model © advocates the absolute necessity of making that child realise that throughout his behaviour, he is making choices via his actions. However, this is not easy to implement. There must be acceptance, via an understanding of what the options are e.g. John this is your first warning, *I am asking you to put that chair down. Dont lean over Jordan to hit David, otherwise you'll have to accept the consequences. It's your choice, you decide''* Adopt a monotone, your voice should be calm, your attitude positive, and one which inspires your trust in him to make the right decision. If he doesn't do as you ask, then don't hold up the entire class, so that he has an audience to perform to, (often that's what he wants), while you appeal to his better judgement.

Figure 8.13: *Teachers Comments*

- See students move from fully hooded to no hoods!
- Pupil managing their own behaviour
- Peer counselling
- Bonding and caring
- Give us a hug syndrome without rewards
- Respond to reasoned guidance
- Willingness to talk about their spirituality without being ashamed
- Morals change
- Students can be trusted and are given opportunities to demonstrate this
- Students take in the happening of each others environment
- Taking control of their learning
- Pupils becoming more confident
- Adhering to instructions and advice
- Accepting Mentoring
- Taking pride in their appearance
- Managing mobile phones
- Apologies are frequent and well meant
- Boys offering to assist teachers

Go around to the other pupils, be sure to remark on those who are working well, giving praise where this is due and later work your way to where John is and again, without drawing the whole class' attention to him, repeat calmly what you asked him to do; only this time, remind him that it's his **second** warning and that you are still giving him another chance to choose to make the right decision. When he complies, give him praise by first thanking him and then reinforcing that he took control of his behaviour by making a positive choice. Use the Reward System which you have in place, (i.e. your Points System) so, that this is demonstrated practically, but also serves as a positive reminder for the other children in the class.

It also encourages John to continue to make positive choices when it is his decision to do so and reinforces your classroom Behaviour Management Strategy, as far as Rewards and Sanctions are concerned. It is important to recognise that children with this type of diagnosis, have additional diagnoses such as ADHD, and other autistic spectrum disorders e.g. Asperger's Syndrome.

Teachers feeling that their job is to teach, not manage the difficulty, may feel frustrated by the disrespectful, loud, physically challenging, loud, disruptive 15 year old pupil. The job of teaching that child is reliant on understanding the underlying problems in order to minimize the impact that the difficulties may cause, not only to the teacher but also others in the environment. Challenging behaviour must be tackled from the point of developing skills to manage it without taking the verbal insult, disrespect, or hostility personally. Time and patience must be devoted to understanding the underlying issues which impact on the child's behaviour problems. This will minimise conflict, encourage progress over a long term, and changes in attitudes (both teacher and pupils), rather than flaring up at the immediate problem and meting out punishment.

Figure 8.14: Visitors Comments

How do you get them to wear uniform?
How do you manage to keep graffiti off the walls?
I don't know how you do it..
I can feel the sincerity here.
If only I had known TCS before..

I am so surprised to see how much work is done in a short time!
It's been a pleasure to talk to the students.
I see your wall displays are not enclosed in glass but they remain undamaged
How can I help you with the work you're doing?
Do you take volunteers?
Thank you for helping the community with the children.
We're all praying for you, keep up the good work!

Conclusion

In considering the findings from the *Antoine Behaviour Excellence Model ©*, and the research around the importance attached to cultural and social values in managing behaviour, it is possible to conclude that its workability relies on aspects of the physical, economic, social and legal environments that act to either constrain or facilitate its outcome. In recommending its application to behaviour management for pupils presenting with emotional and social behavioural difficulties, we must be mindful of the following:

- Provide information and simple guidelines of how ABEM will bring about changes in behaviour.

- Encourage belief in the outcome, that they will have control over their adverse behaviour.

- Emphasize the positive effects of the model and equally.

- Emphasize the negative effects of not changing the present behaviour.

- Describe how ABEM will be employed in their overall plan of development/change and the perceived personal consequences.

- Be committed to the expectation of change in behaviour, when the pupil is shown how to take control of his/her behaviour, rather than control it for him/her.

Additionally, consideration must be given to a variety of measurements that evaluate progress and achievement. While quantitative data.producing hard evidence of attainment is predominant in measuring pupils progress, my advice is that should be an equal appreciation for what I call *Soft Outcomes*. These are less popular but from my experience, they form the basis on which *internal* success is achieved. Therefore, once a feeling of well-being is in place, it becomes a prelude to the more popular, and *external* or hard data, i.e., results based on exam certification. The *Antoine Behaviour Excellence Model* advocates measuring achievement and progress using the following model which has used at TCS Tutorial College for the past 15 years. **(Table 8.1)**

Table 8.1: TCS Behaviour Achievement – Tools For Measuring Soft Outcome

MEASUREMENT TOOLS	REMARKS
Behaviour On Entry – 5% 1st half term – 20% 2nd half term – 25% (learning to manage behaviour – *motto & Mentoring*) End of year – 40% (with ongoing monitoring & incentives)	At this stage pupils are repeatedly rejected, lacking self esteem and confidence. Many would have been at home for long periods of time Many would have been turned down post- interview
Wearing Uniform 100% among Year 7 – 9 pupils 90% - 98% among Year 10 90% - 95% among Year 11 pupils , with persistent reasons for incorrect uniform	Those who have come from Pupil Referral Units would be out of the discipline of wearing uniform Uniform represents a code of conduct which some might have been happy to discard in their previous *Unit, Centre, or Project*. Incorrect wearing of uniforms could be affected by family poverty, (having 1 alternative backup), e.g reasons range from broken washing machines, only set is dirty, torn, parents cant afford items, so periods of time with full uniform finds the child in trouble, but beyond his control. Affordability is a main issue.

Wearing Hoodies Lower Secondary 0% Upper School 100%	Need to wear hoodies, helps to hide their low self esteem – treated as a mask. Therefore can assume any type of behaviour. Operates as a uniform, since it helps pupil to identify with the majority of those wearing hoodies. Applies mainly to 15 & 16 year olds. Have adopted a habit of non-compliance and instead replace it with dominant and aggressive behaviour
Haircut Lower School 100% Upper School 10%	A drop in standards, personal hygiene accompanies the extremely low self-esteem. Non-compliant hair-cut standards used as a sign of defiance. A change is this area signifies a stronger sense of self, pride and invitation for the receipt of praise.
Facial Expressions - daily On Entry to School 90% unhappy After 4 weeks 60% End of Term 85% End of Year 100% happy	Noticeable on first entering the school in the mornings. That facial *picture tells a story*, you use it to find out the *thousand words* behind it! Common causes e.g. conflicts at home before coming to school sibling rivalry, parental reprimands and pupil resentment, anger leading to the need for an outlet. Suggestion: immediate mentoring or a confidential discussion to off-load – a common source of barriers to engaging in the class work.

Bonding (first starting school at TCS) On Entry 40% 1st Half term 50%* 2nd Half term 80% End of Year 100%	Resentment, fear, unknown territory, gauging reaction of other pupils, the need to test the waters first before opening up Remaining aloof before the Post Codes and areas of others are known, Testing attitudes and general quality of acceptance from pupils on school site.
Etiquette On Entry 10% 1st Half term 40% 2nd half term 60% End of year 80%	Acceptable Social manners are lacking Pupils behaviour generally one of staking out the territory and gauging where they can adopt an air of dominance or a "reputation" that has street credibility. E.g. arrogance, extreme rudeness, showing off, clowning, bullying, confrontation – aimed at both teacher and pupil.
Attitude towards Authority teachers, **rules, barriers, school ethos)** On Entry – Disaffected 1st half term – Engaged 2nd half term – Quite Engaged End of year – fully engaged	Pupils continue with their disaffected stance until they are sure they can be themselves. Most adverse behaviours are for the benefit of their peers Creating a "school rep" is demonstrated by firstly breaking rules and gauging reaction from others. Appearing not to care, and expecting reactions they have been used to from former placements.

School Attendance On entry 100% 1st term – 95% (including authorised absence) 2nd term – 80% End of Year – 90% (affecte4d by Year 11 who are go on Study and Exam Leave)	High percentages may form a condition of continued placement, so therefore is high to begin with. E.g. if on a Youth Offending Order, experienced repeated rejection and have experienced long periods with a placement, at home with little interaction with others. The need to prove to others that he can recover former reputation, can be accepted and a need for "normality" in their lives Complacency steps in in 2nd term but with incentive and other measures in place for rewards, serve as constant reminders to adhere to Attendance within the School's Code of Conduct
Punctuality On Entry – 100% 1st half year – 85% (public transport pupils) End of Year – 90%	The pupils who are brought to school by Local Authority arranged transport are helped with punctuality. Those who use public transport are constantly making excuse of late buses and trains.
Work & Progress On Entry – 60% (on Assessments) Termly – 90% (incl. *Weekly* recognition and Awards) *Annual* Graduation 100% (bronze, silver & gold)	Based on pupils' ability levels on entry at TCS, and the Individual Education Plan (IEP), students are given incentives to encourage persistence and steady personal development

Working together as a group On Entry – 5% 1st half term – 20% 2nd half term – 40% End of year – 80%	Due to previous happenings which might have led up to rejection, exclusion and lack of placements, pupils may prefer to walk around to understand the culture of the place before becoming familiar enough to invite closeness. For the 1st half term, distance is maintained and interaction is on a need to do basis. For Years 7, 8 & 9 the opposite is the case. There is more readiness to form friendship and laughter, jokes, playful teasing competing and obvious happiness are good measurements and outward signs of both *internal* and *external* changes..
Peer Counselling On Entry – 0% 1st half year – 2% (boys) 60% (girls) End of year –	This takes place when there is a build-up of trust and respect from teachers and pupils, confidence, a sense of achievement and a need to test/display that achievement. It demonstrates the pupil's independence and own satisfaction, and self-lessness. Therefore he/she is willing to share, pass it on. It is also a sign of maturity and confidence in the School to disseminate and support its rules. .
Respect demanded Self - 100% Given to others- 50% School – 100%	To "DIS" a pupil, is a cardinal sin, according to "street credibility". Therefore respect is demanded. Interpretation can sometimes be trivial and is a source of arguments and conflicts. What is often demanded is sometimes rarely given in return.

The *Antoine Behaviour Excellence Model*, as exemplified in this chapter, is applicable to both British Caribbean pupils and others who are involved in educational processes in Britain and other parts of the world. There is a recognition also that this approach to dealing with behaviour management, educational underachievement as well as underperformance, is a necessary fillip to educational attainment and eventual career prospects, if applied in the manner as recommended throughout this book.

Finally, while this model may appear to be prescriptive in character, it reflects a modern approach that is required to deal with not only symptoms related to adverse behaviour and educational underachievement but also impacts on the overall performance/underperformance of employees in the labour market. Consequently, if this tried and tested approach to behaviour management is maximized, it can enable pupils with behavioural and emotional difficulties, to realise their true potential, thereby taking control of their lives in order to participate and contribute to the wider society.

SELECTED CHAPTER REFERENCES _

Atkinson P. (1990): *The Ethnographic Imagination: textual constructions of reality, London*, Routledge

Clifford J. & Marcus G.E. (1986) *Writing Culture: the poetics and politics of ethnography,* Berkeley University of California Press.

Emery R. E., (1982): 'Interparental conflict and the children of discord and divorce': *Psychological Bullitin*, 92(2), 310-330

Goetz J. & LeCompte M. (1984): *Ethnography and Qualitative Design in Educational Research,* London Academic Press

Grych J. H. & Fincham F. D. (1990): Marital conflict and children's adjustment: A cognitive-contextual framework. *Psychological Bulletin* 108 (2), 267-290)

Hammersley M. & Atkinson P. (1998): Ethnography and Participant Observation, in N. Dezin Y. Lincoln (Eds) *Strategies of Qualitative Enquiry*, London Sage

Hart B., & Risley T. R. (1995): *Meaningful Differences in the Everyday Experience of Young American Children*. Baltimore: Paul H. Brookes Publishing Co.

Patterson G. R (1982) *Coercive Family Process*, Eugene, OR:Castalia Press

Patterson G. R Reid, J.B. & Dashion T.J. (1992): *Antisocial Boys*. Eugene OR: Castalia Press

Risley T. R., Clark, H.B., & Cataldo, M.F. (1976): Behavioural technology for the normal middle class family. In E.J. Mash, L.A. Hammerlynck, & L.C. Handy, (Eds), *Behaviour Modification and Families* (pp.34-60), New York: Brunner/Mazel.

Rutter M. (1985): Family and school influences on behavioural development. *Journal of Child Psychology and Psychiatry*: 26. 349-368.

Saunders M. R. (1992): Enhancing the impact of behavioural family intervention with children: Emerging perspectives. *Behaviour Change*, 9(3), 115-119,

Saunder M.R. (1996): New directions in behavioural family intervention with children. In T.H. Ollendick, R.J. Prinz, (Eds), *Advances in Clinical Child Psychology, Vol. 18* (pp.283-330): New York: Plenum Press..

Saunders M. R., Markie-Dadds C. (1997): Managing common child behaviour problems. In M.R. Sanders, C. Mitchell & G.J.A Byme (Eds). *Medical Consultation Skills: Behavioural and Interpersonal Dimensions of Health Care* (pp. 356-402): Melbourne, Australia, Addison-Wesley-Longman.

9 | Developing Your Own Adverse Behaviour Reduction Programme

Introduction

This chapter presents programmes for evaluating and reducing adverse behaviours which are underpinned by the goals set by the *Antoine Behaviour Excellence Model, (ABEM)*. The programmes are aimed at reducing adverse behaviour rates, by identifying the causes of behavioural problems and implementing effective intervention to deal with them. The design of the exemplar programmes addresses risk factors that help with improving school attendance, academic outcomes, students' social and emotional lives, students and their families' access to services in the community and a reduction of juvenile delinquency and youth offending and re-offending

An Exemplary Model

The goal of the *Antoine Behaviour Excellence Model, (ABEM),* is to reduce the adverse behavioural rate by identifying the causes of behavioural problems and implementing effective intervention in order to give all children the educational opportunities they deserve. Research indicates that exclusion rates stemming from behavioural difficulties often lead to a life of delinquency and crime. To this end, the *Antoine Behaviour Excellence Model* employed at TCS Tutorial College, is taken very seriously and has been rigorously employed in the management of adverse behaviour.

Addressing underlying risk factors for behavioural problems The Model can help:

- Improve school attendance for targeted students,

- Improve academic outcomes for students,

- Improve students social and emotional lives,

- Increase student and family access to services in the community, and

- Decrease juvenile delinquency and youth re-offending.

TCS Tutorial College serves a cross section of London students and adverse behaviour intervention is delivered as a school based programme. We have a multicultural school population, and our focus is on children and families who are faced with issues of Emotional and Behavioural Difficulties (EBD) or Emotional and Social Behavioural Difficulties (ESBD), have Attention Deficit Hyperactivity Syndrome (ADHD), Attention Deficit Disorder (ADD), low literacy levels or learning difficulties; are in the majority. The minority are made up of pupils who are at risk of permanent exclusion from their mainstream school or have been permanently excluded; have become disengagement in education; on the cusp of becoming engaged in crime or are already involved in the criminal justice system or those who have become disaffected and are not engaged in education.

There are many factors to be taken into consideration which parents, teachers and professionals must be aware of when decisions are being made for his/her education management. Firstly, the Special Educational Needs Statement will outline the kind of education provision that the individual is to receive based on the assessment of needs. There is well-documented information on specific learning disabilities, which result in the issuing of a Special Education Needs (SEN) statement that documents the pupil's legal right to special education provision.

Many Caribbean parents view the Statementing process with apprehension, and fear that it attaches a stigma to their children (see **Conclusion**). Such misapprehension which has its basis in a lack of understanding, mistrust, past experience of being labeled and its consequences, cause parents to refuse the help that a child could have in meeting his/her special education need, which therefore could alleviate associated problems later on. Generally, a lack of information and knowledge among parents on the various special needs categories and their presenting symptoms, cause communication problems. This can often result in conflicts arising from the managing challenging behaviours in the classroom among child, school and parents.

What follows is a very brief and general outline of various SEN categories presented in children and checklists for dealing with them.   It is not designed to be definitive and parents should consult with their General Practitioners (GPs), School Special Needs Co ordinator (SENCo), and other professionals involved in the child's welfare, for specific problems relating to their child/ren.

Some Caribbean parents need reassurance that management of the problems is paramount, compared with the pride and shame felt in firstly, acknowledging the problem and secondly, doing something about it. From my experience, the majority of parents who are faced with these problems prefer to ignore diagnoses, state there is no history of it in their family, hope the child will 'grow out of it' and are adamant that accepting medication (as an intervention), is completely out of the question!

ADD/ADHD

Attention-Deficit/Hyperactivity Disorder (ADHD or ADD), is characterized by a majority of the following symptoms. These symptoms are often lumped into two main categories – those being *INATTENTION* and *HYPERACTIVITY.* These symptoms need to manifest themselves in a manner and degree, which is inconsistent with the child's current developmental level. That is, the child's behaviour is significantly more inattentive or hyperactive than that of his or her peers.

INATTENTION

- Has trouble maintaining level of attention when carrying out tasks or play

- Fails to complete schoolwork, chores or jobs (not resulting from failure to understand)

- Fails to pay close attention to detail or makes careless errors in schoolwork or other activities

- Appears not to be listening when given instructions

- Has trouble organizing activities and tasks

- Is forgetful

- Easily distracted by extraneous stimuli

- Dislikes or avoids tasks that involve sustained mental effort, namely homework/schoolwork

HYPERACTIVITY/ IMPULSIVITY

- Appears constantly 'on the go'

- Leaves seat at inappropriate times

- Fidgets or squirms when seated

- Inappropriately runs or climbs (although in adolescents and adults this may only be a subjective feeling of restlessness)

- Has trouble playing quietyly or engaging in leisure activities

- Talks excessively

IMPULSIVITY

- Answers questions before they have been completely asked

- Interrupts or intrudes on others

- Has trouble taking turns

- Acts without much thought beforehand

- Symptoms must be presenting in at least 2 types of situations, such as school, work or home

- The symptoms are not better explained by a mood, anxiety, dissociative or personality disorder

- Symptoms do not occur solely during pervasive development episode or any psychotic disorder including schizophrenia

- Begins before the age of 7

ASSOCIATED FEATURES

- Learning problems

- hyperactivity

The Cause of ADD/ADHD

ADD/ADHD is not caused by poor parenting and/or family problems, as is often thought to be the case. An early theory was that attention disorders were caused by minor head injuries or by damage to the brain. Therefore for many years ADD/ADHD was referred to as 'minimal brain damage' or 'minimal brain dysfunction'. The vast majority of people with ADD/ADHD have no history of either head injury or brain damage. ADHD is more likely to be caused by biological factors which influence neurotransmitter activity in certain parts of the brain and which have a strong genetic basis. Studies have shown a link between a person's ability to pay continued attention and the level of activity in the brain. Specifically, researchers measured the level of glucose used by areas of the brain that inhibit impulses and control attention. In people with ADD/ADHD, the brain areas that control attention used less glucose, indicating that they were less active. It appears from this research that a lower level of activity in some parts of the brain may cause inattention and other ADD/ADHD symptoms.

- Treatments have been known to include:
- Psychotrophic medications (light therapies)
- Psychosocial treatments (talking therapies)
- Dietary management
- Herbal and homeopathic remedies
- Biofeedback
- Meditation

The general advice for parents is, always consult with your GP or medical adviser. Of these treatment strategies, Stimulant Medications and Psychosocial interventions have been the major foci of research.

Psychosocial treatments

Psychosocial treatment of ADD/ADHD has included a number of behavioural strategies such as contingency management i.e. point/token rewards system, timeouts. Clinical behaviour therapy, (parent, teacher or both are taught to use contingent management procedures), and cognitive-behavioural treatment, (e.g. self-monitoring, verbal self-instruction, problem solving strategies, self-reinforcement). Cognitive behavioural treatment has not yet been found to be result in beneficial effects in children with ADD/ADHD. In contrast, clinical behavior therapy, parent training and contingency management have produced beneficial affects.

DYSLEXIA

The word 'dyslexia' comes from the Greek language and its literal translation is "*dys*", meaning difficult, and "*lexis*", pertaining to words. The British Dyslexia Association defines dyslexia as: "*A difficulty with the automatic processing of language based information, especially with the written word. It is important to understand that evidence points to a constitutional origin, possibly genetic, and that it is not related to intelligence. Difficulties with the symbols of written, and possibly mathematical, language may result in a severe loss of self-confidence.*"

Dyslexia is a specific difficulty with language, especially with putting together the symbols of a written language. This results in dyslexic students having problems in demonstrating what they know. It is characterized also by problems with short-term, auditory-sequential or visual-sequential memory. Dyslexia is also expressed differently, and in varying degrees in each affected individual. The pattern of difficulties will often increase when the student is under stress. Some dyslexic adolescents have often evolved effective strategies to deal with their dyslexia, but many experience difficulties in the following ways:

- Reading at speed
- Spelling
- Comprehension
- Reading, particularly the reading of new terminology, or of multi-syllabic words
- Ordering and expressing ideas in essays
- Following complex oral instructions
- Handwriting and presentation skills
- Time management and organizational skills
- Concentration

How Teachers can help Dyslexic pupils

- Recognize the extra effort students may have to put into their studies and the extra fatigue this may cause
- Ensure that a student has got any exam concessions mentioned in the student's dyslexia assessment and give extra time in timed essays were relevant

- Do not ask the students to read aloud, allow them to volunteer

- Encourage students to use the technology available to help – ICT e.g. word processor, photocopier, tape-recorder etc.

- Try to give information through visual as well as auditory channels

- Give handouts to back up teaching

- Write key vocabulary on board, allowing students plenty of time to copy/refer to it

- Ensure that specific instructions, such as deadlines for completion of work, are written rather than simply given orally

- Allow students to submit essay outlines or rough drafts before writing the final version

- Help students with study skills

- Use diagrams where possible

- Be sensitive to students who do not wish their difficulties to be known

Help in the Classroom

Classroom teaching involves taking the needs of the whole class into consideration. The basic principle to remember is that students (dyslexic and non-dyslexic), will have different learning styles, learning needs, learning difficulties and level of skills. The aim is to adopt teaching methods which meet the various needs of all the individuals in the classroom.

Presenting teaching materials - Use different ways to do this

VISUALLY – use pictures, diagrams, colour coding and highlighting. Also good quality and well laid out handouts, with practical demonstrations help.

AUDITORIALLY – Repeating explanations, discussions, dialogues, drama

KINAESTHETICALLY – this involves practical activities, making things, tactile experience and exploration, three dimensional models

Strategies offering 'right brain' activities

- Use of music, drawing, visual-spatial patterns, humour, use of imagery, empathy and intuition
- Also encourage sensory exploration and hands on activities and use of the imagination. Develop visualization skills

Other ways of presenting subject matter

There are other holistic ways that materials can be presented i.e. introduce the whole picture and then the parts within it

- ✓ Make explicit links from particular examples to the general, overall idea
- ✓ Give some concrete examples (e.g. using audio-visual aids or demonstrations where possible), to build up a picture of abstract ideas.
- ✓ Try to understand the student's learning process
- ✓ Explain your actions – why you are doing a particular activity – this will bring out learning objectives e.g.
  - Which skills you are hoping to develop
  - What information or skill the student is expected to learn
  - What the relationship to other learning experiences is.

Some Helpful strategies

- ✓ Using discussion, help students understand how they go about learning something
- ✓ Explore with them, which strategies have worked for them
- ✓ Encourage them to share strategies which have been successful
- ✓ Develop students' analytical skills to decide why certain strategies work and others are less successful
- ✓ Discuss how memory works and the importanceof the motor
- ✓ Relate new learning to successful learning in the past

Encouraging meaningful connections

✓ Link what they are learning by the following:

✓ mind maps, spidergrams, or drawing to plan essays

✓ picture stories, (imaginatively or on paper), especially when teaching facts or events

✓ Use of recording (information can be recorded over music)

✓ Nemonics which are personally meaningful

Students taking charge of their own learning

✓ Offer a variety of methods and approaches for them to select or discover which works best for them

✓ Set up active learning situations where they can explain or demonstrate things to each other, work in pairs or groups, select activities or projects, set goals

✓ Stress self-checking and give plenty of opportunity for self-evaluation

Learning skills through content

✓ Introduce learning skills development via a variety of methods:

✓ Discuss, define, explain and demonstrate language particular to your subject e.g paying attention to common vocabulary, new terminology, expressions, jargon or idioms

✓ Break down processes into steps with opportunity for feedback – this helps to check understanding and develop language skills

✓ Encourage the asking of questions. Asking questions are a way of checking our hypothesis about what's being presented

✓ Give students opportunities to observe models by giving them examples of what they should be aiming for

✓ demonstrate and explain how to do assignments

DYSPRAXIA

Dyspraxia is an impairment of immaturity of the organization of movement. It is an immaturity in the way that the brain processes information, which results in messages not being properly or fully transmitted. The word Dyspraxia literally translates as "difficulty doing/acting". Dyspraxia is a combination of the Greek prefix 'dys', meaning difficult and the Latin word 'praxis' meaning knowing what to do and how to do it. Praxis is the ability by which we figure out how to use our hands and body in skilled tasks such as using a pencil, a knife and fork or cleaning a room. The following are the three elements of Praxis:

- **Ideation** – forming the idea and knowing what to do

- **Motor planning** – organizing the sequence of movements involved in the task

- **Execution** – carrying out the planned movement in a smooth sequence

Dyspraxia affects the planning of what to do and how to do it. It is associated with problems of perception, language and thought. Dyspraxia often overlaps with dyslexia.

Students with Dyspraxia may have a combination of problems that could include any of the following:

Motor co-ordination skills

- Poor balance/poor posture and fatigue

- Poor hand-eye co-ordination

- Lack of manual dexterity and poor at manipulative skills – they may have difficulty with typing, handwriting and drawing

- Clumsy fait and movement and a tendency to fall, trip, bump into things and people

Perception

- Poor visual perception, lack of spatial awareness, poor sense of direction (distinguishing left and right).

- Little awareness of time, speed, distance or weight

- Difficulty in distinguishing sounds from background noise

- Over-sensitivity to noise

Learning, thought and memory

- Difficulty in planning and organization of thought, difficulty with concentrating and a Tendency to be easily distracted

- May have poor memory and forget/lose things

- Can be messy and disorganized

- Difficulty in following instructions, especially ore than one at a time

- Problems with maths, hand-writing, reading, spelling ad writing

- Slow to finish a task and prone to daydreaming

- Poor listening skills

Speech and language

- May talk continuously and repeat themselves

- Difficulty with content and sequence of their language

- May have unclear speech

- Speech may have uncontrolled pitch, volume and rate

Emotion and behaviour

- Difficulty in listening to people, especially in large groups

- May interrupt frequently

- Difficulty in picking up on body language

- Understand things literally and may listen and not understands

- Slow to adjust/adapt to new or unpredictable situations

- Easily frustrated – wanting immediate gratification

- May have erratic behaviour, experiencing 'good days' and 'bad days'

- Often untidy and has problems with dressing

- Might flat or clap hands when excited

- Tend to get easily stressed or anxious and often have low self-esteem

- Prone to emotional outbursts

- Difficulty in dealing with him/herself when there is a feeling of failure and may opt out of activities that are too difficult

NB: *The above is prone to cause high stress levels in Dyspraxic students most of the time because of the perceived demands placed on them exceed their assessment of their ability*

Figure: 9.1   Recognizing Dyspraxic Stress:

Student Statements	Changes often seen in behaviour
Leave me alone!	Angry outbursts
I don't want to!	Unnatural silence
Its hurting me!	Isolation
This is impossible!	Loss of control
I cant do it	Intensity

Teacher strategies to reduce stress

- Make instructions as clear and as simple as possible

- Keep language as simple as possible

- Give clear guidance on what the student is required to do

- Allow for opportunities check students understanding

- Break work down into clear portions and give opportunity for checking work and going feedback

- Explore options of difficult tasks, break them into smaller, achievable tasks

- Constantly changing activities help students to focus and get the most out of the lesson

- Distribute clear, concise handouts

- Use mnemonics, study timetables, flow charts and diagrams may help the students cope with their poor organization and memory difficulties

ASPERGER'S SYNDROME

Identified by Hans Asperger in 1944, Asperger's Syndrome is a form of autism that affects social relationships and communication. People with Asperger's Syndrome have immense difficulties in social situations. The find it very difficult to understand facial expressions and body language. People with Asperger's Syndrome are often clumsy, both in their co-ordination and their articulation. They often have an 'obsessional' area of interest, for example computers, cars, trains, music, that can take over their concentration and their conversation.

Children with Asperger's Syndrome have difficulties with the following

- Managing conversations

- Anticipating appropriate topics

- Giving acceptable amount of information and predicting what may interest the hearer because to to medical reasons, it is virtually impossible to understand that other people think differently from themselves.

- The content of their speech is slightly inappropriate and may be very repetitive

- Speech may contain phrases that they have heard from their peers, parents, tutor, TV, that they can repeat perfectly without understanding what they are saying

- Unusual social styles and limited social skills

- Extreme lack of organization

- Very literal way of thinking

- Lack of eye contact, facial expressions and bodylanguage when engaging in conversation

- Lack of spontaneous speech to relate to other people

- Repetitive behaviour and actions

- Highly sensitive to noises

- Good attention to detail and are very precise

- set routines and ways of doing things and great distress can be caused if they are changed

- Difficulty sleeping at night – may lead ot poor concentration of falling asleep during lessons

- Very literal ways of thinking, they find abstract concepts very difficult e.g. emotions

- Have very good memory and excel at courses that require memorizing lots of facts and figures

- Good attention to detail and are very precise

- Good awareness of time management and are usually punctual

- Have a tendency to be anxious and stressed due to inability to turn their minds off – this may lead to emotional outbursts.

Teacher strategies for students with Asperger's Syndrome

- Do not assume that instructions and information have been understood and always double check that the student understands what has to be done

- Students with Aspergers have a very structured routine and do not like change. If there is going to be a change of venue for a lesson, a change of time or even if the lesson is going to finish early, the student should be prepared in advance

- Encourage the student to brainstorm their ideas onto paper

- If the student is required to complete work, make sure that they know what they are expected to do

- Students with Asperger's Syndrome tend not to pick up on your intonation or tone of voice and often find eye-contact threatening

- Do not be sarcastic or rely on communicating through facial expression and body language

- Students often have difficulty remembering, retaining and making notes from spoken instructions.

- Clear handouts that clearly specify both the main points from the lesson and the tasks to be completed for homework are very helpful

- A checklist of materials needed for homework and lessons is useful

- highlight and organize work in order of priority and break it down into chunks

- encourage the student to sit at the front of the class away from the window as this reduces the distraction of external stimuli and other classroom distractions

- Remind students that they must ask for help

- make sure all relevant teachers are informed of the student's condition and the implications and possible problems that may occur

- students with Asperger's Syndrome like familiarity and hve good relationships with those they trust so it is useful to let the student get to know you.

- Get to know the student and their areas of anxiety and stress

Preparing pupils with Asperger's Syndrome for exams

- Give them as much information as possible about the exam, location, invigilators and peer group, date, time, duration

- Familiarise them with the exam room in advance

- Show where they will be sitting by showing them in advance or drawing a plan, this will help ease any anxiety

- See if the student can have a separate room

- extra time may be required

MENTAL HEALTH ISSUES

Recognizing possible mental health problems

Apart from the Statement of Special Education Needs, a number of behavioural features may suggest mental ill health. A change in behaviour or appearance can be a sign of deteriorating mental health. For example, poor attendance, mood swings, deterioration in standard of work, deterioration in motivation to work, personal hygiene/attention to dress, marked weight gain or loss, bizarre or inappropriate behaviour, disruptive behaviour, or speech, social inclusion or withdrawal.

In addition, marks on arms or elsewhere may indicate self harm. If a student has a significant mental health problem they may need a collaborative approach with may require input from family, medical, pastoral, teamwork and an an agreed realistic plan of action. Do not attempt to challenge any abnormal thoughts or beliefs. and it is also not advisable to arrange meetings with a disturbed or violent student on your own.

Schools have behaviour and emergency policies to help them deal with situations where a student poses potential harm to teachers, himself, or his peers. Additionally, external help from and through GPs and Community Mental Health Teams are able to support/monitor the student in the community. Many teachers will be familiar with dealing with a range of emotional problems that students present, e.g disruptive behaviour. Often these can be resolved with Behaviour support plans, peer support and a range of external intervention e.g. CAMHS (Children and Adolescence Mental Health Service).

Depression & Anxiety

Depression is often accompanied with feelings of anxiety, lowered mood and a feeling that everything seems harder to do and less worthwhile. Students who have had long breaks from mainstream schools due to exclusion, being rejected from more than two alternative placements, loss of friends, feeling of identified with a group/school, stigma attached to rejection, experiences with pupil, immediate and extended family. For some anxiety can become so overwhelming that it takes over their lives. They may experience very frequent panic attacks for no apparent reason. It may be accompanied by an overwhelming compulsion to escape from the situation they are in – called the "fight or flight" reflex, and may also be expressed by aggressive behaviour.

Physical effects

- Individuals breathe more rapidly

- Tense their muscles

- Feel light-headed and shaky or pins and needles can ensue

- Raised blood pressure and can become aware that their heart is pounding

- A cyclical effect results and this increases their anxiety

Psychological effects

- Such anxiety include fear, heightened alertness

- Being on edge

- Irritability and an inability to relax or concentrate

- Talking to someone can help to deal with the problems

- Loses or gains weight

- Seems tired and appears to lack energy

- Has impaired concentration

- Is agitated and possibly aggressive

- Seems out of touch with reality

- Is easily frustrated

LEARNING STYLES

So far we have defined a number of Special Education categories which are included in children's Statement of Special Education Needs, identified as additional learning support given to a learner over and above what is normally provided in a standard learning programme, which leads to their primary learning goal. In other words the additional learning support is required to help students gain access to, progress to and achieve successfully, their learning goals. Taking the different ways that students learn is into consideration, it is necessary to look at some styles to avoid teaching in our own preferred styled, which may exclude some learners. Here is a range of strategies which enable learners to take in information and experience learning in as multi-sensory, multi-dimensional way as possible.

The general assumption is that if learners can understand their own learning preference, they are able to both make choices about ways that they learn and take part in metacognition. We take in information about the world around us through our senses. In order to access information as fully as possible, learning needs to be multi-sensory, accessing these areas: *(Fig. 9.2)*Visual

- Auditory
- Kinaesthetic

It is generally thought that from a classroom of pupils, 34% will be auditory learners, 29% visual learners and 37% kinaesthetic learners. The general characteristics of each preference, *(see Fig. 9.2)*.

Teachers recognize that all learners are constantly perceiving and processing sensory data through hearing, seeing, touching, smelling, tasting and doing. It is also accepted that different nerves (auditory, visual, tactile, olfactory, and gustatory), sends messages to the brain. The brain then decides which messages are important and worth retaining, filtering and unnecessary information is discarded mentally.

Figure: 9.2 Learning Styles

VISUAL LEARNERS	AUDITORY LEARNERS	KINAESTHETIC LEARNERS
Finds spoken instructions difficult	Enjoys music	Uses hands while talking
Likes to read	Talks to self aloud	Enjoys ding activities
Remember faces	Say things like "*That rings a bell!*"	Says things like "*I don't follow*"
Likes to write and draw pictures	Easily distracted	Reading is not especially enjoyed
Say things like, "*I see*" and "*This looks OK*"	Easily distracted by noises	Will try out new things
Usually a good speller	Outgoing personality	Taps things while studying (foot, pen)
Remembers faces	Enjoys talking	Outgoing personality
Has good handwriting	Likes to be read to	Is quite demonstrative
Likes doodling	Likes to hear someone explain	Prefers to wear clothes for comfort
Quiet personality	Likes to explain things to others	Often daydreams
Notices details	Enjoys listening activities	May prefer to walk around than read
Neat in appearance		Likes making things
Activities e.g. (*verbally*) writing, creating, reciting, listing, telling/retelling	**Activities**: diagramming, depicting, cartooning, observing, painting, storyboarding, illustrating, drawing,	**Activities**: (*bodily*): performing, dancing, dramatizing, roleplaying, acting, pantomiming, sculpting, constructing

This process is influenced by our learning styles, therefore, it is important to understand students preferred styles for better performance and more effective teaching and learning. Behaviour management therefore takes all these factors into consideration in creating the pupil's Individual Education Plan (IEP), for his/her development.

For many students presenting an adverse behaviour that impacts on both their learning and learning environment, TCS Tutorial College is their last or second chance to remake or re-model themselves for a positive and productive future. It is hoped that in recognizing that there is a need to develop programmes to remedy adverse behaviour, there will also be determination and consistency, (for all those faced with challenging behaviour), to impart knowledge that would enable students to manage their own their lives, positively. There is no magic wand! My belief is that where there is a willingness and commitment, there will be progress and success. These can be measured in incremental ways that are discussed further in this chapter.

Strategies for Schools - Adverse Behaviour Reduction Programme

Develop a position where the only focus of duties is on improving school behavioural difficulties. This prevents other duties from taking valuable time away from behaviour intervention.

Include the students who will be receiving behaviour improvement intervention services. (Include Social Services, YOTs, EWOs and any other involved area agencies in the development process). All parties will be involved at some point (pre- or post-court stages), and will have valuable input as to how the programme can be most effective. A positive working relationship with all parties involved is critical to a successful programme.

Clearly define the roles or responsibilities of all parties involved in the behaviour intervention process. Depending on the number of students in the school that will be serviced, it may be appropriate to designate some duties to school counsellors, Mentors, Deputy Heads, TAs etc. Divide the caseload up in a way that most effectively reaches as many students as possible at the targeted time.

Document your behaviour intervention protocol. This provides a point of reference if there is any question as to when to intervene with students, and *who* is responsible for *what*. If possible, have behaviour intervention staff located on the school premises. The close contact with students and visibility within the school environment is important. Students need to know *where* they can go if they have questions/concerns regarding behaviour difficulties. This also allows for easy communication with school staff.

Start interventions as early as possible.

1. Involve parents from start during the planning stages and often in the intervention process. Parents appreciate any kind of contact. Parent support is necessary, particularly in cases where behavioural difficulties are chronic.

2. Communication regularly with all agencies involved in the behaviour intervention process. Regular updates on how the programme is going are helpful for all. This will help to maintain a positive working relationship with all, and will greatly increase the effectiveness of your programme.

3. Assign the responsibility of determining **consequences** for adverse behaviour to school staff, (counsellors, assistant principals/heads etc). This allows the Behaviour Intervention Officer to support the pupil by helping students to improve, rather than meeting out negative consequences for , say, poor attendance. This also helps the behaviour intervention staff to maintain a positive relationship with students.

4. When selecting a person to work as your Behaviour Intervention staff member, find someone who enjoys working the age group of students you will be servicing and someone who communicates extremely well with others. This is a critical to the success of the programme.

5. While it's important to be a support person for students who are having problems and are, as a result of displaying adverse behaviour, be careful not to become too "friendly", with students. Pupils are very good at taking advantage of such a situation, and an overly familiar relationship is counter-productive.

6. Work persistently with every student until all resources and opportunities to improve have been exhausted. Don't give up on any student.

7. Understand that school is not the place for every child. There may be a time when you need to suggest an alternative learning programme/environment. If that is appropriate, that is OK. Students need to be in a programme where they are, and will be successful.

8.   Have a clear behavioural policy at the school with which you will be working. Be sure everyone involved has a full understanding of that policy and the consequences associated with it and that the policy is full and consistently enforced.

Services of the programme

Pre-exclusion interventions for all students at school as well as post-court supervision (YOT), for all juveniles referred from court, (who are linked with this school), for behavioural misdemeanours.

Managing the Programme

The Adverse Behaviour Management Programme will require the following personnel: Behaviour Officers, Caseload Managers and Mentors.

Behaviour Officers

To deal with students who are at risk of exclusion due to persistent disruptive behaviour, those who have been placed on probation for being adjudicated habitually with emotional and social behavioural difficulties (especially those without a Statement of Educational Needs -SEN).

The time spent working with these students will vary each week. In an average week, approximately 50% of the Behaviour Officer's time is spent working with the caseload. The Behaviour Officer will ensure that each student completes his/her weekly plan/court order and follows the conditions of any Supervision Order. The Behaviour Officer also assists other Juvenile Behaviour Officers not on site at the School with YOT related matters when convenient.

The Behaviour Intervention Caseload includes all students at the school where the Behaviour Officer is situated. During the school year the Behviour Officer works full time at the school. While working at personal behaviour plans will be the duties of the Behaviour Officer's daily routine, pre-exclusion interventions with the general school population are the primary focus of duties during the school year. Between 50 to 70% of the Behaviour Officer's time is spent working with these students in an average week. Due to the large number of students who the Behaviour Officer will communicate with, visits will be short, though some interventions will be more time consuming.

Behaviour Case Managers

- I have worked with several hundred students over the past 10 years and have experienced successes, for various reasons:

- The student see and experience that someone cares

- Someone is able to explain to these students why it is so important to maintain school attendance without records of exclusions or be permanently excluded, as these behaviours can carry on in later adult life.

- I demonstrate the importance of good school behaviour and draw attention to the behaviour policy, especially in our weekly assemblies, rewards were given.

- Students have been referred to services that they really need which compliment or reinforce behaviour policy at school

- The co-operation I have received from parents of the school and agencies have worked to produce successful results; and

- Communication to share good moments or practices at school with parents, have resulted in whole family pride and student increased self-confidence and self-esteem.

Mentors

Mentors will act as Interventionists who will provide individual or group mentoring, segmented according to pupil's needs. This will be via a range of support and developmental sessions. This is designed to provide intensive support for pupils who need greater input with Expert delivery, to deal with a complexity of needs. These needs are strategically approached as follows:

1. Supporting Behavioural improvement

2. Improving academic attainment levels

3. Personal Development

4. The Main Objectives will be to develop

5. An awareness of self via evaluation

6. Provide confidential opportunities to explore actions and consequences

7. Increase general self esteem and confidence

8. Develop relationship in a trusting and confidential manner

9. Address issues which become barriers to pupil (academically & socially)

10. Provide practical support via Behavioural Improvement Plans (BIP).

Challenges

One of the most challenging cases that I have experienced is one where the student and mother had concluded that another setting was best for the student, not school. The pupil truly did not fit in at the school, constantly remarked on the fact that *no other placement had worked in the past;* did not care whether his placement was successful or not, and the fact that mother was looking for a way to get out of the school and into another programme – a residential placement.

The way that the student, supported by his mother, did this was through chronic adverse behaviours. In our efforts to help them become successful at all costs, they were offered opportunity after opportunity, to allow the placement to work, while trying various strategies and being as creative as we could be. Mother made sure to make suggestions to the vulnerable and easily suggestible boy, so that he became destructive by fire-lighting, dismantling safety equipment and terrorising young pupils. The ulterior motive behind the disruption became obvious and were reinforced by the mother's belief that she would now get her initial request - a residential placement and be rid of the boy. This created an impasse and hastened the boy's exit from school. It is sometimes difficult to realise that a student does not belong in a regular school setting and that keeping him/her could be setting them up for failure. Therefore decisions must be based on long range considerations and with the input of the pupil as much as possible.

Importance of an Effective Programme

Promoting positive behaviour management is so important to all students, not only to their success at school but also in their future. Pupils often do not see how their actions and behaviours during their teenage years will affect their adult lives. It is important to help children to understand the linkages between behaviour in their youth and the positive changes it will make in their lives forever!

Setting up your Programme

PLAN AHEAD

✓   It is best to plan for evaluation at the same time that you design your programme. Consider the time that this might take and be as realistic as possible!

✓   You will need to consider your evaluation at the end of the programme. Therefore, set aside money for evaluation in your initial budget.

✓   Do not give up on evaluation if you did not plan it at the beginning. In any case, the advice is to still design one!

Create a Logic Model of Your program

Decide what outcomes(s) you want. Some possibilities are improved behaviour, improved attendance and punctuality, reduced truancy, improved attainment levels.

Programme components to achieve your goals

Be sure your programme components and your designated outcomes match. In other words, if all your interventions are aimed at a small subset of students with serious behaviour and attendance problems, you may not see measurable outcomes across the entire student body. But that will not mean that your programme is not working – it means your evaluation is not well designed. Decide on measurement tools to be applied.

Know what kind of evaluation is needed

You will need to consider which type of evaluation suits you best from the following examples:

IMPLEMENTATION EVALUATION, looks at the way in which a programme is set up and is operating. It is particularly relevant when an established programme already shown to be effective, is being copied in a new location. Unless the programme is implemented as intended, one cannot expect to achieve the same good result. This type of evaluation lends itself to both qualitative and quantitative data collections.

OUTCOME EVALUATION, measures the effect of a program once it has been established. A programme will not likely be ready for an outcome evaluation until it has been in operation for some time – generally a year or more. If begun too early, an outcome evaluation will likely show no results and may unnecessarily dampen enthusiasm for a potentially good programme.

COST BENEFIT ANALYSIS, compares the cost of a programme as measured in pound sterling to the outcomes of that programme, also measured in pounds. If benefits are greater than costs, then the programme may be said to pay off. Sometimes it is difficult to put a price on benefits, cost effectiveness analysis may be used to compare the cost of a programme as measured in pounds, to benefit measured in something other than pounds. For example, how many pupils have increased attainment levels as a result of a £50,000 exclusion reduction programme? Cost effectiveness analysis is more useful when comparing multiple programmes.

Data and Data collection Methods

Data come in two general forms – *quantitative and qualitative.* Each provides a distinct purpose and you must consider what kind of data will be best used.

Studies of school exclusions lend themselves easily to quantitative analysis but the most thorough evaluation include both. School records can provide data on outcome measures such as attainment levels, fixed term exclusions, poor attendance and Education Welfare Referrals, which can be correlated with race, gender and age.

Students, parents and school personnel can be surveyed. Be careful how you formulate survey questions; borrowing from other surveys is the best way to get meaningful questions. *ABEM*, which focuses on an ethnographic approach, also provides for qualitative and quantitative analysis via a variety of methods. Provide clear directions so that respondents understand how to complete the survey.

Interviews can include structured questions in which respondents select from a set of designated responses; these data are quantitative. Interviews may also include open-ended questions that allow respondents to answer any way they please; these questions provide qualitative data. Direct quotations should be taken. Notice that *ABEM* utilised quotations from pupils, parents, visitors, and teachers.

Focus groups bring together a group of people – usually between 5 and 10 – to discuss their experiences. Questions are open-ended and discussions are encouraged.

Focus groups should be tape recorded and transcribed for analysis. Focus groups provide qualitative data.

Collecting and Analysing Quantitative Data

QUANTITATIVE DATA are numeric, they can be counted and measured.
Obvious examples include student grades on a 4-point scale, days or class periods behaviour and attendance or missed, and behviour points earned.

Quantitative data such as attendance, grades and class credits may be collected from the school's admin records. Quantitative data on the number of students served by the Behaviour Programme or the number of students who receive mentoring or another inter-agency referral may be collected from records e.g. Social Worker. You would need good record-keeping practice. Create a system for recording Inter-Agency interventions (e.g. YOT, Intensive Supervision Surveillance Programme (ISSP) Education Welfare Officers (EWO) on an on-going basis and keep up-to-date. The following is an example of a quantitative survey question.

How to Collect and Analyse Qualitative Data

QUALITATIVE DATA are non-numeric. They can be descriptive text passages, observations, field notes, records or documents, audio or video files.

Qualitative data can come from interviews and focus groups and sometimes from open-ended questions on written surveys. Collecting and analyzing qualitative data is time-consuming, and therefore expensive. It is most practical to collect qualitative data from a relatively small sample of pupils.

While *quantitative data* are best suited for answering the "*what*" question, qualitative data are best for answering the "*how*" and "*why*" questions. Quantitative data may tell you a programme did not work, but you will not know why it did not work without some qualitative data. It is best to tape record and transcribe interviews and group discussions to record actual responses.

The following is an example of a qualitative interview question.
What effect did the mentoring programme have on your class behaviour?

You may find some computer programmes that can help in analyzing large amount of qualitative data. For example, those that allow you to import text files, code electronically and gather all selections with the same code for analysis. This will depend on good database organization at the start of your programme design.

Longitudinal evaluation, measures changes that occur within the same group of students over time. They require taking a "baseline" measurement in other words, measuring the outcome variable(s) **before** the intervention begins, (or in its very early stages if need be), and comparing it to a second measurement of the same variable(s) taken **at the end** of the programme.

Both qualitative and quantitative data may be collected longitudinally, though a longitudinal study is generally thought of as having a quantitative component.

QUANTITATIVE BASELINE DATA:

Number of class periods behavioural disruptions occurred in the month. The total number of disruptions before the intervention began divided by the total number of class periods during a period i.e. a month, would give you a baseline figure – the formula is thus:

$$\frac{\textbf{Before } \textit{Behaviour programme began}}{\textbf{Total } \textit{class periods } \textbf{during } \textit{that month}} = \textit{Baseline data}$$

Based on the above formula, you will now be able to calculate information as follows: *Was there improvement? How much? Was the change large enough to be meaningful?*

You will need to decide if the improvement you have calculated should remain static or whether you would track the improvement beyond the end of the programme. Follow participants over time to find out. For example, you may want to know what happened to pupils over periods of say three months after the end of the programme, six months later or one year

Control Groups and Experimental Groups

The best way to be sure that a program is having an effect is to compare students who participate in the Behavioural Programme with students who do not. Students in the experimental group receive a treatment that is under evaluation. In this case they participate in a Behavioural Programme. Students in the control group, sometimes called the comparison group, do not participate.

Adverse Behaviour Reduction programmes

This section describes blueprints for Adverse Behaviour Management Programmes that address challenging and difficult behaviours, truancy, school attendance and student achievement concerns.   The following programmes become "blueprints" model programmes based on stands of programme effectiveness developed by TCS Tutorial College for the management of difficult behaviour.

The programmes described are grouped by setting:

1.   School based programmes

2.   Community based programmes

3.   School & community based programmes

4.   And programmes offered in other settings

Each listed programme includes: names of the programme, type of programme, age of students targeted, programme goals, programme description, study design, study sample and study outcomes. These programmes offer conclusions based on results gained by TCS Tutorial College.

PROGRAMME 1: PREVENTIVE INTERVENTION

Programme Type: Culturally Sensitive Behavioural Training,
using individual behaviour strategies
Age: aimed at secondary (age 11 to 16yrs)
Setting: School
Program Goals

The Preventive Intervention programme aims to prevent an increase in school failure experiences among students at risk of exclusion, regarded as "high riskers". The programme also strives to reduce school delinquency, including school-based problems, criminal behaviour.

PROGRAMME DESCRIPTION: The intervention consists of 4 components
1.   Collecting up-to-date information about students actions
from interviews with teachers and records of daily behaviours,
difficulties, disciplinary action

1. Providing systematic feedback to students and or parents about the students' actions

2. Attaching value to students' actions (e.g. students could earn points towards a special trip for good behaviour, receiving no disciplinary action and

3. Helping students determine strategies for modifying their behaviour and therefore earn more points.

4. The programme lasts for 1 year, with booster sessions available during the following year.

Study Design

New arrivals to the secondary environment, (a mixture of social and cultural backgrounds, low income, and a mixture of classes - working-class and middle-class); matched into pairs based on relevant behaviour difficulty variables. Each pair is to be assigned to the intervention or control group for a year. The control group is to receive no treatment. During a one year post-intervention period, twice weekly booster sessions will be available to the experimental group.

Outcomes

The study will monitor behaviours in booster sessions, and non-attendees will be sent letters. Sample size will be determined by the School (e.g. mixture of cultures). The programme will also evaluate behaviour improvement among students during intervention stages (receiving communication from the school to attend the Behaviour Officer to the programme end), attendance on sessions, and the effect of participation in the intervention.

The management of adverse behaviour in pupils must involve the participation and development of parents. This enhances and speeds up the rate of positive behaviour and ensures consistency in methods and teamwork necessary for the planned outcomes. The following parent and pupils positive action programme is aimed at working as a group or unit to affect behaviour change that would benefit whole families, and also impacting on the wider society.

PROGRAMME 2: POSITIVE ACTION TEAM (PAT)

Programme Type: School individual strategies, parent training
Age: compulsory school age 5 – 16yrs
Setting: School
Program Goals

Pupils and Parents **Positive Action Team Programme** aims to reduce adverse behaviour, truancy and instil a sense of responsibility in students and their parents.

The project also seeks to increase bonding to the school and reduce school disorder through the implementation of broad-based structural changes; these changes might include adopting different disciplinary procedures, management practices or school activities.

The programme also aims to increase student educational and behaviour attainment as well as enhance the quality of family life, which results in a positive impact on the community.

PROGRAM DESCRIPTION

Positive Action Team (PAT) programme, is a behaviour management programme that requires school personnel to monitor school behaviour closely and contact parents promptly if their children have 3 days of adverse behaviour.

Parents must respond, outlining measures they have taken to ensure that their children understand the consequences of their actions. If a child continues to be disruptive, the school notifies the Education Welfare Officer and Behaviour Officer, who will work out a plan to rescue the situation before other agencies are called in. A diversion programme will need to be designed to strengthen family relationships and encourage children to behave in school.

Study Design

This programme will utilize a non-equivalent comparison group design involving all teachers and students. The school, rather than the individual is the unit of analysis, the individuals Pre-test and post-test study would need to be conducted The entire school and student population will be surveyed in all years with over a 2 year period, to evaluate response rates

Outcomes

Rates of behaviour disruption would be monitored as well as the following: Attachment to schools, school attendance, academic achievement, delinquency rates, drug involvement, exclusions and sanctions, with a sample size that would determine Rates *before* and *after* parents' notification of their involvement on the programme.

THE POSITIVE ACTION TEAM (PAT) PROGRAMME is a school-wide intervention programme, with 6 major components:

1. Staff, student and community participation in managing adverse behaviours and helping to design and manage school behaviour policies.

2. Organizational changes aimed at increasing academic performance.

3. Organizational changes aimed at increasing school attainment levels among low achieving pupils, especially those whose adverse behaviour present a barrier to accessing the curriculum.

4. Vocational preparation, and a community participatory approach to achieving positive behaviour changes.

5. Support and affective services for "at risk" individuals and their parents

6. Special academic and mentoring services for low achieving and disruptive students.

Individual behaviour plans, addressing academic or behaviour objectives will need to be implemented with high risk students by Behaviour Officers, and where relevant, Behaviour Specialists. The programme also calls for a measure of mentoring or counselling sessions. Other activities include peer counselling, personal behaviour evaluation, and referrals to other agencies, where necessary.

Behaviour Passports

Below is an example of TCS Tutorial College Behaviour Management, tracking and measuring device, used to help pupils monitor and take control of the quality of their own behaviour; working in partnership with Teachers and Teacher Assistants, and other staff, on a daily basis. It is called a *Behaviour Passport.* It also enables easy tracking of behaviour patterns, and is further assisted by information gained from pupils' mentoring sessions and parents' evaluations of their children's behaviour. It enables students to be aware of their behaviours in many ways. For example, monitoring patterns which develop, analysing and discussing variables or consistency/inconsistency and allows them to share in the process of planning, controlling and celebrating successful outcomes. **(Fig. 9.3)**

The evaluation is recognised and awarded on a weekly basis in our Friday Assembly, and you can be sure that, whatever their age, each child is expectant of a mention or receipt of an **Award** (tangible recognition and achievement) for having some positive outcomes. This is a short-term goal and the active participation and the sharing of the progress with the whole school is a good management approach to enabling children to self-manage their behaviour. As a medium-term measure, greater rewards are targeted towards the end of term, when more recognition is given and rewarded at an increased level and different from the weekly recognition. Furthermore, a long-term recognition takes behaviour management and achievement on a larger scale which is then made public at our **Annual Celebration of Achievement and Graduation**. At this event, the highlight of our School year, trophies, cups and medals mark overall sustained progress and this is shared with the whole school, families and invited members of the public and Local Education Authority representatives who are able to witness the children's milestones and live performances.

Figure: 9.3 TCS TUTORIAL COLLEGE

STUDENT BEHAVIOUR PASSPORT – BEHAVIOUR TRACKER©

Pupil Name: ....

DOB: ....Year Group: ....

LEVEL	REQUIREMENTS	OUTCOMES					
		1	2	3	4	5	6
Bronze Award 1	• Wearing school uniform • Tools for schools • Punctual for school • Report absence from school • If homework is set … it is completed • Being able to manage mobile phone • Behaviour Award Received						
Bronze Award 2	• Contribution to group learning • Participating in class learning • Respecting others/self by allowing others to air views • Minimize conflicts and follow advice given • Ask for help • Behaviour Award Received						
Silver Award 1	• Set daily objectives in Maths, English and Science and • work at achieving them • Complete set pieces of work in each subject area daily • Work at getting set work marked each day • Achieve set targets for behaviour • Peer mentored a classmate • Behviour Award Received						
Silver Award 2	• Be productive with unstructured time eg using library, internet research, ICT, completing assignments, planning assembly, hobby or project, reading, music, drawing, D&T • Start working at developing individual personal profile, cv, career plan, transition plan • Start assessing training programmes with the idea of making a choice eg work experience, career guidance • Draw on available resources to advance learning eg making presentations, projects						

		I	2	3	4	5	6
Gold Award	• Seek career advice from relevant personnel eg Connexions, career advisor, College prospectus • Work out a mentoring plan for a friend • Reflecting on outcomes…what could be done better • Witness Testimony outside TCS • Achieved at least 3 Awards for behavior (I in each category above) • Assist teacher in planning one Individual Behaviour Plan (IBP) • Behaviour Award received						

Measurement Scale 0–5

0. Cause for Concern   (needing additional interventions)
I. Poor   Never done
2. Satisfactory   Sometimes done
3. Good   Most times done
4. Very Good   Consistently done
5. Excellent   Always done

NB : This Behaviour Passport enables tracking on a six weekly basis

Apart from the above Behaviour tracking device, other forms of data could be collected and used to help in evaluation based on the child's own perception and score on the level of his self-esteem , Resilience, sense of identity, problem-solving skills. A range of statements are made, approximately 20, and these are scored on a scale of I – 5. The pupil is allowed to self evaluate these to test how well he/she understands what is acceptable or not, the level of his judgement and the risk of repetition and offending, as well as where self-denial is obvious. The method is self-reflexive and allows for exploration of areas that need further support. .

One way of managing challenging behaviour is the realistic support for those presenting the difficulties, in the form of ongoing emotional support provided by not only teachers but friends, therapists, relatives who understand and recognize the individual's strengths and weaknesses. Adequate and continuous research and education, help families to cope with their own frustrations and will enable them to be less critical and more supportive of each other. For parents who are only *hopeful* of a positive outcome, without action or an awareness that left untreated, their child/ren's difficulties can impact on their self-esteem, confidence, learning as well as their capacity to manage their future. In many instances, timing is of the essence, because early intervention can make a difference before the child and parents become demoralized, lose all hope of positive changes and become so disaffected, that 'turn-around' approaches are harder to impact.

SELECTED REFERENCES & USEFUL SEN SOURCES

British Dyslexia Association (www.bda-dyslexia.org.uk).   BDA provides a range of useful resources related to dyslexia. It offers advice, information and help to families, professionals and dyslexic individuals.

The Disability Rights Commission (www.drc-gb.org). The DRC has been established to eliminate the discrimination faced by disabled people and promote equality of opportunity. It also produces guides on how to organise disability awareness/equality training.

The Dyslexia Institute (http://dyslexia-inst.org.uk).   The DI specialises in the assessment and teaching of people with dyslexia. It seeks ways to improve the effectiveness of teaching and also focuses on the development of teaching materials.

AFASIC – Overcoming Speech impairments 347 Central Markets, Smithfield London EC1A 9NH Tel: 0207 236 6487 www.afasic.org.uk	Network for the Handicapped Disability Law Service, 2nd Floor, Room 241, 49-51 Bedford Row, London WC1R 4LR Tel: 0207 831 8031 www.mib.org.uk	MENCAP 117 Golden Lane London EC1Y 0RT Tel: 0207 454 0454 www.mencap.org.uk
Advisory Centre for Education, Unit 1C Aberdeen Studios, 22 Highbury Grove, London N5 2EA Tel: 0207 354 8321 www.ace-ed.org.uk	Royal National Institute for the Deaf 19-23 Featherstone Street London EC1Y 8SL Tel: 0207 296 8000 www.mid.org.uk	MIND (National Association for Mental Health) 15-19 Broadway Stratford, London E15 4BQ Tel: 0208 519 2122
Education Adviser Association for Spina Bifida and Hydrocephalus Asbah House 42 Park Road Peterborough PE1 2UQ Tel: 01733 555 988	SCOPE, 12 Park Crescent London W1N 3EQ Tel: 0207 636 5020 www.scope.org.uk	National Association of Citizens Advice Bureau 115—123 Pentonville Road, London N1 9LZ Tel: 0207 833 2181
Epilepsy Action New Anstey House Gate Way Drive Yeadon Leeds, LS19 7NW 0808 800 5050 www.epilepsy.org.uk	SENSE 11-13 Clifton Terrace Finsbury Park LondonN4 3SR Tel: 0207 272 7774 www.sense.org.uk	KIDS 80 Waynflete Square London W10 6UD Tel: 0208 969 2817
Children's Legal Centre University of Essex Wivenhoe Park Colchester CO4 3SQ Tel: 01206 872 466 www2.essex.ac.uk/clc	Special Education Consortium c/o Council for Disabled Children 8 Wakley Street London EC1V 7QE Tel: 0207 843 6000	Royal National Institute for the Blind 224 Great Portland Street London W1N 6AA • Tel: 0207 388 1266 www.mib.org.uk

Council for Disabled Children C/o National Childrens Bureau 8 Wakley Street London EC1V 7QE Tel: 0207 843 6000 www.ncb.org.uk.cdc.htm	Network 81 1-7 Woodfield Terrace Chapel Hill Stansted Essex. CM24 8AJ Tel: 01279 647 415	Spinal Inuuries Association – www.spinal.co.uk This is mainly concerned with supporting individuals with spinal injuries but it does have an information service that colleges may find helpful
DIAL UK (Disability Information Advice Line) Park Lodge# St. Catherine's Hospital Tickhill Road Doncaster DN4 8QN Tel: 01302 310 123 Members.aol.com/diialuk	Parents for Inclusion Unit 2, Ground Floor 70 South Lambeth Road London SW8 1RL Tel: 0207 735 7735	The Mental Health Foundation And Foundation for People with learning difficulties (www. mentalhealth.org.uk) They produce many publications on mental health. www.learning difficulties.org.uk
Down's Syndrome Association 155 Mitcham Road, London SW17 9PG Tel: 0208 682 4001 www.downs-syndrome.org.uk	Pre-School Playgroup Association 61-63 & 69 Kings Cross Road London WC1X 9LL Tel: 0207 833 0991	BCODP (British Council of Organisations of Disabled People) – www.bcodp.org.uk BCODP campaigns to overcome the oppression of disabled people. It can provide access to disability equality training.
I CAN (Invalid Children Aid Nationwide) Babican City Gate 1-3 Dunfferin Street London EC1Y 8NA Tel: 0207 374 4422	Royal Association for Disability & Rehabilitation (RADAR) 12 City Forum 250 City Road London EC1V 8AF Tel: 0207 250 0123 www.radar.org.uk	Skills, The National Bureau for Students with Disabilities (wwwskill.org.uk). The only organisation which works specifically to further the interests of disabled learners in post school education.
IPSEA Tribunal Support Service (for parents appealing to the SEN Tribunal) 4 Ancient House Mews Woodbridge Suffolk IP12 1DH Advice Line: 0800 018 4016 or 01394 382814 www.ipsea.org.uk	For young adults with mental health needs: www.lookingforward.org.uk Targeted at paractitioners, managers and policymakers' but overall intended to promote good practice and raise awareness of young adults with mental health needs.	info@addiss.co.uk presents information about ADHD across the lifespan. Sponsored by the National Attention Deficit Disorder Information and Support Service
www.aspergersadults.co/ aspergrrrlz.html. This is for girls and women with Asperger's syndrome	www.lukejackson.info for people with Asperger's syndrome ALSO books on Asperger's Syndrome by The Jessica Kingsley Publishers at www.jkp. com	Adders.org provides a wide variety of information about ADHD inEnglish, French, German, and Spanish.

CONCLUSION

In Chapter 3, we looked at perceptions, notably, how society conceptualizes images of youth deviance and criminality. However, discussions have shown throughout this book, that the problems of youth crime is also to do with the way society understands and assesses young people's actions. In other words, definitions of "crime" are conceptualized according to the prevailing power relations, based on moral and political judgments. A conclusion is that, at times, criminal acts are defined as *criminal* only when it is in the interest of the ruling class to define them as such.

From a British Caribbean perspective, experience has shown that certain ethnic minority groups are "*criminalized*" to divert attention from the inequalities and injustices, if not exploitation they endure. In some cases, penal laws are passed in reaction to minority groups' behaviour, in order to maintain the position of the ruling class, whilst ensuring that the working classes are subjected to strict and tight control. From this perspective, it can be said that behaviours are criminalized in order to maintain control, (politically and socially), and eradicate any perceived threat to the ruling class. In other words, a behaviour can be categorized by virtue of public and political perceptions and society's reaction to it.

For this reason, it is possible to see how the reality of gang-related disorder discussed in Chapter 6, highlighted activities that have become an expected 'norm' of life in Britain's cities. In fact, the words *young men*, have almost become synonymous with *gang*, particularly so for minority ethnic youths. Other concerns among already troubled communities, is the disproportionate amount of media attention given to certain crimes and the resultant fear of young people which is causing an escalation of social disorder and gang-related crimes. This rising phenomenon runs the risk of a self-fulfilling prophecy, in that young people act out the stigma which is attached to them, even though they may not necessarily be so inclined. For many, the stereotypical *image* has given them the impetus for creative but negative action.

This means that constant media attention can fuel an interest in gang membership and therefore encourage gang behavior. The violence which accompanies gang behavior and the ease of membership acceptance among gang leaders, show this type of activity to be attractive to, and taken up by young people who have no moral conscience, poor education, are excluded, deprived, feel alienated, lack a sense of safety on the streets, and receive poor parenting . There is also a lack of consistent intervention by members of the community at large, in ways which give the impression that these gang leaders and members are unstoppable!

With political will, Britain in the 21st century has to take stringent action to eradicate gang-related activities by getting to their root causes. In order to do so, there will be a need to engage community leaders, members of the public and especially families of gang members, in a range of meaningful advice, imaginative and committed action, that support and strengthen parents, families and especially those gang members who no longer wish to remain in gangs. In fact, some young people view one solution as being a need for the adult population to provide opportunities for young people to voice their fears and concerns, to be listened to, and to have their opinions valued by resultant action.

There is a misconception that young people from in the upper classes have more to say and are more articulate in expressing their views than those from lower classes. Youth Parliament groups and selected members of youth society, many young people feel, are not truly representative of the opinions of the masses, especially those at grass-root level. Indeed, there were among the young people who took part in our 1st National Youth Conference, (October 2008), very articulate young people who had visions of the future of Britain that were admirable. They demonstrated the power of alienated youth who, once empowered to engage positively, were confident, constructive in their solutions of the problems they face and inspired confidence in their abilities, as custodians of the future.

Examples of solutions suggested in our youth surveys included the need to value and show the importance of fathers in helping to mould young boys, especially. It was felt that the influence of peer group pressures on young people could be minimized if male role models and male action counteracted the force of threat among youths. Initiatives such as the *100 Black Men, Black Boys Can, The Roselle Antoine Foundation's Men's Forum, and Boyz to Men,* that targeted development and support of male youths, should be supported at the national level. This is because they are, in the main, community-led and managed by members of the community, with self-financing resources that limit their impact and potential on a larger scale. These organizations should be encouraged to work collaboratively at both the local and national level, to share their expertise and experience with political thinkers and planners, in order to address the factors that underlie problems in the community.

Parental Strategy

My first recommendation for behaviour change is a suggestion for large-scale parenting intervention. Epidemiological studies have shown that family risk factors such as poor parenting, family conflict, and marital breakdown are predictors for the development and maintenance of behavioural and emotional problems in children and adolescents (Cummings & Davies 1994; Dryfoos 1990; Robins & Price 1991). Other risk factors that have a direct impact on children's behavior are insecure attachment, harsh or rigid or even inconsistent discipline practices; parent relationship that lacks warmth and positive encouragement, marital conflict and marital breakdown, lack of or inadequate supervision, parents depression, high levels of stress; all increase the risk that children will develop behvioural and emotional problems, conduct issues, substance abuse, and antisocial behaviours, (Loeber & Farrington 1998: Patterson 1982).

I have shown where circumstances can conspire against families so that they find themselves embroiled within these adverse factors. There needs to be a population based strategy that would support parents and therefore prevent dysfunctional practices so that they will be better able to undertake their role in society. The fact is, beyond the experience of becoming parents, they may have had very little support other than their "learning by doing" or "trial and error". Also the more disadvantaged a parent is, the less likely he/she will be to actively involved in parenting education. Therefore the challenge is to develop strategies that can inspire confidence and competence, to bring up children in ways that would help to reduce behavioural and emotional problems in their lives.

However, such intervention strategies must be able to demonstrate the correlation between improvement in behaviours in children and the increased competence of parents. There is evidence to support the view that teaching parents positive parenting and disciplinary skills results in improvements in the majority of disruptive and adverse behaviours in children. (Patterson 1982, Taylor & Biglan 1998; Webster-Stratton & Hammond 1997).

These mechanisms of interventions need to be able to demonstrate how short-term gains maintained over time cannot only be cost effective, relative to no intervention but are linked to overall satisfaction. These interventions also need to be culturally appropriate. In other words, it must be accessible and relevant to all parents, presenting the positive values of cultural beliefs, traditions and aspirations and above all, they must respond to the need of all racial and ethnic grouping.

- Some factors which interventions must take into consideration are:

- Family structures

- Cultural beliefs and values

- Child raising practices

- Sexuality and gender roles

- Those who are socially, economically and geographically disadvantages

- Must not be viewed as coercive or intrusive

- Take into consideration, the medium of access (internet, and technological media may exclude "hard to reach" groups)

- There are different levels of dysfunction and behavioural difficulties in children

- Parents have different needs (e.g. type of intervention, intensity, method of support)

Mass Media Intervention Strategy

Since the desire is to reach the mass population, a very effective way of disseminating information is to use one of the most powerful and popular tools of information distribution – the mass media. (Egger, Donovan & Spark 1993). This strategy via the television medium, already plays an effective role in safe sex campaigns on *sexual health*, *smoking*, *drink and drive*, use of *mobile phones when driving*, *speed limits* for drivers, *drugs awareness* and *public information sharing* about *disaster fund appeals*.

One objective of a mass media parenting intervention would be to normalize the notion of participation. Other aims would be to increase parents' involvement and reducing the stigma attached to getting help.

A good strategy would be to involve the general mass media, which is television, radio, internet, and news print. However, TV has by far, the greatest appeal and has been known to influence habits, awareness and change in attitudes, people's beliefs and their behaviours. Therefore, it is regarded as one of the most powerful educational tools in our lifetime. (Hofstetter, Schultze & Mulvihill, 1992; Zimmerman 1996).

Figure: C1: Benefits to using TV mass media intervention

• Television is pervasive, (with an average of 3hrs spent watching per parents daily).
• Information can be accessed in the privacy of one's home.
• Can be used geographically wherever parents are.
• Programmes can help parents to recognize early warning signs and therefore seek help early to prevent need for long-term intervention.
• Promote community awareness and understanding of the role relationships play in the well-being and behaviours of children (Sanders 1999).
• Supporting parents education and reduce sensational and alarmist information or the blame culture.
• By parents watching behaviour programmes and putting strategies into place, would give the sense that they contributed and achieved the desired change via their own efforts (Flay 1987). This will increase their self esteem and confidence as well as competence.
• It provides information about the problems and practical advice on how to solve them.

The fact is such interventionist methods not only tackles the problems but are able to develop skills to deal with related behavioural problems. For example, a mother learning how to respond to a child's adverse behaviour will, at the same time, learn how to modify her own behaviour. Behavioural change then requires parents to regulate themselves in ways that require self-monitoring, self identification of their weaknesses and strengths, and self-evaluation based on set goals. (Halford, Sanders & Behrens 1994).

My suggestion would be for TV and Media moguls to consider programming aimed at changing behaviours with parents and children at the heart of behaviour change strategies. There is no doubt that such programmes would increase ratings and popularity: in fact, this has been found to increase viewing by at least 20-35%, (Neilson 1997). The use of celebrities could help here, so would programmes which include a range of parenting strategies designed to encourage desirable behviour in children. These strategies must include the following:

Figure: C2: Behaviour Strategies

✓ Show use of praise and positive attention
✓ Present how to monitor child behaviour with guidelines for using a range of parenting strategies designed to encourage good behaviour in children,
✓ Rule setting,
✓ Provision of clear instructions by up by logical consequences,
✓ Quiet time & time out,
✓ Temper tantrums and how to deal with them,
✓ Encourage creativity,
✓ Help with homework,
✓ Sleeping and eating difficulties,
✓ Celebrate successful outcomes.

Television could additionally be backed up by radio and other forms of print media, so that parents are reminded of the programmes. Furthermore, fact-sheets could be provided to concretize the information and make for ease of reflection and reference. The benefit of our globalized and technologized world is that parents could record and watch the programmes at times that suit them best, with the added use of CD, Videos, and other technical formats, to make carrying and accessing the information easy and accessible.

It must be borne in mind that parents with a severe behavioural child may not find all the answers in the programmes for parents but programmes will go some way towards raising awareness for more intensive forms of interventions. Overall, the general aims and objectives are realistic, despite the cost that may be involved in creating programmes specifically aimed at behaviour change in society. There is no doubt, that the long-term benefit to everyone - individuals, families, the community and society at large, far outweighs the initial financial cost as well as the cost of remedial approaches as presented earlier, in *Chapter 4.*

Education Strategy: The Antoine Behaviour Excellence Model© (A Working Model)

There is a particular value in articulating the merits of the ***Antoine Behaviour Excellence Model,*** at a time of change in the 21st century, or when new initiatives are needed for solutions to underachievement, behavioural management issues and crises involving juvenile criminality in the UK. The ***Antoine Behaviour Excellence Model*** is not a theory but it is a multi-layered strategy, based on the relations between peoples and social groups, with processes that can help parents, teachers and managers/Carers, to develop a way of working with children that reflects their individual ideals and priorities.

The Model can also help to facilitate choices about shaping children's activities, with sensitivity paid firstly, to them as human beings, and secondly, with regard to their cultural and social make-up; all of which direct their ways of thinking, talking and behaving. This counters any trend towards prescriptive, and fixed notions of what those involved in caring for and managing children need to know; some of which have fallen short of children's holistic development.

The ***Antoine Behaviour Excellence Model*** has already detailed in the preceding chapters, (specifically ***Chapter 7***), how its practical application can produce positive behavior management results; having merged the boundaries between teaching, learning and researching. However, this research is an "undetermined journey" or "voyage" since it highlights many problems that have required new frames of references and analyses which need further research. For example, a culturally sensitive approach may prove difficult for those who lack the knowledge of how to apply it. Also the word "culture" has different meanings for individuals and may challenge their own perspectives on what is culturally relevant and applicable in managing adverse behavior. There are also different multilingual communities in Britain, (language itself being integral to culture and tradition); where different cultural input can be linked to the learning process to enhance attainment outcomes. For example, those who have come from an orally based culture may present with poor literacy levels, especially writing, but show a preference for, and excel in the expressive arts as well as practically based subjects. This has implications for assessment methods used to measure a child's total attainment levels in general.

In this context, a highly specialized and multi-media set of practices can be used in teachers and professional development courses, to encourage them to bear in mind that a triangular relationship exists in understanding pupils. For example, as trainee teachers, *their own practices* are set against their **students own** (in and out of the classroom), as well as practices which have a **broader frame of reference for society. (Figure C.3)**

Trainee teachers and professional managers should be constantly focusing on all sides of the triangle, in order to link all three sets of practices for greater understanding of their pupils. It means one is able to consciously build this knowledge into learning programmes, using it as a basis for discussion and learning strategies with pupils.

This does not mean debunking the formal educational settings and practices in favour of culturally sensitive and socially specific approaches. The issues here are that of:

Acknowledging and respecting the existence of culture and social   backgrounds as relevant to a child's learning and development and,

1. The importance they bring to children's learning in motivating pupils and parents;

2. Understanding that the child's learning is not limited only to the classroom or school environment (*Saturday Schools, Mother Tongue Schools* and *Extra tuition in Cultural Studies* are examples) and.

3. Imposing standardized curricular which are not sensitive to local, cultural and social issues may increase the gap between achievers and underachievers, home and school, educational outcomes, and may alienate parents and children from educational practices.

Figure C.3: Some Cultural Factors

Here are some cultural factors which highlight the added value that they bring to children's education:
Cultural emphasis on discipline, obedience to rules, respect for elders, who are the sources of family advice for all matters
The use of humour (or the *grinning mask*), as a means of coping
The value placed on education of children, seen as the models of hope, success for the future

Strength gained from the community cohesion, community representatives, and community organizations that help access support from larger societal bodies
Child-rearing traditions that are different from the host community, children caring for younger ones
The view that "Special Needs" is a blight or curse and therefore could be rejected by families if such a label is attached to their child. Rather than tackle the problem they are likely to ignore or dismiss it.
Social status differences and conflicts within regions (e.g. Caribbean the *"bigger vs. smaller island"* rivalry; (Jamaica vs. the other smaller islands;' bigger', suggesting 'better')!
Styles of communication – avoiding direct eye contact, and use of gestures which are not necessarily seen as confrontational
Family interaction patterns: verbal and non-verbal communication between parents and children
Use of Caribbean vernacular, language of the Caribbean, dialect as well as 'street talk', emergent sense of pride, compared with early 1930-50's references to "bad English"
Strong religious values, customs and the part played by churches, which also reinforces cultural values, supplement group socialization processes and strong spiritual support
Bi-language and bi-cultural competences of the British Caribbean children in adapting to different situations within the host community
Strong loyalty to family in general but family ownership of children can present problems
Extended family (where existing in the UK) provides strong support and sharing of child care – this also extends to family friends and neighours.

However, teachers have limited time to get to know their children's cultural practices, especially children from cultures which are very different from the teacher's. Therefore policy must guide a reflective curriculum which can mediate between home, local communities, schools and teaching and learning programmes. Policy must also inform trainee-teachers' and professional development courses or those caring for children, if it is to make a substantial contribution to the goals set out in the *Antoine Behaviour Excellence Model.*

TEACHER TRAINING: The preparatory training, continuous professional development and the skilling of supply teachers will require some rethinking on strategies to support delivery of innovative models such as the ABEM. It calls for innovative thinking and would mean a need to carefully scrutinize present models of training as well as the delivery of that training – *practice* being the watchword rather than theory. However, moving ahead beyond goals, calls for tremendous effort and commitment to educational practice that improve and motivate practice for teachers. A General Teaching Council (GTC) and Mori poll (2003), highlighted the following issues for which the government must take seriously, if it's vision for 21st century **(Chapter 6),** is to foster, develop and retain a world- class teaching and learning workforce in the West.

TEACHER MORALE: There is a raft of issues surrounding the national picture of teacher employment, morale, retention, and job satisfaction which affect teachers attitude to pupils in school.

BUREAUCRACY: According to the results of the General Teaching Council (GTC) for England/Guardian/Mori survey of 70,011 teachers, .many teachers felt burdened by paperwork and the target-setting culture to the point where they were ready to leave the profession. Unfortunately, the teaching profession is already struggling to recruit enough members to keep going, The poll findings revealed that from a list of three factors which de-motivated teachers the most, 56% of them said that being over-burdened by paperwork was the number one de-motivator.

Other factors cited were initiative overload and the target-driven culture. This suggests that many teachers are unhappy about their treatment by the government and employers. Though the respondents were not sampled or weighted and were by definition self-selective, they appeared to be representative across the gender divide as well as the age of the teaching population nationally.

BEHAVIOUR: Discipline, or the lack of it, is the fourth de-motivator for teachers. In general, younger teachers complain more about behaviour issues whilst the older teachers are more likely to protest at initiatives and the target-setting culture. The survey also revealed that women in primary schools are most likely to complain about target setting. After their first year, many teachers get de-motivated, and 15% of New Qualified Teachers (NQTs), say their morale is lower than when they first started. This makes a figure of 4 in 10 teachers with 1 – 5 years service.

RETENTION: The above factor has an obvious impact on retention levels. The attrition of teachers from service is a concern and therefore the need to redress decline in teacher morale for new teachers is critical.

GENDER DIFFERENCES: The Poll also revealed that factors which most motivate teachers are working with young people, general job satisfaction, and that the role is creative/mentally stimulating/challenging". Men are more likely to be motivated by the idea of giving something back to the community - 24% mentioned that, compared with 17% for women. Black and Asian teachers are also more likely to cite that. But there appears to be a limited sense of a specifically "public sector" ethic.

SUBJECT SPECIALISM: Working with young people was the main reason teachers cited for going into the profession. But "love of my subject", one of the most mentioned motivators for joining the profession, became less important as teachers continued.

PAY: The survey cited 11% of teachers maintained that pay was one of the three factors which most demotivated them.

LONG SCHOOL HOLIDAYS: From the majority of teachers, 56%, say morale is lower than when they first joined the profession. Some 11% say it is higher and 27% say it is about the same. Nearly one in five teachers with low morale said one of the main reasons for keeping going is the long school holidays.

Media: The media was identified as the group which gives the least respect to teachers. Some 21% of teachers believed the media gave them no respect at all; 86% either none or not much. But within their schools, teachers feel largely respected by their colleagues, students and parents. Only 5% of respondents did not feel respected by their fellow teachers; 13% felt that of their students; and 19% of their students' parents. Some 43% of teachers felt they received "a great deal" of respect from their colleagues. Black, Asian and newly-qualified teachers felt less respected.

JOB SATISFACTION: On the whole teachers felt respected by their colleagues, parents and students and generally enjoy working with young people. They felt a sense of personal achievement and believe they are good at their jobs. However, the survey findings showed that teachers in state secondary schools were the most likely to believe they made the wrong career choice, *Table C.1*). Job satisfaction was greater for Heads and those with managerial positions/responsibilities, than it is for classroom teachers. Overall, the survey showed that teachers who are given the opportunity for further training or "professional development" are much more likely to want to stay in teaching. (*guardian.co.uk, Tuesday 7 January 2003*).

Table C.1: Comparison showing differences between
Teacher attrition & Teachers dissatisfaction

REASONS FOR NO. OF TEACHERS DECLINE	REASONS FOR TEACHER JOB SATISFACTION
Bureaucracy	Working with young people
Initiative overload	Creative/mentally stimulating job
Target-driven culture	Giving something back to the community
Behavioural issues	Long school holidays
Pay issues	Love of own subject speciality
Media disrespect	Respect by their colleagues
Low morale	Sense of real personal achievement

INTEGRATION/ASSIMILATION: There have been several approaches and models to intercultural and multicultural education. These have, in social reality, run the risk of touching only the symptoms of problems. Many are presented mainly as providing equality of opportunities to the social and cultural groups. So why haven't these approaches produced the desired outcomes. For example, the early Caribbean migrants approached their development in Britain through assimilation, *(1950's-60's)*. This way they could blend in with the host population by allowing their identity to be absorbed into the dominant or host group. The sense here is that the host group is more advanced and therefore cultural diversity is conceived as a problem that threatens the integrity and social cohesion of the majority.

This thought proved difficult for Caribbeans who were already British colonial citizens and whose social and cultural norm was not so far removed from the host community. There was certainly the idea that the original culture of the minority's children, if left unassimilated, would obstruct the way to integration in school and society. This was seen as something which interfered with both the school and social development of the migrant.

Segregation in the 1970's, was attempted in order to provide the answer to a slow integration and minimal outcomes. *Educationally Sub-normal* schools (ESN), provided a parallel to assimilation and such political moves segregated Caribbeans, racially, socially and culturally – ESN schools reserved for them because of their 'intellectual'/biological characteristics – educationally sub-normal. The disadvantage of such a label to the pupils (of a poor socio-economic situation) as deficient, or disabled due to the social and family environment, also relayed a conscious and unconscious communication of low expectations of pupils, that produced an effect of low stimulation and low motivation; in other words a self fulfilling prophecy.

Multicultural education/curriculum, *(1980's to date)*, recognizes the plurality of cultures. The recognition of the mother language in schools is also a recognition in value, for the cognitive individual development. The cultural curricula as ideological and politically correct, argues for the development of a stronger sense of self and at the same time, helps to prepare all pupils – majority and minority, to be able to understand and adapt in both cultures. What is clear from the application of the **Antoine Behaviour Excellence Model** which was applied to TCS Tutorial College, is that development took place on many levels (I). Cultural contact, (2). Skills developed and adopted from the contact; and (3). Positive attitudes generated for both, with regard to cultural diversity and a sharing of knowledge both ways.

Many of the current British Caribbean parents and families, have experienced all three approaches – from assimilation, to segregation and multicultural - within the British school system. The resulting currency of paradoxes and dilemmas, have been highlighted throughout this book, **(Figure C3)**. However, what is clear from researching the **Antoine Behaviour Excellence Model,** is that a school can contribute to the behaviour management of pupils through the social construction of actions that promote equality, within an environment that has these features:

Figure C.4: ABEM's Educational Philosophy

• The school values and legitimizes cultural and social diversity,
• The school staff has a commitment to democratic attitudes and values each pupil on merit and not via a stereotype,
• The activities promote the value of all social classes and ethnicity,
• That staff teach styles of motivation which are effective and culturally and socially sensitive to pupils needs,
• That teachers acquire skills that are necessary to recognize the different forms of racism (conscious and unconscious),

> The school prepares pupils to live in a society where the cultural diversity is recognized and valued – cultural diversity seen as a value and not a hindrance,.
>
> There is recognition of the right of each child to receive the best education, carefully planned and which includes the formation of his/her personal identity,
>
> Participation of parents in the school activities to develop positive relations between and among the diverse ethnic groups.
>
> That the application of the Antoine Behaviour Excellence Model will not be seen as a marginal and separate need of the school to deal only with the Caribbean or just migrant communities, but would consider the relevant of it as the requirement of good general education of the individual, whatever cultural origin, for the benefit of society.

By encouraging a broader understanding of what cultural sensitivity and socially specific approaches are, help to break down monolithic discourses around the type of "one medicine cures all", notion that actually hide the complexity of behavioural issues in reality. We need initiatives and approaches generated through reflective practices which are workable, to help us engage with current policies on children's development, that will benefit ALL children, equitably. The *Antoine Behaviour Excellence Model,* via an ethnographic approach, can help teachers, pupils, families, Carers and workers with children, to access behaviour management strategies, with good results.

The fact that one is able to count the cost of youth crime in statistical terms, measure behaviour levels, look at society's construction of youth deviance, (shaped by the media, political and public discourses); it is possible to conclude that the problems of the youth go beyond adverse behaviour alone. Although eyebrows are raised when one mentions institutional racism, as if it somehow has disappeared or should have disappeared from Britain as if by magic, there is still a major factor in young people's complaint about how they are treated and that is to do with not being listened to, especially when there is a case of injustice suffered at the hands of those who are supposed to hold the reins of power and authority. Gang formation and action, responds to an element in this factor, that if young people cannot get justice, they will create their own forms – called "street justice". We must therefore guard against developing trends, (seen right across the various racial and cultural divides), that probably imply a lack of trust in the system of justice to administer justice objectively, in favour of individuals taking matters into their own hands. However, it is important to reiterate that not all young people are gang-related, gun-toting and spinning out of control. Sometimes we lose sight of the creative good that are evident among what I would call the *majority* of youth in Britain, who are working towards a positive and productive future.

Over-indulgence in the fears of young people's exuberance, the view that every young person on the street is involved in social instability, with comparatively less attention being paid to the need for youth social justice, or social and media discourses that project them as valuable members of society, then the question would have to be; *In whose hands lie the future of our well being?* Can we continue to misunderstand the functions of the youth in society? Left to fester, as they do at present, many problems will continue to affect, not only our moral, spiritual and economic development but the entire fabric of society. However, by re-establishing our priorities and understanding that each and every one of us is an *Agent of Change*, we can begin the investment in restorative empowerment, and a belief that if we *teach them well and let them lead the way*, the future will be less ambivalent.

SELECTED REFERENCES

Cummings E.M., & & Davies, P. (1994): *Children and marital conflict: The Impact of Family Dispute and Resolution,* New York, Guildford Press.

Dryfoos, J. G (1990): Adolescents at Risk: Prevalence and Prevention, New YUork, Oxford University Press.

Robins, L. N. & Price, R. K. (1991): Adult disorders predicted by childhood conduct problems: Results from NIMH epidemiological catchment area project, *Psychiatry*, 54, 116-132.

Loeber, R., & Farrington, D. P. (1998): Never too early, never too late: Risk factors and successful interventions for serious and violent juvenile offenders. *Studies on Crime and Crime Prevention,* 7(1), 7-30.

Patterson, G. R. (1982), *Coercive Family Process*, Eugene, OR: Castalia Press.

Taylor, T. K. & Biglan, A., (1998): Behavioural family interventions for improving child-rearing: A review of the literature for clinicians and policy makers. *Clinical Child and Family Psychology,* 1(1), 41-60

Webster-Stratton, C., & Hammond, M. (1997): Treating children with early-onset conduct problems: A comparison of child and parent training interventions, *Journal of Consulting and Clinical Psychology,* 65, 91-109.

Egger, G., Donovan, R., & Spark, R., (1993): *Health and the media: Principles and Practices for Health Promotion.* Sydney, Australia, McGraw-Hill Book Company

Hofstetter C. R., Schultze, W.A., & Mulvihill, M. M. (1992): Communications media, public health and public affairs: Exposure in a multimedia community. *Health Communication*, 4, 259-271.

Zimmerman, J.D., (1996): A prosocial media strategy: Youth against violence: Choose to defuse, *American Journal of Orthopsychiatry*, 66, 354-361.

Sanders M. R. (1999): Triple P-Positive Parenting Program: Towards an empirically validated multilevel parenting and family support strategy for the prevention of behavior and emotional problems in children. *Clinical Child and Family Psychology Review,* 2 (2), 71-90.

Halford, K. W., SandersM. R. & Behrens, B.C., (1994): Self-regulation in behavioral couples' therapy, *Behavior Therapy*, 25, 431-452.

Neilson A.C. (1997): *People Meter Rating Analysis*, Sydney, Australia:

ACRONYMS

ABEM	The Antoine Behviour Excellence Model
EBD	Emotional Behavioural Difficulties
ESBD	Emotional and Social Behavioural Difficulties
ADD	Attention Deficit Disorder
ADHD	Attention Deficit Hyperactivity Disorder
ESOL	English for Speakers of Other Languages
EAL	English as an Additional Language
YOT	Youth Offending Team
PAT	Positive Action Team
GTC	General Teaching Council
NQT	Newly Qualified Teacher
ESN	Educationally Sub-Normal
CXC	Caribbean Examinations Council
BME	Black and Minority Ethnic
BMH	Black Mental Health
GCSE	General Certificate of Secondary Education
GCE	General Certificate of Education
BNP	British National Party

CSJ	Centre for Social Justice
MMAGS	Manchester Multi-Agency Strategy
ICT	Information and Computer Technology
SEN	Special Education Needs
LEA	Local Education Authority
PRU	Pupil Referral Unit
OFSTED	Office for Standards in Education
NEET	Not Engaged in Education or Training
UN	United Nations
NSPCC	National Society for the Prevention of Cruelty to Children
UK	United Kingdom
DCSF	Depart for Children, Schools and Families
CARICOM	The Caribbean Common Market
CARIFESTA	Caribbean Festival of Arts
UNESCO	United Nations Educational, Scientific and Cultural Organization
OECS	Organization of Eastern Caribbean States
NSF	National Service Framework for Children
PCT	Primary Care Trust
UNICEF	United Nations International Children's Emergency Fund
CPD	Continuous Professional Development
CSE	Certificate of Secondary Education

GLOSSARY OF KEY TERMS

Adolescence – a term which originates ifrom the 18th century to describe the special status of young people undergoing extended periods of educational training. During the 20th century this has become associated with a period of emotional upheaval which affects all young people (G.S Hall 1905).

Academies - Academies are all-ability, state-funded schools established and managed by sponsors from a wide range of backgrounds, including high performing schools and colleges, universities, individual philanthropists, businesses, the voluntary sector, and the faith communities. Some are established. educational providers, and all of them bring a record of success in other enterprises which they are able to apply to their Academies in partnership with experienced school managers.

Afro-Caribbean - A native or inhabitant of the Caribbean region who is of African ancestry. It is also referred to a combination of African and other, generally European cultural elements as found in the Caribbean region: Afro-Caribbean music; Afro-Caribbean religions. This description is also used to refer to someone, something that is related to Afro-Caribbeans or their history or culture.

African Caribbean – coming after the popular use of Afro Caribbean is used interchangeably to mean the **British African-Caribbean** or simply **British**

BME – Black and Minority Ethnic communities – indicated all groups of people who who are categorized as black as well as those from other minority cultural groups in the UK.

Caribbeans. Nowadays, it is referred to include Indo-Caribbean (Caribbean Indians), and other Caribbean categories. Generally they are residents of the United Kingdom who are of West Indian background, and whose ancestors were indigenous to Africa. As immigration to the United Kingdom from Africa increased in the 1990s, the term has been used to include UK residents solely of African origin, or as a term to define all Black British residents, though this is usually denoted by "African **and** Caribbean".

Creole - The term "*Creole*" was originally applied to people born in the colonies to distinguish them from the upper-class European-born immigrants. Originally, therefore, "Creole language" meant the speech of those Creole peoples. As a consequence of colonial European trade patterns, many Creole languages are found in the equatorial belt around the world and in areas with access to the oceans, including the Caribbean as well as the north and east coasts of South America, western Africa and in the Indian Ocean.

Crime – described as a violation of the criminal law, but contested by some to include all social injuries and social harms (Michael and Adler, 1933;Hulsman, 1986).

Delinquency – described loosely as misbehavior among young people.

Deviance – a social term used to describe youthful rule breaking behavior.r

Discourse – a particular way of talking, thinking and writing. It could be personal, media, political or academic.

Ethnographic research – research which is directed towards in-depth and detailed understanding of the lives and personal meaning of subjects.

Gang – described as involving a group of people who over time, crate rules of membership and identifiable leadership.

In loco parentis* -** The term ***in loco parentis, Latin for "in the place of a parent" or "instead of a parent," refers to the legal responsibility of a person or organization to take on some of the functions and responsibilities of a parent. Originally derived from British common law, it is applied in two separate areas of the law. The *in loco parentis* doctrine is distinct from the doctrine of ***parents patriae***, the psychological parent doctrine, and adoption. In the United States, the parental liberty doctrine imposes constraints upon the operation of the *in loco parentis* doctrine.

Institutional Racism (or **structural racism** or **systemic racism**) refers to a form of racism that occurs specifically within institutions such as public bodies, corporations, and universities. The term was coined in the late 1960's by black Panther and pan-Africanist, Stokely Carmichael. He defined the term as "the collective failure of an organization to provide an appropriate and professional service to people because of their colour, culture or ethnic origin."

Mods – As a subculture, Mods originated from the East end of London and working-class estates in the suburbs of the capital. They were engaged in semi-skilled manual labour which gave them relative affluence. Their preferred drug was amphetamine, so they lived for the nights, weekends and bank holidays. They were characterized by short hair, smart Italian designer suits and an obsession with neat appearance. They emulated the cool and sleek style of their West Indian counterparts (the shades and pork pie hats).

Motherland - generally this means one's native land or, sometimes, the land of one's ancestors. Used in this book it refers to a country thought of as originator or source. Therefore, on one hand, Africa is the motherland of all Negroes, from where all Negroes in slavery were taken against their will. On the other hand, and conversely, for some, England is also seen as the *motherland* because ancestrally, politically, and culturally it was instrumental in the part production of peoples' and their history in the Caribbean.

Multiple Intelligences is a theory which was proposed by psychologist Howard Gardner in 1983, to define the concept of intelligence and to address whether methods that claim to measure intelligence (of aspects of it) were indeed scientific. He suggested that an array of different kinds of "intelligence" exists in human beings and that each individual manifests varying levels of these different intelligences. Therefore each person has a unique "cognitive profile."

OFSTED – Office for Standards in Education in the UK, it is a regulatory body which inspects and regulates the achievement of education excellence and skills for children, young people and adult learners . OFSTED brings together the wide experience of four inspectorates.

Pupil Referral Unit (PRU) - A Pupil Referral Unit is a centre for children who are not able to attend a mainstream or special school. Each local education authority has a duty to make arrangements for the provision of education in or out of school for *all* children of compulsory school age. If children may not receive suitable education for any period for reasons such as illness or exclusion from school, these arrangements can be made through Pupil Referral Units - which are a mixture of public units and privately managed companies.

Racial Discrimination – Simply called racism, is the belief that a particular race is superior or inferior to another, that a person's social and moral traits are predetermined by his or her inborn biological characteristics. In the case of institutional racism, certain racial groups may be denied rights or benefits, or get preferential treatment by public institutions or other statutory agencies working for the public benefit.

Rights of the Child - The Convention is a universally agreed set of non-negotiable standards and obligations. These basic standards—also called human rights—set minimum entitlements and freedoms that should be respected by governments. They are founded on respect for the dignity and worth of each individual, regardless of race, colour, gender, language, religion, opinions, origins, wealth, birth status or ability and therefore apply to every human being everywhere.

Role Model – In general this term is used to mean any "person who serves as an example, whose behaviour is emulated by others".

Rude Boy – A style developed in the mid 1960's by Afro Caribbean youth in Britain based on the subculture of West Kingston, Jamaica. In Britain the style evolved based on self-assurance, coolness, smart clothes and ska music. Theirs was also a style of 'resistance', brought about by a response to economic inequalities and the situation of black youth. They were demonized in Britain as lazy, criminals, who lived by dope dealing and dependent on Welfare.

School League Tables - Every year the Department for Children, Schools and Families (DCSF),publishes information on the achievement and attainment of pupils in all schools. These tables provide a guide to how well a school is doing. They list National Curriculum test results for each school in England and show how they compare with other schools. There are four tables published each year: Test results do not give a complete picture of a school..

Skinheads - named for their close-cropped or shaven heads, the first **skinheads** were greatly influenced by West Indian (specifically Jamaican) rude boys in early 1968. Characterised by their almost uniform style of dress e.g. cropped hair, braces, half-mast trousers, and Doc. Marten 'bovver boots'. They were associated with violence, football hooliganism and '*Paki*' and '*queer*' bashing, in an attempt to take control of their territory, the streets.

Special Education Needs (SEN) - The term '*special educational needs*' has a legal definition. Children with special educational needs all have learning difficulties or disabilities that make it harder for them to learn or access education than most children of the same age. These children may need extra or different help from that given to other children of the same age. Children with special educational needs may need extra help because of a range of needs, such as in thinking and understanding, physical or sensory difficulties, emotional and behavioural difficulties, or difficulties with speech and language or how they relate to and behave with other people..

Social exclusion - a concept that described the way in which the poor are marginalized from the economic mainstream and isolation from relationships and sources of identity.

Su-su, partner, giving "hands", conubite or sociedad – a form of community banking among traditional Caribbean families. Money is amassed by individuals forming a group and each member contributes a fixed sum per wek. Each week one member from the group receives the total contributed, until everyone has had a turn, then the cycle starts again. Freed slaves from slave plantations used this method to buy their freedom and many Caribbean families have used this method to purchase their homes in Britain; more prevalent in the 60s and 70s.

Teddy Boys - Some groups of gangs of the 1960's who gained notoriety following violent clashes with rival gangs. The most notable was the <u>Notting Hill riot of 1958</u>, in which Teddy Boys were conspicuous within <u>racist</u> <u>white</u> mobs who roamed the area attacking <u>black people</u> and damaging their property Inspired by the Edwardian styles of dress, Teddy Boys were the first youth group in England to differentiate themselves as <u>teenagers</u>, thus helping to create a youth market.

The Great House - A **great house** is a large and stately <u>residence</u> occupied by Slave masters and colonial land owners with their elaborate hierarchy of domestic staff, on plantations in the Caribbean.. The name refers to the makeup of the <u>household</u> and the size of the structure which is often huge and imposing, compared with the homes of the rest of the population. Every Caribbean territory has either traditional or modern structures of 'The Great House' which accommodates Heads of State or Prime Ministers.

Windrush - On June 22, 1948, the **SS Empire Windrush** docked at Tilbury in Essex. This steamship brought the first generation of migrant workers from the Caribbean to England. There were 492 passengers from Jamaica, most of whom were ex-servicemen seeking work. This therefore played an integral part in the making of modern multicultural Britain.

Youth – a loosely defined , it refers to a period of a young person's lifespan between infancy and adulthood.

Youth Justice System – Governed by the Youth Justice Board, it is set up to tackle youth offending, in three ways:

- Prevent youngsters from falling in to crime
- Provide the criminal justice system with more sentencing choices
- Focus sentencing on preventing repeat offending.

Vandalism - is ruthless behaviour, committed by vandals, who destroy other people's property. Such actions may include criminal damage, defacement, and graffiti. Although it is often considered one of the least serious common crimes, it can become quite serious and distressing when committed extensively, violently or as an expression of hatred and intimidation.